The Practice of Writing

Edited by Valerie Ross

Taken from:

A Short Course in Writing: Composition, Collaborative Learning, and Constructive Reading, Fourth Edition
Kenneth A. Bruffee

Revising Prose, Fourth Edition
Richard Lanham

PEARSON
Custom
Publishing

PEARSON
Longman

Cover Art: *Chairs at Getty Museum*, by Arkady Nemerovsky

Taken from:

A Short Course in Writing: Composition, Collaborative Learning and Constructive Reading, Fourth Edition
by Kenneth A. Bruffee
Copyright © 1993 by Kenneth A. Bruffee
Published by Longman Publishers
Originally published by HarperCollins
New York, New York 10036

Revising Prose, Fourth Edition
by Richard Lanham
Copyright © 2000, 1992 by Allyn & Bacon
A Pearson Education Company
Boston, Massachusetts 02116

Printed in the United States of America

10 9 8 7 6 5 4 3 2 1

ISBN 0-536- 97554-X

2005240312

MR/RR

Please visit our web site at *www.pearsoncustom.com*

Table of Contents

Preface

The text before you is not quite a book, but neither is it a reader. Conversations, writings, research and seminars, along with the creation of Penn's Critical Writing Program, prompted it. Penn undergraduates played a significant role, particularly those enrolled in John Lessard's critical writing seminar on film and my own on peer tutor training, which I taught with the help of Andrea Kushnick Rubin. Our students drew their assignments from Kenneth Bruffee's *A Short Course in Writing*s. John's students wrote essays on the films they were viewing; my students chose their own topics. Together we explored approaches to writing best suited to the needs, talents, and interests of Penn undergraduates.

Faculty in the Critical Writing Program have one goal: to help students write well. Like our founder, Ben Franklin, we also want everyone to "employ time well." Thus our writing seminars are a practicum on writing, but also an introduction to the scholarly, professional or avocational interests of our faculty. Offered a wide range of topics across disciplines, students can be adventurous and yet assured that they are doing something unimpeachably practical: working on their writing.

What faculty in the program learned over the past two years is that Penn students like Bruffee's nuts-and-bolts, hands-on, collaborative approach to writing. They appreciate his attentive, nonjudgmental, intellectually-driven way of conducting peer reviews. With a little practice, and ensconced by the writing community that is fostered by Bruffee's consensus-building approach, our students discover how liberating formal constraints can be. They reach for similes to express the experience: "like writing a sonnet;" "like designing software;" "like playing jazz; like learning a sport."

Faculty and students alike noticed something else over the course of the "Bruffee semester": improvement with each paper, each peer review; revisions generated by a desire to connect or dazzle, clarify or transcend. Somewhere along the way our students stopped being students. They became writers. No longer dutifully dispatching "A" or "B" papers, their assignments became occasions to stretch, experiment, refine, or otherwise practice their art. And as they transformed from student to writer, their increasing fluency in form and function led to an affectionate restlessness with Bruffee's workmanlike approach to writing. They graduated from building a sturdy chair (to borrow Bruffee's metaphor) to crafting an artful one, and their attention turned to the matter of style.

This is where our work-in-progress ends and begins for now: this customized text, *The Practice of Writing*, an outgrowth of the work, desires and successes of our students. We include some chapters by Bruffee that have been especially effective for our students and, at their request, have added some chapters by Richard Lanham that focus on style.

We are excited that your seminar will be participating in this year's adventure in writing. With such talented faculty and students, who knows what this book will look like in coming years. Stay attuned.

Valerie Ross

Valerie Ross is Director of the Critical Writing Program, Center for Programs in Contemporary Writing at the University of Pennsylvania.

Section I

Selections from *A Short Course in Writing*
by Kenneth Bruffee

PART ONE

Remembering, Questioning, Generalizing

The essay exercises in this book ask you to write essays, but they do not tell you what to write those essays about. They give you a form, but not a topic. For each essay exercise you have to come up with something to write about on your own.

That may be a disturbing prospect. It may even seem unfair. You may wonder "What have I got to write about?" and you may find yourself answering "Nothing."

If so, then this book chooses not to believe you. It believes that you do have something to write about. In fact, it believes that you have a lot to write about and have a lot to say. The purpose of Part One is to prove it to you. Part One is about *invention*. That means inventing topics to write about and inventing what to say about them. If you already know what you want to write about, you can skip exercises 1 and 2 and begin with exercises 3 and 4. If you already know what you want to write about *and* what you want to say about it, you can skip Part One entirely and begin with exercise 5 in Part Two.

Exercises 1, 2, and 3 ask you to write about yourself in different ways: to reminisce about old times, tell family stories, describe changes in yourself and your life, and recall things you have learned in school and elsewhere. Exercise 4 explains how to discover what may be worth writing about from the material you produce in exercises 1, 2, and 3.

What you write in these invention exercises is not an essay. It is raw material. It is like oil when it first comes out of the ground—an unclear, undifferentiated mass that is potentially very valuable, however unpromising it may look. To make that raw material valuable, you have to analyze it.

3

When you do that, you wind up with general observations, judgments, or statements of opinion based on your raw material. These generalizations can become the main point, or proposition, what some people call the thesis statement, of any essay in Parts Two to Five (exercises 5 through 11).

There are many other kinds of invention exercises you could do besides the ones suggested in this section. But these alone, if you worked through them carefully, could give you enough interesting topics to keep you busy writing essays for years.

The best way to use these invention exercises is to combine them with essay exercises 5 through 9. When you set out to do exercise 5, for example, begin by using exercise 1, 2, or 3 to generate raw material and then use exercise 4 to discover some of the issues implicit in that material. When you do that, your essay is sure to be about a topic that interests you, because it grows out of your own experience. Some of that experience may be experience reading. The topic you settle on in any case will probably be one that you know something about, will like writing about, and can explore, explain, or defend in your essay with a good deal of feeling.

In short, the invention exercises in this section can help you learn to explore your ideas through writing. They may even help you discover ideas you never knew you had. A few of these ideas may be entirely your own, because no one has experienced exactly what you have experienced. These ideas will probably be the hardest to get across to people. Other ideas will be more familiar to people who share some of your experiences and background. These ideas will therefore be easier to explore, explain, and defend in writing.

Discovering issues in this way is the first thing to do in learning to write. If you start by discovering issues based on your own experience, including your experience reading, your writing will help you understand yourself better. It will also make your readers more willing to consider what you have to say and maybe even agree with you. These are two of the most important uses of writing.

▷ EXERCISE 1   MINING THE PAST

You can do this exercise in one or more of the following three ways:

REMINISCENCE

Write a true story about something that happened to you once that deeply moved you, upset you, or made you angry.

Write in language that fits the experience. Tell the story in the most forceful way you can, explaining how you felt about what happened.

Give plenty of details, but write only as much as you need to in order to tell the story as you feel it must be told. Don't pad it. And for this exercise, don't worry about spelling, punctuation, usage, or grammar. Don't worry about being correct or "proper" in any way.

Just begin at the beginning and tell the whole story: what happened, in the order that it happened, and how you felt about it. Finally, when you have completed the reminiscence to your satisfaction, skip to exercise 4 to discover issues based on your reminiscence and write a generalization you can use in writing an essay.

☐ EXAMPLE REMINISCENCE ─────────────────

Arnie and the FBI

A few years ago while we were sitting at the dinner table one night an awful thing happened. The whole family was there, my mother and father and I, and my three sisters, my younger brother, and also my older brother Arnie. Arnie was there because he had run away from the Army. He was AWOL—absent without leave.

Arnie joined the Army on his eighteenth birthday, just as soon as he could. They sent him to basic training right away and we didn't see him for a couple of months. We didn't hear much from him, either. He called once or twice, but he didn't say much. He sent a couple of postcards. Everything seemed okay.

But one day he turned up home. He said they'd given him leave for a few weeks. He seemed glad to be home and just settled down again.

Then one day he told me that he didn't really have a leave. He was AWOL. I didn't know what to say. I told my mother and father, and they didn't say much either. After a while, when nothing else happened, we just sort of forgot about it. We were happy Arnie was home. He's a great guy, always kidding around. But we were scared for him really. I could tell he was scared too, although he tried not to show it. He even got a job in a dry cleaners.

Then at supper that night, with all of us there around the dinner table, we heard a knock on the door. Not a loud knock. It sounded like the lady downstairs when she wants to borrow something. When my sister opened the door, two men in brown suits pushed her into the room saying "FBI." They showed their badges and walked right over to the table.

They looked at Arnie and said, "Your name Arnold Jones?" He said, "We're just having supper, can't you wait?" One of the men interrupted him and said, "Come along." He took Arnie by the elbow, almost picked him out of his chair, and pushed him ahead of the two of them out the door. My father shouted, "Hey, wait a minute," and got up, but they were out before we knew it. There was nothing else we could do.

We got a letter from Arnie a few days later saying that they put him in jail. He said he wished he was home. When he gets out of jail, he said, they're going to send him overseas. He didn't know where. □

A FAMILY STORY

Tell a family story. A *family story* is one that a member of your family tells when everyone gets together for holiday dinners, parties, picnics, or other celebrations. It is the story Aunt Joan tells about how Uncle Fred stripped the gears on the old Ford during their honeymoon. The story Grandma tells about meeting Grandpa on their first day in America. Your sister's story about how Gavin sat on the Thanksgiving turkey. Uncle Fred's story about the barn burning down.

Tell your family story with as much detail as you can remember. But keep in mind that *your* audience is not your family. It is a class full of strangers. You may have to explain to them as you go along why things happened as they did, the conditions people were living in or working under when the event occurred, the personal peculiarities of the people involved, and some of your family or ethnic traditions that are related to the story.

Begin by describing the occasion when the story is usually told, and who usually tells it. Tell the whole story as people tell it in your family. Then explain how you feel about it.

When you have finished telling your family story skip to exercise 4 to discover issues based on your family story and formulate a generalization you can use in writing an essay.

☐ EXAMPLE FAMILY STORY ──────────────────────

I Like Ike

My father only gets to see his favorite cousin, Jack, once a year on the Fourth of July. That's when our whole family gets together— all my aunts and uncles and my cousins and my mother's cousins and my father's cousins—everybody turns up at somebody's house, usually ours, and we have a barbecue.

My father looks forward a lot to seeing Jack. One reason he likes him is that they are exactly the same age. They both voted for the first time when President Eisenhower first ran for president. They liked Ike and they both voted for him. Back in those days, Dad says, some people thought Eisenhower was a great president. But some others thought he wasn't so good and not even very smart.

So whenever my father and Jack get together they tell old Eisenhower jokes. Dad's favorite Eisenhower joke starts, "Did you know that President Eisenhower was a literary man?" Whenever he starts with that my mother says, "Oh, no, not again," and laughs. Then she gets up and goes into the kitchen. But of course my father keeps on telling the story, because Jack always laughs at it. He's the only one who ever does laugh at it besides my Dad.

The story goes this way. "Did you know that Eisenhower was a literary man? Yes, he was. It's a fact. He read all the time. In fact, he read every night when he went to bed until his lips got tired."

Frankly, I think it's a dumb story, but you ought to hear Dad and Jack laugh when my father tells it. Sometimes I go out to the kitchen to get away from them, and then I catch my mother laughing too. But I never think she's laughing at the story. I think she's laughing at my father and Jack. She thinks *they're* funny. I think they're funny too, so I laugh with her.

But, you know, I don't think either of us are making fun of Dad and Jack. I think when we laugh at them telling their old stories we feel very fond of them. In fact, I don't think the Fourth of July would be quite the same, or quite as nice, if they didn't tell their old stories and my mother didn't leave the table and go out in the kitchen and laugh. I'd miss it a lot if that didn't happen. □

ACCOUNTING FOR CHANGE

Write a story about some aspect of your life that has changed quite a bit during the past year. Describe yourself as you were. Describe yourself as you see yourself now. Then try to describe how you think the change came about.

The sort of change in your life that you are likely to find most valuable to write about might include changes in things that interest you, changes in things you do, changes in things you like or don't like, changes in the way you feel about who you are, changes in your relationships with people, or changes in your ideas about what you want to do with your life.

☐ EXAMPLE ACCOUNTING FOR CHANGE

How I Got to College

Most of my school years were spent during an era when society, including my family, felt a college education was necessary for a prosperous future. The trend was for everyone, men and women, to attend college. But my father maintained society's older values regarding women. He believed that a woman's place was in the home, and since a woman would ultimately become a housewife despite a college education, it was not necessary for her to obtain one. A man had to become a breadwinner, so my father believed an education was integral to a man's future. The quality of that future depended on a college degree.

I internalized these values as my own, and I directed my life toward marriage and that ultimate role of housewife. During my junior year in high school I took courses geared for future homemakers. They included Home Economics and Clothing and Foods. In my senior year I took Advanced Clothing and Foods.

All this time, while I was preparing to become a housewife, my three brothers got college degrees. Then my brothers married teachers. All these degrees constantly reminded me that I lacked one of my own. As a result, I always felt inadequate—stupid, really—when I was surrounded by all the professionals in my family. When I hung my husband's sheepskins on the wall, I realized that I was the only member of the entire family who didn't have a degree, the only one who "didn't know anything."

Finally, thirteen years after I graduated from high school, I applied for admission to college. My acceptance had an immediately positive effect on my self-confidence. And attending college has continued this positive effect. ☐

(See "Going Back to School," by Kathleen Wilson, p. 323.)

COLLABORATIVE LEARNING

Work in a group of five to seven people. Have one person record the views expressed in the group and the consensus that the group arrives at collaboratively. Try to arrive at answers most people in the group can live with. Make sure the recorder makes note of any differences of opinion. Finally, review the recorder's notes. They should accurately state what the group has decided, and include differences of opinion and dissent. When you have finished the task, the recorder will report the results of the group's discussion to the rest of the class.

Task 1   *Personal Experience Story: Practice Analysis*

Have one person in the group (not the recorder) read aloud to the others in the group "How I Got to College" (p. 20). Then, working together, answer the following questions:

1. **What did the story mean to you** when you heard it for the first time? Explain in a sentence or two.
2. Now have someone read the story aloud again. Then, working collaboratively,
   a. **List the characters** in the story and describe the relationships among them. What does each relationship look like from the point of view of each character?
   b. **List the incidents** in the story. What does each incident look like from the point of view of each character?
   c. **List the settings** (the places) in which the incidents occur, and explain their significance to the story.
   d. **List the key words** (the most important words, or repeated words) used in the story. What do they tell us about the most important characters in the story, about what happens, and about how the events affect people's attitudes or feelings?
3. **Does the story seem complete?** Does the narrator seem to be leaving anything out that you want to know more about?
4. Focus on the person who is telling the story—the narrator.
   a. **How does the narrator seem to feel about the experience now?** How can you tell? How does the narrator's attitude differ from the way he or she seems to have felt about the experience when it occurred? How can you tell?
   b. If there is a difference between the narrator's present and past feelings about the experience, what does it mean to you personally that people's feelings about something that happens to them can change?
5. Reread what you wrote in answer to question 1 (what the story meant to you when you first heard it or read it). **What does the story mean to you now, after reading it more carefully and answering these questions?** What do you see in the story now that you didn't see before?
6. Review your answers to questions 1 through 5. Based on these answers **decide what you think the narrator feels is the most important aspect of the story.**

Task 2 *Personal Experience Story: Exchange and Analysis*

Exchange one of the stories you wrote for exercise 1 with another member of the class. Answer the preceding questions 1 through 6 about your partner's story.

When you get to question 6, this analysis of a real experience may produce some results that go quite a bit beyond those of the practice analysis. You may discover that your partner's understanding of your story differs from your own understanding of it, and that your understanding of your partner's story differs from his or hers. What happens to you may not mean the same thing to other people or be as important to them as it is to you. The reason for these differences is that people have different experiences and belong to different ethnic and cultural discourse communities—those groups of people we agree with and trust. As a result, they have different values and expectations.

These differences can mean that you may find out something new about your story and what it's about. That is, you may learn something new about yourself.

The differences between the way you understand your story and the way other people understand it can also mean, however, that in order to share with other people what your personal experiences mean to you, you have to find ways of talking about those experiences and explaining them that other people will understand.

When you and your partner tell each other what you see in each other's personal experience stories, you will find some aspects of your experience that are sharable and some that are not. You will begin to discover that you have had some experiences in common or that there are aspects of your partner's experience that are similar or related to your own.

On the basis of these common, similar, or related aspects of your experience, you will eventually be able to formulate the sort of generalization explained in exercise 4, a generalization that you can turn into the proposition of an essay. You will find points along the boundaries of the communities that the two of you belong to where it is possible to translate from the language your partner speaks to the one you speak, and vice versa. (For the dangers inherent in generalization, see Assumptions, p. 132.)

▷ EXERCISE 2   FREE WRITING (BRAINSTORMING)

This is an exercise in letting your mind run wild. It can be useful any time you want to find out what you're thinking. Sit down with plenty of paper and several well-sharpened pencils or a pen you can be sure won't run out of ink. Then let your mind go.

Begin by remembering what happened earlier today or during the past week—what you read, what you did, where you went, what other people said and what you said yourself. As you recollect, begin making lists. Don't try to make coherent sentences or paragraphs. Don't try to make sense. Write words and phrases, just as they come to you. Let your mind go as fast as it wants, where it wants. Keep writing things down in lists; keep up with your mind as best you can.

Write *everything* down, even if it seems silly or offensive or repetitious. Just scribble away.

Try doing this several times, perhaps at different times of day and in different places, until you get the knack of it and find the conditions that suit you best for doing this kind of work. If you draw a blank sometimes, don't force yourself. Relax. Come back to it later and try again.

When you have collected several pages of material, read them over all at once. Try to make some sense out of what you have written. Compare lists. Group words and phrases that appear in them. See where your mind went when you were not consciously controlling it. See what the material reveals about what your interests and ideas are. You may find some interests and ideas that you did not know you had.

Finally, write a short paragraph saying how your free writing turned out and the topics that came up in it. You might also say what you learned, if anything, about yourself.

COLLABORATIVE LEARNING

Brainstorming or free writing is an unfamiliar activity to many people. It may help to introduce yourself to free writing collaboratively. A group of writers can learn a lot about it in a single pleasant, if chaotic, hour.

Task   Collaborative Brainstorming

Have someone start the hour off by writing a single word on the blackboard or at the head of a sheet of paper. It should be a concrete word (satellite, dog, rifle, street) or an abstraction with powerful associations (money, fear).

From then on the rule is that everybody tosses in words and phrases that they associate with the original word or with any word that has been added to it by association. Try to keep your contributions concrete, but if you have to choose between abstractions and stopping the flow of association, by all means include the abstractions. The recorder—the person writing down words and phrases—may need a helper as people begin to catch on and the pace picks up. Everything should be written down as quickly as possible and totally at random.

After ten minutes or so, stop. Working together, classify into sets the words and phrases that you have collected. Many groupings will be possible and some will overlap. You can rearrange and add to the material as time permits.

Use the last fifteen minutes or so of the hour to begin making connections and drawing relationships among the sets of words. These connections and relationships can lead to ideas that you haven't thought of before, some of which may be a long way from the word you started off with.

The material you produce in this group is not likely to be very coherent. The incoherence results from the fact that group members have had different experiences, many belong to different communities, and everyone knows different things and talks about things differently. Writers have to develop their ideas in order to get through to people who differ from themselves.

▷ *EXERCISE 3   DRAWING ON WHAT YOU HAVE LEARNED*

One excellent source of topics for essays in a writing course is what you have learned in other courses, what you have learned in educational organizations that you belong to (such as scouting, 4-H, museum programs, science clubs, and so on), what you have learned at work, and what you have been reading. Some of the best sources of topics are introductory courses in subjects such as psychology, history, chemistry, sociology, anthropology, biology, music, mathematics, and art. Interesting material for essays can also be found in specialized courses such as forestry, engineering, business management, public administration, home economics, philosophy, nursing, and computer science.

Another excellent source of topics is an essay assigned to you to read in your writing course or some other course. Here the range of possible topics is if anything even greater than what you have learned in other courses. You can read any of the professionally written essays included in this book, you can read one in any anthology of essays, or you can read some student-written example essays in the Anthology of Student Essays, p. 319.

This invention exercise may be so fruitful and instructive that you can return to it more than once, if you like, drawing on several courses you have taken and analyzing several essays to develop topics for writing position papers.

When you are just starting out generating ideas and material, don't worry about whether someone else will understand you. Just explain what you know to yourself, in a way that satisfies you, in any order and in whatever language that comes most easily to you. Eventually, when you write an essay about something you have learned from another course or from what you have read, you will have to translate that specialized language into clearer, more familiar language, so that people who may not know what you know (other students and your writing teacher perhaps) can understand you.

RECALLING SOMETHING YOU HAVE LEARNED

Pick a course that you have taken or some other learning experience you have had. Write down everything you can remember learning. At this stage you can also say why you think it was a good thing to learn and why other people should learn it. But stress *what* you learned about: what caused the American Revolution, seven ways to stop erosion, how to repair a carburetor, the functions of DNA, why Hamlet puts off revenging his father's murder.

Second, read through this preliminary material and separate your statements about the subject matter itself from your remarks about the value of learning it. Put aside for now what you said about how valuable it was to learn the subject and why other people should learn it. You can use that later to introduce the essay you write that explains what you learned.

You have now isolated the part of your preliminary material that has to do with the subject itself. Exercise 4 will show you some ways to develop issues based on this method of exploring what you have learned and to formulate generalizations you can use to write an essay.

☐ EXAMPLE RECALLING SOMETHING YOU HAVE LEARNED

What I Learned in Film 1

Last semester I took Film 1: Basic Filmmaking. It was a terrific course. Everyone should take it because everyone likes to take pictures of their family and show them to their friends. Film 1 shows you how to do that on film, not just videotape. The advantage of film is that you can edit what you've taken and make it into a movie. The result of editing is that you get a real story, not just a string of miscellaneous shots of Junior jumping on the dog and Lucy falling over in the wading pool.

Film 1 taught me how to be a real amateur filmmaker. I learned how to write a treatment and sketch a storyboard. I learned how to plan out a movie with these two devices too, so that I wouldn't waste time and film. I learned the difference between long shots and close-ups and pans, and I actually had a chance to make a short movie using one of the school's super-8 cameras, use my own treatment and storyboard, and take different kinds of shots.

I guess it was learning how to plan making a movie with a storyboard and shooting script that was the most exciting part of the course for me. The teacher told us that, although we could use one of the school's cameras, we had to buy our own film. When she told us that, and told us how much film *cost*, she also said that since we were spending our money, we should try to figure out how to make our movie using the least amount of film.

Then everybody got scared. Nobody in the class knew how to plan like that. So then she explained how movies are made efficiently by shooting several scenes at one time that take place in the same location, whether or not they will occur in sequence in the movie. To do that they write a shooting script. Then they edit the film, splicing the scenes in where they belong.

So we all wrote shooting scripts, and I can tell you that writing mine saved me lots of money on film. And it also saved me lots of time when I shot the movie. □

Based on this free-written recollection of what he had learned in his film course, this student wrote the following essay:

 EXAMPLE ESSAY ——————————————————

The Role of Planning in Making Films

Greg Suarez

Making home movies on TV camcorders showing family members playing ball, celebrating birthdays, or having picnics is a popular hobby in the United States. All anyone has to do is aim the camera at what is happening and push the button. The story tells itself. But a small number of these amateurs shoot movies that tell a more complex story or that convey information in a more complex way. To do this, many of them still work with film. They use super-8 movie cameras and cut and splice their footage on inexpensive home-editing machines. To these die-hard filmmakers, filmmaking is more than just a hobby. It is an art medium and a medium of communication. It is not just something they enjoy doing. It is something they enjoy doing well. And it is a complicated process that requires several steps in order to produce the kind of film they aim for. The most important of these steps is planning.

There are two reasons why planning is essential to making good super-8 films. The first reason is that planning ensures that each shot (each segment of film recorded in one continuous run of the camera) and each sequence of shots will have the desired effect on viewers. Drawing up a storyboard ensures this. A storyboard consists of a rough sketch for each shot. Each sketch indicates the camera angle of the shot (high, low, eye level), camera distance (close-up, medium, long shot), and camera motion (pan, tracking, stationary). Each sketch also estimates how long each shot will last. The result—the storyboard—is an ordered collection of filming instructions that represents consecutive shots of the film as they will appear to the viewer.

The second reason planning is essential to making good films is that it ensures that the actual filming of the movie will be as uncomplicated and efficient as possible. Filming is governed by a shooting script. To write a shooting script, the filmmaker has to figure out the order in which to film the shots. A movie is seldom filmed in the order we see it in the final version. With most films it is not convenient to film the shots in the order they run in the story. Consider, for example, a film about a runner that begins at the beginning of the race, cuts to a scene with his family at home before the race, and ends with the finish of the race. It would be expensive and inefficient to shoot the film in this order. The sensible way to shoot the film would be to shoot the beginning and the end of the race all at once, film the scene at home, and then cut the race scene in two and splice the home scene between the two halves. A shooting script would tell the director and camera to do just that. □

DETAILED DESCRIPTIVE OUTLINE

PROPOSITION   Planning is essential to making a good film.

PLAN   Develop two reasons supporting the proposition.

PARAGRAPH 1   *says:* Many Americans make home movies on camcorders, but a few make more serious, complex films using super-8 film and equipment.

does: Introduces the proposition by identifying an activity and the group of people who engage in it. Distinguishes between two subcategories in this group according to their attitude toward the activity and the way they do it.

PARAGRAPH 2   *says:* Planning ensures the effect of the film on viewers. Writing a storyboard is the main technique in planning this effect.

does: Supports the proposition by subdividing it into two techniques. Identifies one technique. Describes the device used in the technique and lists four ways that device is used. States the value of the end result.

PARAGRAPH 3   *says:* Planning also ensures that shooting the film will be done efficiently. Writing a shooting script is the main technique in gaining efficiency.

does: Supports the proposition by identifying a second technique. Describes the device used in the technique. Explains how the device is used with an example that contrasts two ways of accomplishing a goal and shows how one way is more effective than the other.

ANALYZING SOMETHING YOU HAVE READ

First Step

In developing a topic from something you have read you have to become more familiar with it than you can be when you have read it only once. To become more familiar with something you have read, reread it and then analyze it by writing a basic descriptive outline of it.

First, number the paragraphs of the assigned essay lightly in pencil.

Then, working on your own, write a descriptive outline of the essay. If the essay is longer than five or six pages, treat clusters of related paragraphs as units. Your descriptive outline will explain how each cluster of paragraphs fits into the essay as a whole.

In writing your descriptive outline, use the following guide:

1. Write out the sentence in the essay that you think states the essay's position or main point most succinctly, or write the main point of the essay in your own words.

If you are not sure at first what the essay's main point is, write down two or three possibilities and continue with the descriptive outline. When you have finished writing your descriptive outline, decide which of your possible propositions now seems correct.

2. **Describe the essay's introduction.** Where does the introductory part of the essay end? Why do you think it ends there? How many paragraphs are in it?

Write the sentence in the introduction that you think states the introduction's main point most succinctly, or write what you think the introduction's main point is in your own words. Consider that sentence as being what the introduction *says*. (There is more about what an essay *says* on p. 154.)

3. **Describe the essay's ending.** Where does the essay begin to end? Why do you think the ending begins there? How many paragraphs are in the ending?

Write out the sentence in the ending that you think states the ending's main point most succinctly, or write what you think the ending's main point is in your own words. Think of that sentence as expressing what the ending *says*.

4. **Describe the middle of the essay—how the essay explores, explains, or defends its position or main point.** Begin by mapping the middle of the essay. First, subdivide it into parts, or chunks that seem to hang together. Then write out the sentence in each subdivision that states its main point most succinctly, or in your own words write what you think the main point of each subdivision is. Consider that sentence as being what you think each subdivision of the essay *says*.

5. Now **describe the essay's overall plan.** The essay's overall plan is what the essay *does* as a whole to explore, explain, or defend its position or main point. (There is more about what an essay *does* on p. 158.)

6. Based on this rereading and analysis of the essay, **revise your initial statement of the essay's proposition.**

COLLABORATIVE LEARNING

In groups of three, confer with other students who have written a descriptive outline of the same essay. Compare the descriptive outlines each of you have written, marking where they differ. Discuss why each of you described the essay in different ways. Then write a single descriptive outline that you can agree on and that represents your combined efforts.

Second Step

Having familiarized yourself with the essay in this way, to develop a topic from something you have read, treat what you have read as something you have learned.

Put the essay and your descriptive outline of it away. On another sheet, **list everything you can remember learning for the first time in reading that essay.** Add to the list everything in the essay that reminded you of something you already knew.

This is the material that you will use in exercise 4 to develop issues based on reading the essay and to formulate a generalization that you can use in writing an essay. That essay will be a position paper based on the essay you read. In it you can oppose or take issue with the essay. You can agree with or support the essay. Or you can use the essay as a point of departure or point of reference to develop a related idea of your own. (This exercise is similar to the collaborative learning task called Practice Descriptive Outline: Long Essays, p. 168. See also Part Three: Constructive Reading, p. 147.)

COLLABORATIVE LEARNING

No one knows how we get ideas. We know less about creativity than about any other aspect of the human mind. But we do know that conversation helps. Talking a topic over with sympathetic, like-minded peers can often lead to new and interesting thoughts. This probably happens because thought uses language that we learn by internalizing conversations we have with each other.

Other people don't get an idea for us when we talk a topic over with them. But we have all heard ourselves say when we're talking with someone, "Hey, that gives me an idea." Talking with other people can help us construct or assemble new ideas. So in the process of working up a topic for an essay, you can bring fellow students, friends, relatives, and teachers into the process. You can use them as sounding boards for ideas, as resources for information, and as prods that push you to explore, explain, and defend your ideas.

Task   *Topic Interviews*

Working in a group of three, tell each other what you think you are going to write about (your topic) and what you think you are going to say about your topic (your position).

Then, ask each other two questions:

"What do you want to know about my topic?" and

"What do you know about my topic that I can use in my essay?"

Your partners in this topic interview don't have to know anything about the subject that you expect to write about. That's your job. Their job is to help you recognize that you really do know something and that you really can explain it to other people.

In fact, it sometimes helps if your partners play dumb and ask obvious questions in order to draw you out. They can sometimes help you in this way to realize what you have to say and to help you put it into words that other people can understand.

▷ *Exercise 4   Questioning and Generalizing*

Exercises 1, 2, and 3 ask you to explore some of your private feelings, memories, and experiences (including learning experiences), and to express them in a loose, personal way without caring whether anyone will understand you or not. This is a first step in writing. Taking two more steps will help you understand yourself even better and also make your thoughts available to other people. These two steps are to discover issues implied in your experience and to draft generalizations that address those issues.

An *issue* is a *sharable concern*, a topic that people talk, read, and write about. Issues grow out of concrete experience and connect several similar or related experiences. You can state an issue in two ways. You can state it as a *noun phrase* (such as "water pollution" or "the relationship between governmental agencies and people's private lives") that identifies or labels the issue. Then you can restate it as a *question* that expresses relationships implied in the noun phrase (such as "What are we doing to pollute the oceans?", "How polluted are the oceans today, anyway?", "What can we do to keep the oceans clean?", or "How can people protect themselves from interference by governmental agencies?").

Some Ways to Question and Generalize

Suppose you are the manager of a store. Three people who work for you begin coming to work late three or four times a week. The similar or related concrete experiences that the issues grow out of are those late arrivals. It is easy to see what some of the issues are. **Noun phrase:** punctuality. **Questions:** Why have several people at one time been late to this job instead of just one at a time? Can this store succeed without punctual personnel? Does the need to be punctual cause employees disabling emotional stress?

Suppose then you find out that the first question may have a factual answer: All three people who are frequently late take the same bus to work, and recently the bus hasn't been running on time. This fact answers the question. But the factual answer about the bus not running on time leads to new issues. **Noun phrase:** public transportation. **Questions:** What can be done to make the buses run on time? What kind of service should bus companies provide? Should public transportation be a business or a government service? And so on.

Here it is probably worth noticing that most factual answers don't generate issues directly. Questions such as the following can be answered with numbers: How many tons of PCB enter the Atlantic Ocean annually through the Hudson River? At what rate does silt accumulate at the mouth of the Mississippi? How many barrels of crude oil are spilled annually on the high seas? But even questions with factual answers can lead to more questions (What are the sources of this information? How reliable is it? Who gathered it? Where does all that PCB come from? How many tons of PCB can the oceans absorb before human beings are affected?).

Here's another example. Suppose you remembered the time when you were very little and an older child cheated you out of a dime you were saving to buy something you wanted very much. That experience is just a private memory. But the issues implied in it may be of interest to many people. Everyone was once a child, vulnerable to the wiles of older children. As children, many people have had experiences similar to yours. Almost everyone takes care of children or deals with them in some way at some time, as a parent, a teacher, a shopkeeper, a camp counselor, a social worker. So as adults we may be faced with a similar situation occurring among the children we meet. And anyone, child or adult, may be taken in sometimes by an unscrupulous person who happens to be stronger, shrewder, or more experienced.

Although your own private experience is inevitably different from other people's experience, it also coincides with other people's experience at many points. At each of these points issues arise that are of direct interest to many people. Some of these issues are about relationships among small children. **Question:** What makes children selfish and cruel? Other issues concern relationships between adults and children. **Question:** How much should adults interfere in relations among small children? Still other issues concern socializing young children. **Question:** When should adults allow children to learn by experience, and when should adults protect children against injury and exploitation? There are also issues such as the nature of cheating, the seriousness of various forms of cheating, how cheating should be punished in children and adults, and so on.

Each of these issues can be turned into several generalizations by answering the questions they generate. A *generalization* is an observation or judgment that says something about more than one person, object, or experience. It says something about many similar people, objects, or experiences. A generalization is always a complete sentence.

For example, the issues implied in your experiences dealing with people coming in late for work lead to several possible generalizations.

ISSUE	GENERALIZATIONS

Punctuality

Why have several people at one time been late to this job?

Can this store succeed without punctual personnel?

Does the need to be punctual cause employees disabling emotional stress?

Service on Sluggard Bus Lines has gotten a lot worse.

Driving conditions on Route 7 are awful.

Most punctual people are successful.

Punctuality has nothing to do with success in business.

Employees' worries about being punctual make their sales decline.

Customers are willing to wait for cheerful, efficient service.

ISSUE	GENERALIZATIONS

Public Transportation

What kind of service should bus companies provide?

Should public transportation be a business or a government program?

What other aspects of people's lives are affected by a lack of public transportation?

Are some groups of people more affected by a lack of public transportation than others?

Can the government run an adequate transportation system?

What alternatives are there to public transportation?

Bus companies should concern themselves with their customers' needs, not their own.

All public transportation should be run by the government.

If the government ran public transportation, nobody would get anywhere on time.

Businesses should run transportation services for their employees.

The issues that arose out of your experience as a child also yield dozens of generalizations.

Children are cruel sometimes because they are selfish.

Children are sometimes cruel when they become afraid.

Children are cruel because they cannot conceive of the feelings (or the rights) of others.

Parents should let children learn by hard knocks.

An adult who stands by and watches a child get cheated without intervening is committing a crime.

Children who get away with cheating are on their way to becoming adult criminals.

Children who allow themselves to be cheated by another child are on their way to becoming adult criminals.

Trying to get away with something is only human.

And so on. You can probably think of many more.

Each of these generalizations may be stated in several different ways. They may be stated in clear, simple, concrete language, as they are expressed here, or they may be stated in language that is more vague, verbose, or abstract. For example, the clear generalization, "Children are cruel sometimes because they are selfish," may also be expressed in an unnecessarily complex way like this:

Young human progeny occasionally evidence lack of concern for the rights and feelings of peer group members because of a tendency to exclusivity and acquisitiveness.

And the sentence "Trying to get away with something is only human" may be expressed in a similarly verbose way:

The urge to discover means by which to avoid penalties for increasing one's own advantage at the expense of others is a fundamental characteristic found in all human beings.

In each case, the simpler way of expressing the idea is more precise and easier to understand. Since the purpose of drawing generalizations from personal experience is to share that experience with other people, always try to express yourself in the simplest, clearest, most precise way possible.

Another reason for stating a generalization succinctly and clearly is to preserve the power and human value that comes from intensely personal experience. To express an idea in simple language does not make it a simple-minded idea. Simple language just makes it easier for you to know what you mean and communicate it exactly. It helps you make up your mind and helps readers understand you. (There is more about writing clearly in Style, p. 137, and about issues in Contexts of Issues, Shareable Concerns, p. 197.)

WHAT TO DO

The purpose of exercise 4 is to discover some of the issues implied in the material that you developed for exercise 1, 2, or 3, and to formulate some generalizations that address these issues. These generalizations can then become propositions (what some people call thesis statements) for essays assigned in exercise 5 to 11. They state the position you are taking in the essay. So in preparing to write an essay there are three steps you can take.

First Step: Make a List

Make a list of issues that interest you. Read the work you did for exercise 1, 2, or 3. Think about what that material taken together says about you, your opinions, your beliefs, your interests, and your relationship to other people and the world you live in. Look for things about yourself that you didn't know before, and don't be surprised if you find some.

Then, list as many issues as you can think of based on the material in each exercise.

Some of the issues you draw from exercise 1 (personal experience) may be about the story you told in your reminiscence, family story, or account of change. Some of the issues may have to do with the way you or other people acted or what they may have felt or thought. Some issues may have to do with the choices people made or the situation people found themselves in. You may also feel that there are some issues in exercise 1 that are relevant to you as a writer.

Here are some examples.

Examples of issues drawn from personal experience. You might draw several issues from the example account of change in a person's attitude toward going to college, p. 20. How does the narrator's father feel about her? How do her brothers feel about her? How does the narrator feel about herself? How are each of these people likely to feel about the kind of change she underwent?

The example might generate the following issues, among others:

NOUN PHRASES

the value of a college education

changes in family attitudes toward women

relations between brothers and sisters

relations between fathers and daughters

roles of men and women at home

the difference between stupidity and ignorance

QUESTIONS

Why should women go to college?

Why shouldn't high schools teach everyone, boys and girls, about clothing and food?

Why should high schools bother to teach anyone, boys or girls, about clothing and food?

What is there about going to college that tends to make people feel better about themselves?

Examples of issues drawn from free writing or brainstorming. The issues you might draw from exercise 2, Free Writing (Brainstorming), p. 22, could be suggested by any number of words and phrases, and any combination of words and phrases, that appear on your lists. What did you find out about yourself and your interests from doing this exercise? What issues are implied in combining lists or contrasting them? What issues are implied by individual objects, places, people, or actions mentioned in your lists? You could also find some issues if you thought about the activity of brainstorming itself—how it affected you, why it worked or did not work in your case, and so on.

Examples of issues drawn from explaining something you have learned. The issues you draw from exercise 3 (explaining something you have learned) might be about the nature of what you learned (What is a benzene ring? What was the main cause of the American Revolution? What is erosion?). Other issues may have to do with a process (How is methyl alcohol synthesized? What were the immediate effects of the Boston Tea Party? How do various techniques to stop erosion work?). Still others may concern ways of applying or generalizing a key object, idea, or event (How can gasohol be made efficiently enough for use in automobiles? Was the Boston Tea Party an act of terrorism? Which methods for limiting erosion have worked best along the California coast-line?).

The explanation of something a person had learned about taking home movies (What I Learned in Film 1, p. 25) might generate the following issues, among others:

NOUN PHRASES

> film versus videotape
>
> making films efficiently
>
> making films cheaply

QUESTIONS

> What do a treatment, a storyboard, and a shooting script have to do with making a movie?
>
> What are long shots, close-ups, and pans?
>
> Why do you edit film?
>
> How do you edit film?

Second Step: Choose and Restate

After you have listed all the issues you can think of that are suggested by one of these invention exercises, choose several issues, restate them as questions if they are stated as noun phrases, and write two or three answers (generalizations) for each question.

Don't feel that you have to agree with every generalization you write. Remember that what you are doing here is trying to discover possibilities. You are not committing yourself to anything you say at this point. For the fun of it, you might try including some generalizations that you absolutely do not agree with. Some of these could negate each other. Others could oppose each other. For example, to *negate* the generalization "It's a nice day out," you would say "It's not a nice day out." To *oppose* the generalization "It's a nice day out," you would say "It's raining hard," or "It's snowing," or "We're having a dust storm."

Generalizations that negate and oppose

> **Issue stated as a noun phrase:** Punctuality
>
> **Issue stated as a question:** What good is being punctual?
>
> **Generalization:** Most punctual people are successful.
>
> **Negation:** Most punctual people are not successful.
>
> **Opposing generalization:** Punctuality has nothing to do with success.
>
> **Issue stated as a noun phrase:** Well-trained service personnel

Issue stated as a question: Why do businesses need well-trained service personnel?

Generalization: Customers have a right to skilled service.

Negation: Customers do not have a right to skilled service.

Opposing generalization: Skilled service is worth waiting for.

Issue stated as a noun phrase: Children's cruelty

Issue stated as a question: Why are children cruel?

Generalization: Children are cruel because they are selfish.

Negation: Children are not cruel because they are selfish.

Opposing generalization: Children are cruel because they cannot yet imagine other people's feelings and needs.

Ask yourself which of these generalizations you could explore, explain, or defend in a short position paper. A position paper (such as those assigned in exercises 5 through 9) does not set out to prove a statement. It sets out to explore its possibilities. It sets out to find out how true, convincing, or useful the generalization might be in a given situation or under given conditions and to persuade people that the position taken is worth considering.

Third Step: Choose and Discard

Finally, choose one of the generalizations to use as the proposition of the position paper you are getting ready to write. Notice when you do this exercise that drawing generalizations from exercise 1, 2, or 3 leaves behind a great deal of concrete material—details of the experience, names, places, words and phrases, things people said, particular characteristics of people, things, and events. You will be able to use some of these generalizations as the propositions of position papers.

COLLABORATIVE LEARNING

Work in groups of three, taking turns stating the issue to be discussed.

Task   Issues and Generalizations

State an issue in question form. Then ask your partners to write out two or three possible answers to that question in the form of generalizations.

26

Finally, decide as a group whether or not each generalization could be explored, explained, or defended in a short position paper. What would you have to know about the topic in order to do that? How do you think you might go about learning what you would need to know in order to do it? Could the topic be explored, explained, or defended in a short position paper? What would you have to know about the topic in order to do that? How do you think you might go about learning what you would need to know in order to do it?

Writing Position Papers

The purpose of Part One was to help you learn how to make your own experiences accessible and useful to other people by drawing issues from them and stating those issues in clear, well-expressed generalizations. In Part Two each exercise asks you to choose one of those generalizations (or make up another one), commit yourself to it for the time being, and develop it in a position paper. A *position paper* explains what your own position on the topic is at the moment: what you think about it, what you know and can explain about it, what your views on it are, and why.

The purpose of a position paper is to explore your position in a well-developed, well-planned way and convince other people that your position is worth considering. Its purpose is to begin a conversation or to enter a conversation that's already going on. Its purpose is not to end conversation by proving your point. It is to get other people to join you in thinking about a topic you are interested in and about a position you have taken on it. The response you want from your readers isn't "By George, you're right." The response you want is "Gee, I never thought of it that way. I'll have to give that some thought."

Writing a good position paper begins with committing yourself tentatively, for the time being, to a generalization—maybe one of the generalizations you worked out in exercises 1 through 4. When you commit yourself for the time being to a generalization, you turn it into a proposition. A *proposition* is the most important sentence in a position paper. It succinctly states the position you are taking. It says in a nutshell what the whole essay says.

Once you have stated your position, the next step is to develop it. **You develop your position by exploring, explaining, or defending it.** To help you learn a simple, commonly used way to develop almost any position on almost any topic, exercises 5 through 9 ask you to practice the same basic form: an introduction and two paragraphs of exploration, explanation, or defense. But they also show you how to vary the way you explore, explain, or defend your position within that form. Each exercise offers you a different template or pattern to use as a guide in choosing reasons to support your position, in arranging them effectively, and in relating or linking them to each other and to the essay's proposition sentence.

That is, one thing essay exercises 5 through 9 have in common is that each one introduces you to one kind of *explanatory subordination*, one way of subordinating one part of an exploration, explanation, or defense to other parts. The reason for learning these different kinds of explanatory subordination is that, in the long run, you will be able to choose among several options whenever you set out to think through and develop a position you are taking. They give you a repertoire of organizational types that frees you to support different positions in different ways, or in some cases, to support the same position in different ways under different circumstances.

When you choose among templates or patterns of explanatory subordination, you are deciding what you have to say and how much you have to say. For example, if you think you have *two* good reasons in support of your position, you would choose the template introduced in exercise 5. If you think you have *several* pretty good reasons, some better than others, you would use Nestorian Order (exercise 6). If you think there may be some *disagreement* about the position you are taking, you would choose one of the templates that takes disagreement into consideration explicitly: a straw man argument or a concession (exercises 7 through 9). When you write longer essays, you may find use for several of these kinds of explanatory subordination in different sections of the essay. (There is more about writing long essays in Length: Term Papers and Other Long Writing Assignments, p. 231 and Practice Descriptive Outline: Long Essays, p. 168)

The three-paragraph form these essay assignments require is not the only form to write an essay in. But it is a good one. And it can teach you how to construct reasons that effectively synthesize and subordinate concrete experiences so as to give them new significance, a significance that affects other people as well as yourself. (See Reasons, p. 96.) When you can write easily in this form, you will be able to write many different kinds of essays with confidence—not just position papers, but also examination essays, term papers, and reports. Eventually you will be able to make up your own ways to vary the basic form, explore other common forms, and even invent forms that are entirely new.

But for now, please stick to this one form.

Each of the five essays should be about five hundred words. You don't have to count words. Anywhere between 480 and 520 will do just fine.

Make an estimate. The average will be about two pages typed, double-spaced.

Write each five-hundred word paper in three paragraphs: one paragraph to introduce the proposition and two paragraphs to defend it, with transitional generalizations at the beginning of paragraphs 2 and 3 tying each paragraph to what went before. Don't write a "conclusion" for any of these first five essays. Don't even write a "concluding sentence." When you get through defending the proposition, stop. That may hurt at first, but let it hurt. Resist the urge to "conclude." (See "But Why Can't I Write a 'Conclusion'?", p. 131.)

Every essay you write from now on should take a position. State your position as a proposition in the last sentence of the first paragraph. Explore, explain, or defend it in paragraphs 2 and 3.

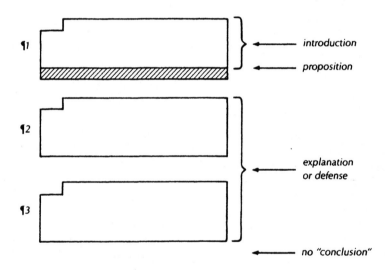

Notice that these essay exercises do not ask you to write from the top down. They ask you to write from the inside out. Your finished essays will begin at the top with an introduction. But do not begin writing the essay where the essay will begin when you are finished with it—don't begin writing by trying to write an introduction. Warm up for a while at first if you like, writing whatever comes into your head. But when you finally get down to business, begin as far inside as you can go, at the very core of the essay, by writing a proposition. Next, continue working on the "insides" by exploring, explaining, or defending the proposition.

Then go back to the top and write a paragraph introducing the proposition. Your introductory paragraph is the essay's "outsides"—its wrappings.

31

When you have written your essay in that order, you will have written it from the inside out. (There is more about writing introductions beginning on p. 81, and in Part Four: Reaching Out to Members of Other Communities, p. 189.)

▷ EXERCISE 5   TWO REASONS

Exercise 5 is a five-hundred word position paper in three paragraphs: an introductory paragraph ending with a proposition, and two paragraphs of exploration, explanation, or defense. Each paragraph develops a single reason that supports or explains the proposition. Don't write a conclusion. But write a descriptive outline that explains what the essay *does* and *says*.

Write the essay from the inside out. Approach it this way:

THINK OF A TOPIC

Draw upon some of the material you developed in the invention exercises 1 through 4, or develop a topic in your own way, on your own. Write about anything, as long as it means something to you and is something you feel you can take a position on and make interesting to other people. (For topics based on personal experience, see Exercise 1. Mining the Past, p. 16. For topics based on a reading assignment, see Analyzing Something You Have Read, p. 28, or Recalling Something You Have Learned, p. 25.)

In most cases it is entirely up to you what to write about, although there are some limits. One limit is an external one. You may sometimes find that it will save time if your class or your teacher defines a general area of choice, such as entertainment, politics, family, or something you learned in another course, or if your teacher gives you a reading assignment and asks you to base your essay on what you read. Then you are not likely to feel quite so totally at sea trying to find a topic to write on. Or the class may agree that you will write on a topic that everyone in the class knows something about, so that you will be able to discuss the substance as well as the form of your essays. (See Essay Exchange and Descriptive, Evaluative, and Substantive Peer Review, p. 185.)

Another limit is more personal. You may find that you write better on some topics than on others. For example, experience suggests that it is hard to learn much about writing when you try to explore topics that trouble you emotionally or topics that do not engage you at all. When you write on topics that trouble you, you may become so involved in the topic that you find it hard to pay attention to craftsmanship: the *way* you are writing the essay. When you write on topics that don't engage you at all, you are likely to be too bored to produce a readable essay. It's almost impossible to interest someone else in a position that doesn't interest you.

But within these very broad limits, you are free to choose your own topic, decide the position you want to take on that topic, and explore, explain, and defend your position in a way that will convince your readers to take it seriously and give it some thought. If you find that you cannot explain or defend your position, at least you have learned that. So you can change your position, or you can give it up and take a position on another topic entirely.

Be a little adventurous in picking topics. Take some risks. Avoid the Groucho Marx effect. The story goes that when Groucho was invited to join a club, he turned it down, because he didn't want to belong to any club that would have him as a member. As a writer you may sometimes feel that way too. You may feel that you don't want to write on a topic that interests you because, if it interests you, it must inevitably be uninteresting to other people. That simply isn't true. Your friends at least will be interested in what you're interested in just because you are interested in it. And later in this book you will find out how to interest people other than your close friends. (See Speaking Other People's Language, p. 191.)

In another version of the same attitude, you may feel that everybody must already know about anything that you happen to know. What's the point of telling them? That's not true either. You know a lot that other people don't know and would be fascinated to discover. You just don't know yet that you know it, or else you just don't know yet that they don't. Not only is it not true that everyone already knows what you know, but one of the biggest problems you are likely to have in writing is that people do not know enough about what you know to follow what you have to say about it. Then the question is, how much background do you have to give your readers, and what should you explain so that they'll be able to follow?

Overcoming these feelings of self-deprecation can be the most important step you take toward becoming a good writer. It may be the first and most important step you take toward beginning new conversations and joining conversations already in progress.

Suppose, for example, you happen to be very interested in transportation, in particular the future of automobiles and highway systems. Boring, right? Who cares, right?

Maybe. But there is a lot to write about on that topic. You could write about safety, for instance. More people are killed every year on American highways than in airplane crashes. That's pretty interesting. The Federal Interstate Highway System is pothole city. I bet you know a lot of people who hate the national 65 m.p.h. speed limit. And maybe you even know one or two who ignore it. You could also write about bridge design and repair or energy conservation. Cars and transportation are *your* interests. Choose a topic you would most like to write about and choose a position you would like to take on that topic.

THINK OF A TENTATIVE PROPOSITION

Write a generalization on the topic (see Exercise 4 Questioning and Generalizing, p. 31). Pick an aspect of the topic that interests you most and relates to your own experience in some way. You might write down several generalizations and then pick the one that you like the best and that you think you have the most to say about. Make a tentative commitment to it for the time being. That generalization, until you decide to change it, will be the proposition of your essay.

Suppose you decide to write about the future of cars as a means of transportation. What can you say about that? What position could you take? You might say, "Cars are obsolete." Or, "In ten years there will not be a quarter of the cars on the road that there are on the road today." Or maybe you could take the other side: "Cars are here to stay because we can't get along without them." You could make any of these into a strong proposition. (See Propositions, p. 85.)

THINK OF WAYS TO EXPLORE, EXPLAIN, OR DEFEND YOUR POSITION

As you think about what position to take, also think over what you could say to defend or explain your position. Draw as much as you can on immediate personal experience. Reading is of course one kind of immediate personal experience, so one source of things to say to defend your position might be something you have read. For these exercises it is important to stay as personally involved as possible in what you are writing. If you like, you can reuse some of the material you produced in exercises 1 through 4.

The essays you write for this first set of exercises are not research essays. But if you need more material to develop your explanation than you have at hand, you can draw upon popular and easily accessible material: TV, newspapers, news magazines, and so on. If you do use information from one of these sources, be sure you indicate in your essay what that source was. For example, say something like, "*Time* magazine reported last week that . . ." or "The president said in his last news conference that . . . ," and so on.

WRITE A TENTATIVE PROPOSITION AND EXPLORE, EXPLAIN, OR DEFEND IT IN THE FORM THE ASSIGNMENT REQUIRES

Now begin writing. Write your tentative proposition (the position you are taking in the essay) in a single sentence. Beneath it, write an explanation or defense of the proposition in two paragraphs. For exercise 5, put one supporting reason in each paragraph, and develop each reason separately.

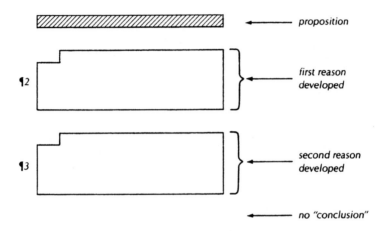

Let's say you decided to defend the following proposition: "Cars may be on the way out as our major means of transportation." And you decided that the two best reasons for thinking that cars may be becoming obsolete are that (1) our oil supply is going to diminish so much in the next hundred years that we will not be able to afford to waste it by burning gasoline to get around, and (2) people want to get places faster than cars can possibly take them.

In that case, you would **develop one of these reasons in paragraph 2** by saying how much oil scientists estimate is left on earth, and by matching that figure with the equivalent amount of crude oil automobiles burn up as gasoline every day. In the long run, you might say, whether the supply lasts one hundred years or one thousand years does not matter much. As the supply diminishes it can never be replaced. Its price will rise so high that no one will be able to afford it. You might also refer to the inefficiency of internal combustion engines: how they waste more oil than they turn into power.

Then, you would **develop the other reason in paragraph 3** by calling on your own experiences traveling and the experiences of your family or friends. Some statistics might be useful here, but you can certainly get along without them. Instead, you could tell an anecdote about, say, somebody you know who used to drive from Chicago to Omaha every week on business. Now, you say, he can't be bothered. Last year he hooked up his Omaha office by modem to his computer in Chicago, bought a fax machine, and needs to go to Omaha only once a month. And he flies there in a quarter of the time it used to take him to drive. (See Paragraph Development, p. 111, and Reasons, p. 96.)

In writing these two paragraphs of explanation, remember that your proposition is not sacred just because you committed yourself to it for the time being and wrote it down. It's tentative. It is the position you have taken in order to explore it and see what sense you can make of it. As you write and think further about the idea, you may want to change your mind. If you do change your mind, change the proposition. The only thing to make sure of is that when you have finished the essay, the explanation and the proposition match. Adjust one or the other of them until they do. (See Propositions, p. 85.)

When you have finished defending the proposition at the end of paragraph 3, stop. Resist the urge to write a "conclusion." (See "But Why Can't I Write a 'Conclusion'?", p. 131.)

WRITE AN INTRODUCTION

Now think about what you could say to introduce readers to the position you have taken. Try to put yourself in your readers' position for a moment. Assume at first that they are not much interested in what you are writing about. What could you say that might catch their interest?

For starters, you could try to show them that they really are interested, whether they know it or not. In the essay about cars, for example, you could say that there are more cars on the road today than ever before, and yet there are signs that the public is not entirely happy with that situation. You could bring in air pollution, government investigation of car safety, and recent experience with high-speed trains. That could lead you to speculate that travel by car may have reached a high-water mark, and that the future trend will be for people to use cars as we know them less rather than more. Indeed, you could say, it looks like cars may be on the way out. And there you would be, back to your proposition. (See Introductions, p. 81, and Part Four: Reaching Out to Members of Other Communities, p. 189.)

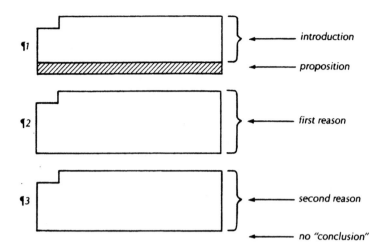

CHECK THE PARAGRAPH TRANSITIONS

Paragraphs in an essay do not stand alone. They are related to each other and they are related especially to the proposition of the essay. One of a writer's most important jobs is to show these relationships very clearly so that the reader will always know what the writer is up to. Writers have to very clearly lead, so that readers can very easily follow.

The first major transition in an essay is between the introduction and the proposition at the end of the first paragraph. You have to make sure that the reader understands just how the introduction is related to the proposition that it introduces.

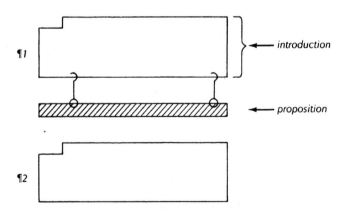

end of ¶1
transition
proposition

. . . the trend will be for people to use cars as we know them less rather than more. In fact, it looks as if cars may be on the way out as our major means of transportation.

The second major transition in an essay is between paragraph 1 and paragraph 2. Usually writers show the relationship of each paragraph to other paragraphs and to the proposition at the beginning of each paragraph. That is, the transition to paragraph 2 should occur in the first sentence of paragraph 2, not in the last sentence of paragraph 1. And the transition to paragraph 3 should occur in the first sentence of paragraph 3. Transitions reach back, not forward.

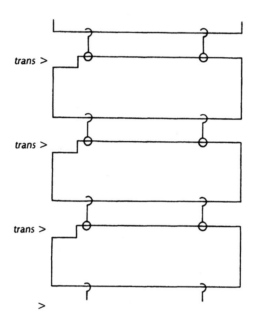

end of ¶1
   proposition

... the trend will be for people to use cars as we know them less rather than more. In fact, it looks as if cars may be on the way out as our major means of transportation.

¶2 transition

And it is high time they were. The world oil supply, which cars depend on for fuel, has been diminishing at the rate of. . . .

The first sentence of paragraph 2 is the transition sentence. The words *and* and *they* in that sentence connect the first element of the explanation or defense with the last sentence in paragraph 1. The last sentence in paragraph 1 is the proposition. It expresses the central idea of the whole essay.

Because the proposition is nearby, the transition sentence for paragraph 2 is relatively easy to write. The third major transition in an essay, the transition to paragraph 3, is a little harder. It has two jobs to do, not just one. It has to connect the second element of the explanation or defense with two parts of the essay. It connects paragraph 3 with the end of paragraph 2. It also connects paragraph 3 with the proposition.

But the proposition is way back at the end of paragraph 1.

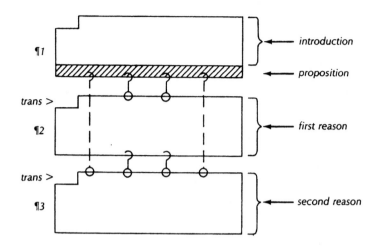

end of ¶1 proposition	. . . the trend will be for people to use cars as we know them less rather than more. In fact, it looks as if cars may be on the way out as our major means of transportation.
¶2 transition	And it is high time they were. The world oil supply, which cars depend on for fuel, has been diminishing at the rate
last sentence in ¶2	of. . . . But we travel these super routes at speeds that threaten our lives no matter how safely our cars may be built.
¶3 transition to proposition, to ¶2 third reason	*Cars will become less important in the future <u>not only because they waste fuel and are dangerous</u>,* but also because they waste time and human energy. The man I worked for last summer used to drive from Chicago to Omaha on business once a week. It would take him on the average. . . .

Notice, finally, that a transition sentence at the beginning of a paragraph is usually also the topic sentence of the paragraph. That is, a paragraph transition sentence is usually a transitional generalization. A *transitional generalization* does two things. It states succinctly what the paragraph goes on to explain. *And* it shows how the paragraph is related to the proposition of the essay. (See Reasons, p. 96, and Unity and Coherence, p. 116.)

WRITE A DESCRIPTIVE OUTLINE AND REVISE

You have now written the first draft of your essay. **Before you revise it, write a descriptive outline of the essay** as it stands. Writing descriptive outlines is a way of learning to read constructively. One purpose of writing a descriptive outline is to make both writing and learning to write more actively collaborative. In writing descriptive outlines and conferring about them, you learn the language that readers and writers use when they talk constructively with each other about reading and writing. (There is more about constructive reading and about writing descriptive outlines in Part Three: Constructive Reading, p. 147.)

Set your descriptive outline up in this way:

PROPOSITION

    PLAN

PARAGRAPH 1 *says:*

         does:

PARAGRAPH 2 *says:*

         does:

PARAGRAPH 3 *says:*

         does:

For the **proposition,** write the proposition sentence as it appears in your essay, the last sentence in the first paragraph. For the **plan,** say how the parts of the essay are arranged. In exercise 5, your plan is to explore, explain, or defend two reasons supporting the proposition.

For **what each paragraph** *says,* write a one-sentence paraphrase or summary of the paragraph; put the paragraph in a nutshell. (See What an Essay *Says,* p. 154.)

Up to this point, a descriptive outline differs little from a conventional sentence outline. What distinguishes descriptive outlines is the second item in the description of each paragraph, **what each paragraph** *does.* What a paragraph *does* is not what it *says.* It is not the point the paragraph makes or its message. When you say what a paragraph *does* you explain

- how the paragraph is related to the essay's proposition,
- how the paragraph is related to preceding paragraphs,
- the function the paragraph serves in the essay, and
- the way the paragraph is organized internally to perform that function.

The idea that every paragraph *does* something in an essay can be difficult to grasp. But to become a good writer, you have to understand this important concept. Every part of an essay serves a function in the essay as a whole, just as every part of a sailboat, an airplane, or the human body serves a function in the sailboat, airplane, or body as a whole. Sails and motors propel boats and planes. Rudders steer them. The heart pumps blood. Nails protect the ends of our fingers. And paragraphs explore, explain, or defend the proposition or main point of an essay. These functions are the "work" that each part does. Each part is designed and constructed to do that work effectively.

Paragraphs can of course do many things and serve many functions. For example, they can argue logically, analyze, and explain. They can list or catalogue objects, events, scenes, witnesses, problems, and so on. They can tell stories. They can describe things, people, places, or processes. They can show the logical relations among the parts of an argument.

But no paragraph does any of these things for its own sake. Every paragraph serves some purpose in the essay as a whole. Paragraphs analyze, describe, argue, and so on, in order to help explore, explain, or defend the main point of the essay, the position expressed in the essay's proposition. When you explain in a descriptive outline what a paragraph *does*, you are explaining how it is organized in order to explore, explain, or defend the proposition. So, **a basic *does* statement has two parts:**

1. it *names* the work that the paragraph does relative to the proposition, and
2. it *explains* how the paragraph does that work.

For the essay on cars, for example, a basic descriptive outline might look something like this:

PROPOSITION   Cars may be on the way out as our major means of transportation.

PLAN   Support the proposition with two reasons.

PARAGRAPH 1   *says:* Use of cars is at a peak, but there are signs of change.

does: Introduces the proposition by describing the present situation.

PARAGRAPH 2   *says:* Our oil supply is diminishing, a loss made worse by the way cars waste gas.

does: Develops the first reason by citing comparative statistics.

PARAGRAPH 3   *says:* Cars waste time and human energy.

does: Develops the second reason by telling an anecdote.

Notice that the *does* statements in this descriptive outline do not mention the content of the paragraph. They say nothing about cars. All reference to the essay's content, cars, is saved for the *says* statements.

Does statements only explain paragraph organization and development. A *does* statement such as "introduces the proposition by discussing how car use may be changing" would be incorrect because it both describes form and paraphrases content.

The example is a *basic* descriptive outline because its *does* statements explain the paragraph's relation to the proposition and only very succinctly explain how the paragraph works. A more *detailed* descriptive outline would explain further, for example, how the statistics cited in paragraph 2 are organized, classified, and compared (in summaries, in tables, in lists, or whatever), how the examples are related to the rest of the paragraph, and so on. (There is an example of a basic descriptive outline and a detailed descriptive outline written for the same essay on p. 77 [exercise 9]. Also, see What an Essay *Does*, p. 158, and Getting Ready to Write a Detailed *Does* Statement, p. 165.)

By writing a descriptive outline that explains the function and organization of every paragraph, you will learn exactly what is going on in the essay. This is the long-range reason for writing a descriptive outline: to gain some objectivity on your writing. A descriptive outline written after you have written a first draft of the essay, but before you write out the final draft, gives you a way to check how well the essay is organized.

After you write a descriptive outline, reread the essay and compare each paragraph with what you say it *says* and *does* in the descriptive outline. Do they match? If they do, write out the final draft of the essay. If they don't match, change the outline to match the essay or change the essay to match the outline. It makes no difference which, as long as in the end the descriptive outline accurately describes the final draft of the essay. *Accurately* means that the descriptive outline describes what is really going on in the paper, not what you think should be going on or what you want to be going on.

You should write an accurate descriptive outline for every essay exercise you write for this book. Remember, write your descriptive outline between drafts, not before you begin writing the essay or after you have finished writing the final draft. Correct the outline as you revise the essay. **Use your descriptive outline as a tool for rewriting.**

READ THE ESSAY ALOUD AND POLISH IT

The last thing to do before you copy or type the final draft of your essay is to read the whole thing aloud to yourself.

Listen to what you have said and how you have said it. Make what you have written sound as much as you can like standard written English. If it doesn't, change it. If it sounds as if you have tried to make it seem grand or impressive, change it. Try to make your writing sound clear, so that someone you know could easily understand what you mean. (See Style, p. 137.)

Reading your essay to yourself is also practice for reading it aloud to your fellow writers. One purpose of reading aloud to each other in class is to make both writing and learning to write more actively collaborative. Read slowly and clearly, and after paragraph 1 announce the number of each paragraph before you begin to read it ("Paragraph 2 . . . ," "Paragraph 3 . . ."). Ask your listeners to restate in their own words the position they think you are taking in the essay. Compare what they say with what you want your position to be. Consider revising the way you state your position (the essay's proposition) if your listeners haven't gotten the main point you intended to make. Then ask them what else they think you could do to improve the essay. (There is more about reading aloud in Part Three: Constructive Reading, p. 147.)

MAKE A FINAL COPY

The last thing to do in writing an essay is to copy or type it neatly, double-spaced. Give it a title. Leave ample margins at the top, bottom, and sides of each sheet. Check your spelling and punctuate correctly. Try not to leave blotches or smudges on the essay. In general, prepare the copy so that the reader will be favorably disposed to reading it. (See the section on preparing a manuscript in a standard writing handbook.)

COLLABORATIVE LEARNING

Task 1   Reading Aloud

Read your essay aloud to the other students in the class.

To prepare, read your essay aloud at home to yourself or to a friend or a member of your family.

Read slowly and clearly so that the people listening can understand what you are saying. Read the title first. Then, as you go along, announce the number of each paragraph following paragraph 1.

Task 2   Essay Exchange and Peer Conference

Exchange essays with another writer in the class, but keep the descriptive outline that you wrote of your own essay.

Write a descriptive outline of your partner's essay.

In the next class, confer with your partner. Examine the two descriptive outlines of your essay, your own and your partner's. Underline where they differ. Try to discover why the two of you described the same essay in different ways. Discuss how to make both descriptions more thorough and accurate. But at this stage please do not try to evaluate each other's essays.

At the end of your descriptive outline, write a note explaining how the conference went from your point of view. If you think now that you would like to make some changes in your essay, in the descriptive outline you wrote of it, or in both, say so in your note and explain. (There is an example of essay exchange and peer review in Example Descriptive and Evaluative Peer Review, p. 177.)

☐ EXAMPLE ESSAY ─────────────────────────────

To Number or Not to Number

Barbara Pleener Sackrowitz

Modern advances in technology and science have increased the amount that students have to learn. In order to help students learn all they have to learn, society has had to revise its educational programs and its teaching methods. Society has also had to raise standards in the schools in order to ensure the highest degree of scholastic excellence. Unfortunately, this effort has led to competition for grades among students, rather than a desire to perfect skills. One result of this competition is that the alphabetical grading system has become more important than any subject taught, and is therefore undermining the educational system rather than improving it. One solution to this problem is to do away with grades entirely. Many people feel that this solution would be impractical. Another is to make the grading system reflect more accurately the differences in quality among student work. To make grading more fair in this respect, the alphabetical grading system should be replaced by a number system.

The alphabetical grading system, consisting of grades A, B, C, D, and F, is by no means a subtle or fair way to represent the quality of students' work. At best it is a rough guideline. Teachers must translate fine distinctions into awkward blocks of evaluation. Plenty of personal bias is involved in evaluating student work in the first place. Add to that the need to make alphabetical equivalents, and evaluation becomes impossibly biased. To one teacher a grade of 79 is a low B, but to another it is a high C. The result is that grading becomes a serious point of contention between student and teacher. Assigning a numerical grade to begin with does not pose this problem. If students get a 79, that is their mark. No adjustment or interpretation is possible. Teachers are saved from an onslaught of student protests, and from the additional agony of trying to be fair to students through a system that is inherently unfair. And students are not likely to want to contest the fairness of their grades, since they will feel that the grades they have received represent accurately their teachers' estimate of their work.

Because of its greater accuracy, the numerical grading system also gives a more reliable account of a student's potential. If alphabetical grades do not give a clear picture of what students have achieved in the past, how can they possibly give an idea of what they are likely to achieve in the future? The main reason for this lack of clarity is that grades are computerized. Besides teacher bias, there is computer bias. Students who get Cs for a near-80 average wind up looking just like students who barely made 70. But can one honestly say that these students have the same potential? Obviously some students could do 10 percent better than others, yet the computer inevitably ignores this significant difference. The graduate schools or businesses that the student applies to are not aware of the discrepancy. So not only do student and teacher lose, but society as a whole loses as well. □

BASIC DESCRIPTIVE OUTLINE

PROPOSITION To make grading fair, the alphabetical grading system should be replaced by a number system.

PLAN Develop two reasons supporting the proposition.

PARAGRAPH 1 *says:* Grading has become competitive, but doing away with grades is impractical; a middle ground is to make grading more accurate and fair.

does: Introduces the proposition by explaining the problem.

PARAGRAPH 2 *says:* Numerical grading is fairer to students and less agonizing for teachers.

does: Develops the first reason by comparing two systems.

PARAGRAPH 3 *says:* Numerical grading represents students' career potential more accurately.

does: Develops the second reason by speculating about long-run effects.

 EXAMPLE ESSAY ————————————————————————

Haiti: The Need to Unite

Annemarie Edwards

The early leaders of Haiti wanted their country to be free, humane, and peaceful. But from its inception, Haiti's politics have been violent, its wealth has been unfairly distributed, and living conditions for most Haitians have been poor. Three major issues underlie the country's problems. One is the question of color. Distinctions between blacks and mulattoes arose during slavery and have always been a source of conflict. The second issue is economic. Haiti's economy is dependent on agriculture. Most peasants own the land they work, but they lack the knowledge and equipment to use their land productively. And foreigners doing business in Haiti spend most of their income overseas, limiting reinvestment in the country and keeping unemployment high. The third issue is education. Most Haitians are illiterate and few speak the official language, French. Instead, most speak creole, a dialect of French. David Nicholls's *From Dessalines to Duvalier: Race, Color, and National Independence in Haiti* shows that these problems, which have always been a part of Haitian life, can be solved, but all of the possible solutions require Haitians to unite. It is clear that unity of purpose has been rare in Haitian history. Yet it is also clear that Haitians can unite effectively.

For one thing, history shows that Haitians have united at crucial times in the past when their freedom and independence were threatened by external force. In 1802, blacks and mulattoes put aside the question of color and stopped fighting each other long enough to crush the French, who intended to enslave both groups. They united again after the invasion of Haiti by the United States in 1915. This intervention was brought on by civil unrest throughout the country. The peasants and members of the elite worked to rid their country of foreigners. The peasants, armed with machetes, attacked American military personnel. The elites attacked the Americans in local journals and refused to work with them. Together, they made the economic situation that created the unrest in the first place even worse, making it clear to the Americans that their presence was unwanted. The Haitians' attacks, although they did not drive the Americans away, made them realize that they were doing more harm than good.

Haitians have also demonstrated their ability to work together outside their country. In fact, ironically, Haitians abroad have united in ways that they have been unable to do, or have refused to do, at home. Haitian-Americans are among the most unified of all Caribbean-Americans. They have created publications such as *Haiti Progress* and *Haiti Insight*. They have established organizations, such as the Haitian American Alliance, that help Haitian-Americans cope with situations arising from mass migration such as employment, language acquisition, and family disruption. They have taken advantage of public education in the United States, reducing illiteracy. Although most Haitian-Americans continue to speak creole with each other, increasingly adults and of course children born in the United States speak, read, and write English. Haitian-Americans are also a fast growing economic force. Whereas in Haiti itself Haitians have rarely reinvested in their own people, in the United States reinvestment is common. As a result, unemployment among Haitian-Americans is very low. In New York City, for example, Haitian-Americans have established themselves in the dry-cleaning and catering businesses by helping new arrivals accumulate the capital they need in order to buy going concerns or build entirely new business establishments. □

WORK CITED

Nicholls, David. *From Dessalines to Duvalier: Race, Color, and National Independence in Haiti.* Cambridge: Cambridge Univ. Press, 1979.

▷ EXERCISE 6   NESTORIAN ORDER

Exercise 6 is also a five-hundred word position paper in three paragraphs: an introductory paragraph ending with a proposition and two paragraphs of exploration, explanation, or defense. Each paragraph develops a single reason that supports or explains the proposition. Don't write a "conclusion." But write a descriptive outline that explains what an essay *does* and *says*.

In these respects, exercise 6 is just like exercise 5. In another important respect, though, exercise 6 differs a good deal from exercise 5.

Begin your work by thinking of a topic. You might reread the material that you generated in exercises 1 through 4 to see what new ideas it may suggest. Or you might do one of those invention exercises again, in your head or on paper, in order to generate new material and new ideas. Once you have a tentative topic, decide what position you want to take on it—that is, decide on a proposition. (For a topic based on personal experience, see Exercise 1   Mining the Past, p. 16. For a topic based on a reading assignment, see Analyzing Something You Have Read, p. 28 and Recalling Something You Have Learned, p. 25.)

Then, instead of giving two reasons to support your position as you did for exercise 5, think of several reasons and develop them according to Nestorian order. In Nestorian order (named after the character Nestor in the *Iliad*), you **create a climax by putting the best reason last.** The *best reason* is the strongest or most effective explanation or defense, the one that explores the position you are taking most deeply, or the one you can develop most fully and convincingly. **Put the second best reason first. Arrange the rest in between.**

For this exercise, present your arguments this way: Begin paragraph 2 with the second best reason and finish the paragraph with minor reasons. Develop the strongest argument, the major reason, in paragraph 3.

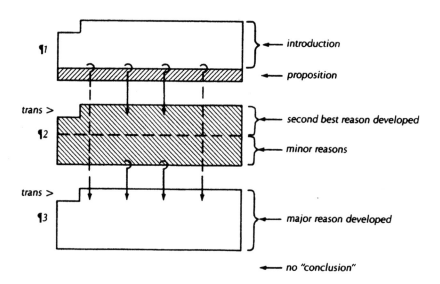

Notice that this exercise adds a new difficulty. Paragraphs 1 and 3 are formally the same as they are in exercise 5, but paragraph 2 is different. It presents a new problem in coherence. You have to make paragraph 2 coherent, despite the fact that you are giving several reasons in it, not just one. You have to avoid just giving a list. You have to show that there is a relationship among the parts of the paragraph. That is, **you have to create coherence among the parts of this paragraph** just as you have to create coherence between paragraphs.

You can make it easier to gain coherence in paragraph 2 by arranging the minor reasons in a sequence that will make them easy to connect. Then you can find ways to relate them so that they will not seem to the reader to be just dumped in. (See Unity and Coherence, p. 116.)

Read through the procedure outlined in exercise 5. Follow it again. Remember, the difference this time is that you have to settle on a proposition that you can defend in paragraphs organized as this essay exercise requires: several reasons, not just two. To find a topic for this exercise, think about things that interest you for a lot of different reasons, think about things you like to do for a lot of different reasons, or think about things you think people should do for a lot of different reasons.

For example, the essay supporting the proposition on cars (Exercise 5, p. 44) develops two reasons. But suppose you had in mind more than two reasons—say, five. Then you could write the essay in Nestorian order. To do that, in paragraph 2 you would shorten the first reason, giving the statistics on oil depletion more briefly, and then give several minor reasons in support of the proposition. Those reasons might be the air pollution caused by cars, lack of safety at high speeds, and discomfort driving on long, straight superhighways.

You might create coherence in paragraph 2 in the following way:

end of ¶1 *proposition*	. . . the trend will be for people to use cars as we know them less rather than more. In fact, it looks as if cars may be on the way out as our major means of transportation.
¶2 transition *second best reason*	And it is high time they were. The world oil supply, which cars depend on for fuel, has been diminishing at the rate of millions of barrels a year. Some geologists estimate that at the present rate of increase in use of oil, we will have drained off almost all the earth's oil by the year 2000. The worst of this
transition	situation is that because of the poor efficiency of the internal combustion engine, most of that oil won't even produce useful
first minor reason	energy. Most of it will pass off in exhaust from car motors. This exhaust is still another reason cars may disappear, that is, because they pollute the air. Eighty percent of Los Angeles's pollution comes from cars, and the worst of it cannot be
transition	trapped by any known exhaust cleansing device. And the new superhighways throughout the whole country do more than
second minor reason	choke our lungs. Their monotony stultifies our minds with boredom when we drive on them. Gone are the days of pleas-
transition	ant drives over the bridge and into the woods to grandmother's house. Today it's through the mountain and around the city.
third minor reason	But we travel these super routes at speeds that threaten our lives no matter how safely our cars may be built.
¶3 transition	Cars will become less important in the future not only because they waste fuel and are dangerous, but also because
major reason	they waste time and human energy. The man I worked for last summer used to drive every week from Chicago to Omaha. . . .

Remember:

- Think of a subject.
- Think of a tentative proposition.
- Think of ways to explore, explain, or defend your position.
- Write the proposition and explore, explain, or defend it in the form required by the assignment.
- Write an introduction.
- Check the transitions.
- Write a descriptive outline and revise.
- Read the paper aloud and polish it.
- Make the final copy.

COLLABORATIVE LEARNING

Task 1   Reading Aloud

Follow the instructions for reading aloud on p. 55.

Task 2   Essay Exchange and Peer Conference

Follow the instructions for essay exchange and peer conference on p. 55.

☐ EXAMPLE ESSAY ─────────────────────

The Sea Gull: A Great Play Makes a Bad Movie

Dana Wenger Morris

I was excited to read that a movie had been made of Chekhov's *The Sea Gull. The Sea Gull* seems very contemporary, even though it was written over ninety years ago. It is what teachers would call a perfect example of "universality." Two very "now" terms, isolation and alienation, although not used in the play, describe the situation of all the characters. The play begins with talk that exposes the narrowness of contemporary theater and dramatic arts. Before the play is over, talk between the major characters pries open their inner lives. That the play dramatizes these many levels of human experience makes it great. But though *The Sea Gull* is a great play, it makes a disappointing movie.

The fault is not all the play's. Sidney Lumet, the movie's director, fails in several respects. His greatest mistake is in casting. Although the cast includes fine actors and actresses, it is all wrong for the play. One of the problems is that many of the performers are so well-known that it is hard to picture them in the roles Lumet casts them in. Vanessa Redgrave seems out of place and unconvincing as Nina, a young, naive, and stagestruck country girl. Simone Signoret plays Arkadina, the aging actress who will not believe she is getting old. Arkadina arouses mixed feelings when we read the play, among them sympathy, but Signoret's film portrayal leaves us with only ill feeling. Lumet also interfered with the author's intention in directing the movie. The visual quality of movies has to be used very subtly in filming an understated play like *The Sea Gull*. Yet Lumet exaggerates with visual effects. By showing the dead body of Konstantin, who everybody knows has shot himself, the effect of the moment is lost. Between the third and fourth acts two years pass, but in the movie, the characters seem to have aged ten years. And the dialogue of the play, which gets philosophical quite often, seems unreal on the screen. On stage, the lines are believable because the human relations involved seem natural. Close-ups of people talking isolate characters and destroy the effect of the scene as a whole.

Probably the best explanation for the failure of the picture is that Chekhov is a playwright who uses little action, the very stuff that movies are made of. The stage does not allow much movement, but a film demands it. Movies also tend to shift scenes rapidly, in order to show different people doing different things. Chekhov, of course, does not allow for these shifts of scene. The play has four acts. Each act takes place in the same place. The scenery remains the same. The actors enter and exit. Finally movies have their own ways of showing change and passage of time. All a playwright has to do is announce passage of time in the program, but the same device used in movies is absurd. The most ludicrous moment in the movie version of *The Sea Gull* comes between the third and fourth acts when the words "Two Years Later" appear on the screen. At this point the viewer cannot help but be convinced that this play belongs where it was born, on the stage. □

BASIC DESCRIPTIVE OUTLINE

PROPOSITION   *The Sea Gull* is a great play but it makes a disappointing movie.

PLAN	State a proposition and develop six reasons supporting it, arranged in Nestorian order.
PARAGRAPH 1	*says:* The theme of *The Sea Gull* is very contemporary.
	does: Introduces the proposition by telling why the play is great.
PARAGRAPH 2	*says:* It is the director's fault that the movie is miscast, unsubtle, technically poor, and reproduces the philosophical dialogue badly.
	does: States five reasons for the movie's failure.
PARAGRAPH 3	*says: The Sea Gull* is a play without much action.
	does: States the main reason for the movie's failure.

☐ EXAMPLE ESSAY

Euthanasia: A Violation of Human Life

Karen Dickman Friedman

Over the years, medical science has progressed until it has provided us with cures for many diseases that were once considered terminal. Polio is gone. Small pox is gone. Tuberculosis has become less of a threat. Yet we are still left with many incurable diseases, and our modern age has provided us with a whole slew of new diseases yet to be explored: new viruses, new cancers, and, of course, AIDS. As a result, the issue of euthanasia is still with us as well. Euthanasia is defined in the clean, clinical way typical of the medical profession as "the mode or act of inducing death painlessly or as a relief from pain." More commonly, we know it as "mercy killing." Ending a person's pain seems on the face of it such a kind and humane thing to do, for the benefit of the victims of pain and for the benefit of their loved ones watching them suffer. But it is not what it seems. Euthanasia, a violation of human life, cannot be justified.

One of the most serious problems involved in the practice of euthanasia is the difficulty of determining the validity of a person's request to die. When terminally ill but mentally competent patients choose to die, do they do so because they are depressed, and might later change their mind? Or do they choose this course because they believe that the relatives who care for them can no longer afford that care either emotionally or financially? Are the people closest to dying patients subtly coaching them, perhaps without being aware of it, to exercise the right to die by choice? Or is the request truly genuine: the patients who ask for relief really are in intolerable pain, really want to die, and are giving their rational and thoroughly considered consent? Another serious problem is the possibility that a cure for the patient's illness may soon be found. In 1921, a man diagnosed with diabetes was told that there was no hope. For two years he fought a losing battle against the disease. Then, in 1923, insulin became widely available. The man survived. Besides the last minute discovery of a cure, there are also many incidents of the remission of disease, including cancer, for no apparent reason. Prognosis is fallible. We know for certain that only death is irreversible. Where there's life, there's hope.

To many people, the most persuasive argument against euthanasia, though, is religious. One deeply rooted religious objection is that to choose death is to play God. It is God's prerogative to determine the end of life, not man's. Religious people believe, furthermore, that the proper attitude towards life is awe and reverence. Tampering with life or ending it prematurely is a profanation of the sacred. There are also those who believe that suffering is part of the divine plan for the good of man, and therefore we must accept it. They look at suffering before death from a spiritual point of view, as a time of absolution. People who suffer undergo punishment in this world instead of the world to come. Even secularized, this spiritual argument is significant. As a famous British lawyer once said with regard to euthanasia, "the final stage of an incurable illness ... can be a vital part of a person's life, reconciling him to life and to death and giving him interior peace." □

▷ *Exercise 7   Straw Man*

Exercises 7 and 8 are designed to give you further practice in paragraph development.

Begin once again by exploring issues raised by your own experience, as in exercises 1 through 4. But this time look for a controversial topic, one about which you think other people's opinions may differ a great deal from your own. In this exercise, you will set up one of those opposing opinions as a straw man and knock it down.

The assignment asks for a five-hundred word position paper in three paragraphs: an introductory paragraph ending with a proposition and two paragraphs of exploration, explanation, or defense. Each paragraph develops a single reason that supports or explains the proposition. Don't write a "conclusion." But write a descriptive outline that explains what the essay *does* and *says*. Write the essay from the inside out.

The difference between this exercise and exercises 5 and 6 lies in the way you defend the proposition in paragraphs 2 and 3. In exercises 5 and 6 you argued positively. You presented the best reasons you could to explore, explain, or defend your proposition. Here you argue negatively. You acknowledge that yours is not the only possible position to take on the issue, and you oppose those who think differently. This means that in paragraph 2 you will give reasons *against* the position you take in the proposition. Set out in paragraph 2 to show that the position you have taken is wrong. Then in paragraph 3 support the proposition by refuting the argument against it made in paragraph 2.

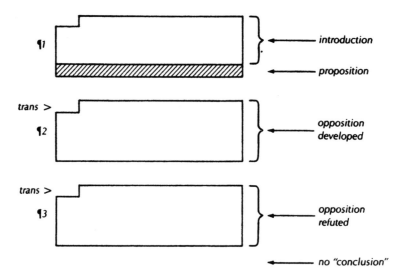

The transition sentence at the beginning of paragraph 2 should indicate clearly that the position you take in that paragraph is not your own but someone else's—someone who would disagree with your proposition. At the beginning of paragraph 2 you can say something like the following:

There are two schools of thought on this issue. One says . . .

Some people take exactly the opposite position. They say . . .

That, in any case, is what Democrats would say. Republicans, on the other hand, would object strenuously . . .

The lumber industry opposes this environmental position as being extreme . . .

In contrast, the National League resisted the temptation to use designated hitters on grounds that . . .

The transition sentence at the beginning of paragraph 3, then, should indicate clearly that you are now going to support the proposition directly by refuting the position taken in paragraph 2. At the beginning of paragraph 3 you can say something like the following:

The other school of thought finds all of these arguments untenable. It says . . .

But that position is obviously illogical . . .

Throughout the campaign, the Democrats have refuted these arguments, saying . . .

Naturally the environmentalists regard every one of these arguments offered by the lumber industry as biased in favor of business interests . . .

The American League says that all these reasons against using designated hitters are old-fashioned in the age of television . . .

Review the assignment for exercise 5 again before you begin. Go about writing this essay as you went about writing that one. By now you should be getting in the habit of approaching an essay in the following way:

- Think of a topic.
- Think of a tentative proposition.
- Think of ways to explore, explain, or defend your position.
- Explore, explain, or defend the proposition in the form required by the assignment.
- Write an introduction.
- Check the transitions.
- Write a descriptive outline and revise the essay.
- Read the paper aloud and polish it.
- Make a final copy.

COLLABORATIVE LEARNING

Task 1   Reading Aloud

Follow the instructions for reading aloud on p. 55.

Task 2   *Essay Exchange and Peer Conference*

Follow the instructions for essay exchange and peer conference on p. 55.

☐ EXAMPLE ESSAY ————————————————————

Keep NASA Going

Eric Raps

"Man has always gone where he has been able to go," said astronaut Michael Collins after successfully completing his moon mission. Many people share this belief. People should go to the moon, and beyond, because now for the first time in history we *can* go. We can at last satisfy our curiosity about bodies in space other than Earth. Without NASA, the United States space program, we would never have been able to explore this new frontier. Our moon landing was truly the climax of modern science and technology, and yet space exploration is only just beginning. We must keep NASA going, but not just to satisfy our pride and curiosity. NASA is important for the welfare of us all.

Not everyone agrees with this point of view. Ever since the space program began, it has been criticized as humanly irrelevant. Some people have called a moon shot nothing but a big toy for grownups. Others have called the space program an example of American middle-class conspicuous consumption in a category with oversized cars, water skiing, and snowmobiles. Worst of all, some say, not only has the space program accomplished nothing of value, it has wasted money that should have been spent on overdue social programs. According to this view, our cities, our national parks, our educational and health programs, our legal systems, have all been deprived of funds they need to modernize and serve people properly. People who take this position are fond of quoting figures that show how many hospitals, school lunches, playgrounds, drug addiction centers, or reforestation plans could be financed with the money spent on one moon shot.

What these people fail to understand is that space projects are exactly the sort of activity human beings should be spending their money on to advance knowledge and technology, so that the many human problems we have can get solved. The amount of money spent on a moon shot is trivial compared with the amount of money the United States spends in even a few months on warfare and defense weapons. And that money really does go down the drain, because war is unproductive, weapons are continually becoming obsolete, and killing people is, to say the least, a corrupt and self-defeating activity. In contrast, what space exploration does is help improve the conception human beings have of themselves. It creates a belief among people all over Earth that the world is small, vulnerable, and absolutely unique. As a result people will become impatient with poor living conditions and a polluted environment. In short space exploration has the effect of centering our attention on the quality of human life. It contributes to man's understanding of the human condition, of the interdependence of all people, and therefore of the need, to put it in very simple terms, to be better housekeepers here on Earth and to take better care of each other. ☐

BASIC DESCRIPTIVE OUTLINE

PROPOSITION   NASA is important for the welfare of us all.

PLAN   Oppose the proposition, and then refute the opposition.

PARAGRAPH 1   *says:* Space exploration satisfies our curiosity and pride.

does: Introduces the proposition by quoting an authority and discussing the quotation.

PARAGRAPH 2   *says:* Space exploration is wasteful.

does: Opposes the proposition with one argument.

PARAGRAPH 3   *says:* Space exploration changes our awareness of ourselves and what life is about.

does: Refutes the opposition by showing that it is narrow-minded.

(The difference between basic and detailed descriptive outlines is explained in Part Three: Constructive Reading. See also the example basic and detailed descriptive outlines written for the same essay on pp. 77–78.)

▷ EXERCISE 8   STRAW MAN AND ONE REASON

This assignment, like the last one, asks for a five-hundred word position paper in three paragraphs: an introductory paragraph ending with a proposition and two paragraphs of exploration, explanation, or defense.

Each paragraph develops a single reason that supports or explains the proposition. Don't write a "conclusion." But write a descriptive outline that explains what the essay *does* and *says*. Write the essay from the inside out.

What distinguishes this exercise is that it combines two types of exploration, explanation, or defense, the one used in exercise 5 and the one used in exercise 7. You recognize here, as you did in exercise 7, that there are other positions that can be taken on the issue, but you refute them. Then, as you did in exercise 5, you argue in favor of your own position.

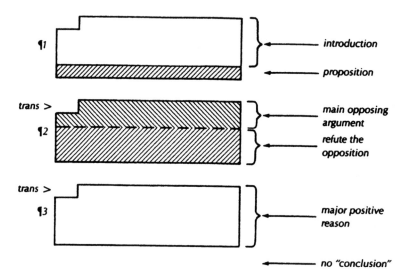

In this essay begin paragraph 2 as you began paragraph 2 in exercise 7, with an argument that opposes the position you have taken in the proposition. **In the rest of paragraph 2 refute that opposition.** Then in paragraph 3 develop a positive reason in support of your position, just as you did in paragraphs 2 and 3 of exercise 5.

The transition sentence at the beginning of paragraph 2 should make clear that the position taken in that paragraph is an opposing position, not your own. Later in the paragraph include a transition sentence or phrase that indicates that what follows supports your position by refuting the opposing position. That is, paragraph 2 in this exercise does in a single paragraph (paragraph 2) what you did in paragraphs 2 and 3 together in exercise 7.

The transition to paragraph 3 should indicate that this paragraph supports your position in a different, more positive way. You can say something like the following:

But this conflict misses the point. The real reason that . . .

The most logical argument is clearly that . . .

Whatever the two national parties say on this issue, most voters today seem to have it pretty much figured out for themselves. The position most people seem to take is . . .

Reasonable people are likely to take the environmentalist position today, however, because . . .

Since the two leagues have now gone their own way on the issue of the designated hitter, the fans have gotten the best of the deal because . . .

Begin once again by thinking over your own experience and what you have learned in other courses in order to find an issue that you can see has two sides (even though you may agree with only one of them). Write a descriptive outline and use it to help you revise.

COLLABORATIVE LEARNING

Task 1   Reading Aloud

Follow the instructions for reading aloud on p. 55.

Task 2   Essay Exchange and Peer Conference

Follow the instructions for essay exchange and peer conference on p. 55.

☐ EXAMPLE ESSAY ——————————————————

A Flood of Debate

Jay Blickstein

Curt Flood was one of baseball's finest outfielders. Or at least he was until the 1970 baseball season. That year, Flood was traded from the Saint Louis Cardinals to the Philadelphia Phillies. Rather than be separated from his home and business interests in Saint Louis, Flood sat out the entire season and legally challenged one of the pillars of baseball's establishment: the so-called "reserve clause." The clause, which bound a player to a team until the team chose to release him, was used by the Cardinal management to justify Flood's trade. Flood argued, however, that the reserve clause was a form of "involuntary servitude," and reduced baseball players to slaves, to be bought and sold at a team's discretion. I could not agree with him more. Baseball's reserve clause had to be abolished.

The management of almost every big-league team defended the validity of the reserve clause. They claimed that it kept ballplayers on the teams that had spent so much time and money developing their talent. The clause also prevented a bidding war between teams for big-league talent and lent order and stability to the game. But these arguments lose all validity when the reserve clause is considered from the player's viewpoint. Even though a team spends time and money developing a ballplayer's talent, he amply repays the team by drawing in the huge crowds that come to see him in action. Certainly the big-league teams can agree among themselves to prevent a bidding war, even without the reserve clause. The baseball establishment's claim that a reserve clause gives the game order and stability is disproved by such incidents as the 1919 "Black Sox" scandal, in which eight players were expelled from baseball for accepting payoffs from gamblers. The reason for the players' actions: woefully inadequate salaries, thanks to the reserve clause.

But baseball's reserve clause had to be abolished for a much more important reason—the way it affected ballplayers as human beings. When a player signed a major-league contract, he was in effect signing away his soul and was reduced to being bought or sold at a club owner's whim. Often, a ballplayer was sent against his will to a city far away from home, family, and friends. A player also could be kept in a city he did not like, and with a team he did not want to play for. Consequently, the player suffered and his performance on the field suffered as well. The team lost, baseball lost, and so did the fans. □

BASIC DESCRIPTIVE OUTLINE

PROPOSITION   Baseball's reserve clause had to be abolished.

PLAN   To oppose the proposition, refute the opposition, and develop one positive reason in support of the proposition.

PARAGRAPH 1   *says:* Because he was traded against his will, Curt Flood began a court fight against the reserve clause.

does: Introduces the proposition by telling the story of one man's struggle against an oppressive rule.

PARAGRAPH 2   *says:* Baseball's establishment had its reasons for supporting the reserve clause, but they lose their

validity when considered from the player's viewpoint.

does: Opposes the proposition and then refutes the
opposition.

PARAGRAPH 3   *says:* The reserve clause had to be abolished because
it adversely affected ballplayers as human beings.

does: Develops a major positive reason in support
of the proposition.

(The difference between basic and detailed descriptive outlines is
explained in Part Three: Constructive Reading. See also the example
basic and detailed descriptive outlines written for the same essay on pp.
77–78.)

▷ *EXERCISE 9   CONCESSION*

This is the last assignment in Part Two, offering you the last in the series
of templates or patterns to use as a guide for choosing reasons to support
your position, for arranging reasons in an effective sequence of explanatory subordination, and for relating or linking reasons to each other
and to the essay's proposition. Like the rest, it is a five-hundred word,
three-paragraph position paper with a descriptive outline and no
"conclusion."

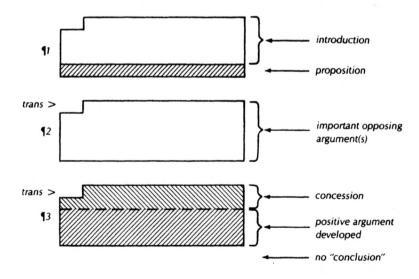

The diagram indicates that this paper is like exercises 7 and 8. You
present an important argument against the position you have taken in

your proposition. But in this exercise, instead of refuting this opposing view, at the beginning of paragraph 3 you **concede the validity of the opposing view.** Then you offer your own defense of the proposition in spite of this concession, and explain that your position is also valid, and is, you believe, the stronger of the two.

This is a more tactful and practical explanation or defense than the one used in exercises 7 and 8. In those exercises you acknowledged that other points of view exist, but you treated the people who hold those views rather badly. You implied or stated flatly that they were wrong, and you showed why. For writing practice, that was acceptable. The purpose was to learn to discover the opposing views and find out in what way those views were vulnerable. But simply to refute other people's views abruptly is obviously not the best way to change their minds, not to mention remaining friends with them.

A more tactful and therefore more friendly and politic approach is to acknowledge that there might be something to another person's position. So in this exercise you show that you do realize that many issues may be approached and resolved in two (or more) reasonable ways. In most of our everyday affairs, you imply, other people's opinions are often just as sensible and legitimate—from their point of view—as your own. In this essay you take this fact into consideration, even as you strive to make those who may oppose you willing to consider your opinions and judgments.

As in exercise 8, the transition at the beginning of paragraph 2 in this essay should make clear whose argument you are giving: someone else's, not your own. You should then develop and explain that opposing view thoroughly and fairly. In a concession essay it is important not to misrepresent or understate the opposition's case. The reason for this is that in the transition to paragraph 3 you will be conceding that the alternative position you have just outlined is neither unreasonable nor irresponsible. You are taking it seriously. Nevertheless, your transition continues, there is more to be said in favor of the position you have taken in the proposition of this essay. This is the position that the rest of paragraph 3 supports.

To find a topic for this exercise, think carefully about your own interests, and especially about why and how your interests seem to conflict with the interests of other people whom you respect.

Don't forget to write a descriptive outline and use it to improve your essay.

COLLABORATIVE LEARNING

Task 1   Reading Aloud

Follow the instructions for reading aloud on p. 55.

Task 2   Essay Exchange and Peer Conference

This collaborative learning exercise takes a step beyond those offered in exercises 5 through 8. It asks you to evaluate your classmate's essay after you write a descriptive outline of it.

Exchange essays with another writer in the class, but keep the descriptive outline that you wrote of your own essay.

Write a descriptive outline of your partner's essay.

Then **write an evaluation of your partner's essay,** following the instructions for peer evaluation in Part Three: Constructive Reading and the Example Descriptive and Evaluative Peer Review, p. 177.

In the next class, confer with your partner. First, examine the two descriptive outlines of your essay, your own and your partner's. Underline where they differ. Try to discover why the two of you described the same essay in different ways. Discuss how to make both descriptions more thorough and accurate.

Then read your evaluation of each other's essay aloud to each other. Help each other plan a revision that will improve the essays in every way you can. As a reader, help the writer know what you think the essay needs to help you understand it. As a writer, ask your reader to help you improve parts of the essay that you are still not satisfied with.

Write a note at the end of your descriptive outline explaining how the conference went from your point of view. If you think now that you would like to make some changes in your essay, in the descriptive outline you wrote of it, or in both, say so in your note and explain.

Revise the essay if you think it needs it.

☐ EXAMPLE ESSAY ───────────────────────────

Project Head Start

Lucille Tornatore Orlando

No project for disadvantaged children has received the public attention given to Head Start. Project Head Start is a program for preschool children that was developed and funded by the Office of Economic Opportunity. It was created with the idea of helping young children overcome the deficiencies of their early environment. Children were to come from the ghetto areas of cities, rural areas, Indian reservations, and Eskimo villages. The program was conceived in November 1964, and it began in June 1965. While it was being planned, the project was referred to as the Kiddie Corps. It was expected at that time that fifty to one-hundred-thousand children would be involved in the eight-week summer program. By late February 1965, the response was so great that the estimated enrollment was raised to between five and six hundred thousand. The project also eventually involved a hundred-thousand adults: parents, teachers, physicians, psychologists, and social workers. Experts from every branch of social studies, medicine, and education teamed up to give culturally deprived children a better chance at learning. The philosophy of the program came from the belief of those who initiated it that disadvantaged children need not fail in school or in life. In pursuing this goal, Project Head Start has become a necessary part of our present-day system of education.

Despite its promise, Head Start still meets with a great deal of resistance. Many local school boards and teachers complain that they sometimes do not get the money the government promised for supplies and salaries. The general public complains that disorganization in the program wastes public funds. Then, although the idea of the program generates much enthusiasm, in some places parents at first refuse to help. This is a great handicap, and members of the program struggle valiantly to overcome it. Parents simply have to help if Head Start is going to work. If children leave their preschool center only to return home to a suspicious and uninterested family, much of the progress they have made is lost. One of the things parents object to most is the age of many Head Start teachers. Some parents and community leaders feel that youthful teachers mean inexperienced teachers. Parents also complain that the grouping in classrooms is too homogeneous, an inevitable effect since the program was of course developed specifically for poor people. And finally, cynical observers note that once Head Start children enter primary school the gains they register during the preschool period tend to disappear.

Much of this criticism of Head Start is fair, factual, and substantial. Some of it is unanswerable. Like any government sponsored program, Project Head Start has had its pitfalls and imperfections. Its gains, however, have outweighed its shortcomings. The project recognizes, for example, that many American children are deprived in many ways, and that the lack of intellectual stimulation is only one of these ways. This is the main reason for its success. The program provides health services, information for parents, food for undernourished children, and means for organizing communities. Nevertheless, teaching children is its main aim. Something that helps Head Start do this job is its teacher-pupil ratio, which in general is one to thirteen. Young, fresh, innovative teachers can capitalize on the opportunity that small classes provide. Activities include art, stories, science activities, creative play, and visits to museums, parks, and landmarks. The teachers' youth also has a tendency to enhance the communication between them and their pupils. And once the initial misunderstanding and antagonism between parents and teacher are overcome, Head Start provides room for parent involvement in education. In some instances it also provides jobs for those who are unskilled but who are eager to work to help their own people. Parents serve on committees and become teacher's aides, storytellers, cooks, carpenters, and secretaries. But the biggest sign of success is the response of the children themselves. Many things middle-class children take for granted, Head Start children experience for the first time. There have been some dramatic instances of children who have never seen themselves in a mirror before or used a telephone. But for nearly all children there was a first in painting, using crayons, visiting a zoo, a supermarket, and a fire station. And to a child, these things are more than education. They are life itself. □

BASIC DESCRIPTIVE OUTLINE

PROPOSITION In pursuing this goal, Project Head Start has become a necessary part of our present-day system of education.

PLAN Raise arguments opposing the proposition, and then, conceding the validity of some of these arguments, offer reasons in defense of the proposition.

PARAGRAPH 1 *says:* Project Head Start began in 1964 to give culturally deprived children a better chance to learn.

does: Introduces the proposition by describing a public program.

PARAGRAPH 2 *says:* Head Start has met with a great deal of resistance.

does: Gives the arguments against the program and points out its failures.

PARAGRAPH 3 *says:* The achievements of Head Start in helping children learn outweigh its shortcomings.

does: Concedes the validity of some criticism, and then argues in favor of the proposition.

DETAILED DESCRIPTIVE OUTLINE

PROPOSITION In pursuing this goal, Project Head Start has become a necessary part of our present-day system of education.

PLAN   Raise arguments opposing the proposition, and then, conceding the validity of some of these arguments, offer reasons in defense of the proposition.

PARAGRAPH 1   *says:* Project Head Start began in 1964 to give culturally deprived children a better chance to learn.

does: Introduces the proposition by describing a government program. Sentences 1 through 4 state its goal and give a general description. Sentences 5 through 8 trace its early history. Sentences 6 through 8 state expectations and outcome. Sentences 9 through 10 describe the program's human resources. Sentence 11 restates its goal as a general principle.

PARAGRAPH 2   *says:* Head Start has met with a great deal of resistance.

does: Gives the arguments against the program and points out its failures. Sentence 1 makes a transition by introducing arguments against the proposition. Sentences 2 through 10 classify criticism of the program by source. This section has two parts. Sentences 2 through 3 describe criticism from two sources. Sentences 4 through 10 detail criticism from a major source and are subdivided still further: sentences 4 through 7, criticism by passive resistance and its effects; sentences 8 through 10, complaints. Sentence 11 describes evidence of failure.

PARAGRAPH 3   *says:* The achievements of Head Start in helping children learn outweigh its shortcomings.

does: Concedes the validity of some criticism, and then argues in favor of the proposition. Sentences 1 through 3 concede the limitations as explained in paragraph 2. Sentence 4 is a transition that reevaluates the opposition. Sentences 5 through 8 define the program's rationale as a list of goals. Sentences 9 through 21 analyze its success in achieving these goals. Sentences 9 through 12 define one cause of success. Sentences 13 through 15 define a second. Sentences 16 through 21 describe a sign of success, giving striking details in sentences 18 through 21 and showing why this particular supporting point is so important.

(The difference between basic and detailed descriptive outlines is explained in Part Three: Constructive Reading, p. 147)

☐ EXAMPLE ESSAY

The Blessings of Urbanization

Annette Brill

I have always enjoyed living in a big city. There is a constant feeling of activity, movement, hustle and bustle. There is a sense of things happening: theaters and music halls, brightly lit streets, busy crowds. At lunch hour, when I walk down the streets of the city I live in, it seems to me that I can feel the pulse of the city in my veins. People walk faster in the city, talk faster in the city, and always seem to have someplace to go and something to do. I take these blessings of city living so much for granted that it's hard for me to imagine what life must have been like before big cities existed. And all the really big cities that I know simply didn't exist two hundred years ago. Most of them became what they are today during the rapid urbanization of the nineteenth-century Industrial Revolution. In those days, urbanization was a symbol of progress and optimism. It meant that, for the most part, the world was getting better and better for more and more people every day. And urbanization still means that today.

Of course there are many people who hate city life and will do anything to get out of town into the country. They think that urbanization was a disaster. And they are right about the beginning of urbanization. Throughout the middle of the nineteenth century there was not room enough for everyone who wanted to live in cities. Cities became overcrowded. Developers built long rows of the smallest possible buildings, stuffed with the smallest possible apartments, crammed onto the smallest possible lots. These buildings lacked sun and fresh air, they had no backyards or front yards, and only an alley separated one row of houses from the next. Living conditions were unsanitary and unhealthy, with open drains and sewers running down the middle of the streets. Water became contaminated. People died of diseases that spread like wildfire. People could only accept these life-threatening, overcrowded conditions fatalistically.

People who condemn these horrible conditions are right to do so. No human being should be expected to live in them, including the millions still forced to do so. And yet, for all its limitations, in the long run urbanization has had more positive effects on modern life than negative ones. Many of these benefits are so familiar today that it is easy to forget that not long ago they were novelties. Two of them are fresh running water and sanitary plumbing. Lack of drink-

67

able water and the difficulty of disposing of human waste in big cities finally forced reformers to realize that many of the diseases that regularly wiped out urban populations could be overcome by piping clean water in and piping out the waste. These simple changes in the way people thought about disease were related to some much more sophisticated changes. Belief in the theory that diseases are caused by germs and the effort to improve hospital hygiene also arose at about the same time in urban settings to meet urban needs. Soon mortality rates began to decline. On the average people actually began living longer in cities than in the country. Longer, healthier life meant more need for greater mobility within cities and between them. Horse-drawn vehicles added to the urban filth, but electrified streetcars and trains turned out to be fast, comfortable, and convenient. Today, not even people who love the country could get along without such improvements in health and mobility as these, designed originally to make life in big, modern cities safe, lively, and satisfying. □

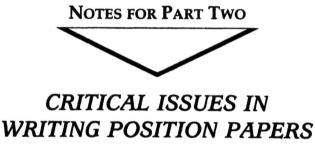

NOTES FOR PART TWO

CRITICAL ISSUES IN WRITING POSITION PAPERS

TOPICS

This course limits the form you write in by asking you to write five-hundred word essays in three paragraphs and to arrange their formal elements in predictable ways: proposition, transitions, and reasons. This formal limitation, assuring your readers that they will always know where to find those formal elements, frees them to concentrate on what you have to say.

The course compensates for these formal limitations by giving you freedom to write on any topic you choose. As Part One says, all that limits the range of topics that you can write about in this course are your opinions, your feelings, and your experience, including your experience as a reader.

But the freedom the course gives you as a writer to write on any topic limits your freedom as a reader. If *you* can write about almost anything you want to write about, your classmates can too. So all of you have to be willing to read about anything any one of you decides to write about.

To put it another way, just as the course asks you to try writing on some topics that may be new and unfamiliar to you, it also asks you as a reader to be receptive to some new and unfamiliar topics and some opinions that you don't necessarily agree with. Moreover, the course asks you to be a constructive reader. That is, it asks you to learn how to help your fellow students write effectively on topics that may be familiar to them but unfamiliar to you and maybe even help them explain opinions that you do not agree with.

The course asks you to learn to work with your fellow students on unfamiliar topics and opinions not only to help others but to help yourself. Helping other students work on unfamiliar topics and ideas may help you learn how to understand and come to terms with topics that are new, strange, complex, maybe even troubling. But it may turn out that you will someday find some of these very topics and ideas interesting and rewarding yourself. (See Collaborative Learning Task: Topic Interviews, p. 30.)

INTRODUCTIONS

When you read a finished essay, the first thing you read is the introduction. But an introduction is not usually the first thing that writers write. The purpose of this note on introductions is to help you begin thinking about writing introductions in a way that may differ quite a bit from the way you are in the habit of thinking about writing them.

WARMING UP

Like most writers, when you first sit down to write you usually have to warm up. You have to write something that will get you into the topic, get your mind working, and get your words flowing. Some writers may take a sentence or two to warm up, others may take several paragraphs, some may take several pages. Invention exercises, such as free writing, brainstorming, and other exercises found in Part One can also be used to warm up for writing.

But the writing you do to warm up seldom makes a good introduction to an essay. Although you may eventually include some warm-up material in your introduction, that material usually needs a good deal of cutting and revision. A lot of it may never get into the finished essay at all. But it has served its purpose if it has helped you discover a tentative position that you want to explore, explain, or defend in the essay you are setting out to write.

In contrast, an essay's introduction is not what *you* needed to warm up to a topic. An introduction is what *readers* will need to warm up to a topic. Warm ups begin wherever you need to begin. Introductions begin wherever you think your readers need to begin. An introduction is calculated to lead readers to the proposition of an essay. You can't lead people when you don't know where you're going yourself. So you can't introduce readers to what you're saying until you know what you're saying yourself. You can't introduce readers to a proposition before you've written it, and maybe not until you have explored, explained, and defended it.

WRITING AN INTRODUCTION

That's why this book teaches you to write essays from the inside out. It asks you to think of an introduction not as the first thing to write in an essay but rather the third thing. After you warm up, **the first thing to write is a tentative proposition.** A *tentative proposition* states the position that you think you will take in the essay. **The second thing to write are some paragraphs that explore, explain, or defend the proposition.** Then, **the third thing to write is an introduction.**

Once you understand this principle of writing from the inside out you will find it fairly easy to write good introductions. The main purpose of an introduction is to make contact with your readers by providing them with a context of issues that they will recognize. What you are trying to do is help readers see how the position you are taking in the essay is related to their own experiences, what they are interested in, or what they already know.

To do that, you have to acknowledge that most readers have other things on their minds than you have on yours. They are likely to use language that is somewhat different from the language that you are using in the essay. They are interested in ideas, issues, and events that are not quite the same as the ones you want them to turn their attention to by reading your essay.

Your task in the introduction is to make your readers feel willing to put aside their own interests and concerns for a moment and consider your interests and concerns, or put aside their normal way of understanding something for a moment and consider your way of understanding it. To do that, you have to talk about ideas, issues, or events in the introduction that your readers are likely to be familiar with and find language that your readers will respond to.

So to write an effective introduction, you have to find points where your position is related to the experience, interests, or knowledge of your readers. You have to prepare them to care about the topic and to be receptive to your position by appealing to their normal, everyday way of thinking about things, what they are likely to know, how they are likely to be feeling, or their general sympathy for their fellow human beings. In an introduction you may also want to appeal to your readers' sense of sound reasoning by making your assumptions explicit, by stating the facts that lie behind the position you are taking in the essay, or by defining important terms. The best introductions assume that the reader is thinking, "Why should I bother to read this? What's in it for me? How does it affect my life? How is it related to what I already know or what interests me?"

Another way to define introductions is to say that they set the scene for the position you are taking in the essay. You may want to take this definition literally. Tell a story or write a description that vividly establishes the situation or problem that the proposition addresses. You may already have written some material of this sort if you wrote personal or family stories for exercise 1. Because these stories are likely to be lively and distinctive, they may become an important part of a lively and distinctive introduction. (There is more about contexts of issues in Assumptions, p. 132, and in Contexts of Issues, Shareable Concerns, p. 197.)

Suppose, for example, that we set out to write an introductory paragraph for the essay about cars that we used as an example in exercise 5 (p. 44). First, we could describe a current situation that everyone would recognize (there are cars everywhere). Then we could point out something wrong with that situation (some people complain about cars). Finally, we could suggest what the solution to the problem might turn out to be (people may find other means of transportation). This solution then would lead to the position we took in the paper: Cars may be on the way out.

the current situation   Cars seem to be everywhere today. We find them in the desert and the mountains, the forests and the plains. They jam the city streets. They flow like rivers along our superhighways. There are more cars on the road today than ever before. Yet, *a problem* there are signs that people are not entirely happy with this situation. We complain about air pollution and high accident rates. We worry when we read the news that even though domestic cars have improved a great deal in recent years, still another manufacturer has had to recall thousands of cars because the brakes are defective or the gas line leaks. More and more people are traveling by plane and train. Bicycles are increasingly popular in many cities and towns. Some two-car families are selling their second car because they simply can't afford the cost of insurance and upkeep. Of course, it is hard to imagine how we could get along without cars entirely. But it is certainly reasonable to speculate that, as people choose other ways of getting around, travel by car may have reached *transition to proposition* its high-water mark and begun to recede. It seems fantastic

proposition	and unlikely, yet it is now possible to say that in the future the trend will be for people to use cars as we know them less rather than more. In fact, it looks as if cars may be on the way out as our major means of transportation.
¶2 *transition*	And it is high time they were. The world oil supply, which cars depend on for fuel, has been diminishing at the rate of . . .

Some Types of Introductions

It is impossible to list all the types of introductions that can prepare readers to consider what you have to say and encourage them to read your essay with interest. Here are a few to consider:

- **Explain the assumptions you are making** in a way that shows that your readers probably make them too or could easily agree with them. (See Assumptions, p. 132, and paragraph 1 of "Family and School," p. 319.)
- **Define key terms you will be using** in language that your readers are likely to be familiar with. (See paragraph 1 of "The Pluralist Model of Power and Modern Society," p. 332.)
- **Tell an amusing or striking story or an anecdote** that will make your readers interested in your topic. (See paragraph 1 of "Going Back to School," p. 323.)
- **Give some historical background** that shows how the problem you are addressing got started. (See paragraph 1 of "Project Head Start", p. 75.)
- **Describe the problem** that you will be suggesting a solution to. (See paragraph 1 of "Kingsgate High School," p. 240.)
- **Describe a place, object, person, or event** relevant to your topic. (See paragraph 1 of "What Should Patients Be Told?", p. 220.)
- **Quote an authority** whom your readers are likely to respect and explain the relevance of the quotation. (See the beginning of "Substitutes for Violence," p. 367.)
- **Summarize** the main points of something you have read and will be drawing on in exploring, explaining, or defending the position you are taking in the essay. (See paragraph 1 of "Aspects of Political Crime," p. 263.)
- **Describe an existing situation** that you think people would (or should) like to change. (See "Euthanasia: A Violation of Human Life," p. 64, and "The Benefits of a Writing Community," p. 325.)

(There is more about introductions in Part Four: Reaching Out to Members of Other Communities, p. 189.)

Follow the instructions for working in consensus groups on p. 20.

Task   *Descriptive Outline of an Introduction*

Choose two or more example essays in this book that do not have a descriptive outline attached and read the first paragraph of each one aloud.

Draft a detailed descriptive outline of each introductory paragraph. The outline should explain how the paragraph introduces the proposition in each case. Be sure to explain how the paragraph makes a transition between the introductory material and the proposition.

Then classify the introductions by type. What sort of introduction is each one? Are they all different? Or do some of them do the same sort of thing in a somewhat different way?

PROPOSITIONS

Suppose you were told after you had just finished writing an essay, "Don't hand that essay in. Tear it up. Save only one sentence—the sentence that states most succinctly the position you are taking in the paper. Throw the rest away."

That would be a cruel thing to do to any writer, and it is not likely to happen to you. But if it did, the one sentence you should want to save would be your essay's proposition sentence, the sentence that states your position. In all of the essay exercises assigned in this book, that sentence would be the last sentence in the first paragraph.

The proposition of an essay is important because it states the point of the essay. A proposition, or position sentence, is a generalization that you can explore, explain, or defend. It is also a sentence that someone else could agree with, challenge, deny, or oppose. *Proposition:* "Cars may be on the way out." *Response:* "Hey, wait a minute, no they're not! What makes you think so?" or "I'm not so sure. Look at it this way." or "Gee, you know, I think you may be on to something there. Just the other day driving home I began to think. . . ."

A proposition is a statement that you explore, explain, or defend in a way that will lead readers to think it is convincing, worth considering, or persuasive enough to refute. A proposition states your opinion. In writing an essay that explores, explains, or defends that opinion, you turn your opinion into a proposal or a position, your feelings into ideas, your hunches into judgments worthy of the reader's consideration. To be judgmental does not have to carry a negative connotation. You make judgments all the time, whenever you decide which color shirt to buy, what to have for lunch, which movie to recommend to a friend. A judgment is a decision. It is what, for the moment, you want to say.

The proposition is therefore the essay's most important sentence. Your introduction prepares readers to consider the proposition. The defense explores, explains, or defends the proposition. Transitions relate paragraphs to the proposition and to each other. The proposition is the key to every transition you write, since every part of your essay has to refer to it in one way or another.

Because the proposition is so important to an essay, you should concentrate on writing short, clear, simple propositions. A proposition should not have more operative words, and should not establish more relationships between those operative words than you can explore, explain, or defend adequately in the length of essay you are going to write. *Operative words* are the words that do the work in a sentence. They are the words that carry the most weight and require the most explanation. For example, in the sentence "Operative words are the words that do the work in a sentence," the words that need explanation are *operative words*, *work*, and *sentence*. The verb phrase *do the work* establishes a relationship that needs explanation between two of those operative words.

That is another way to think about the proposition of an essay. It creates the most important relationships in the essay: between the introduction and the rest of the essay, among the paragraphs of the essay, and among the essay's operative words.

Consider the following examples. Most of these sentences, if you used them as a proposition, would probably be limited enough to explore, explain, or defend in a five-hundred word, three-paragraph position paper in *Short Course* form.

> Cars may be on the way out.
>
> This school should replace the alphabetical grading system with a pass—no credit system.
>
> Although Caesear dies in the first scene of Act III, his character dominates the whole play.
>
> The city is an excellent place to bring up a family.
>
> A farm is an excellent place to bring up a family.
>
> The suburbs are a terrible place to bring up a family.
>
> Children are cruel sometimes because they are selfish.
>
> Peacekeeping, as the UN practices it, is doomed to failure.
>
> We can solve the smog problem by keeping cars out of our cities.

UNCLEAR PROPOSITIONS

These sentences are short, clear, and simple. They are also relatively limited in scope. That is, their operative words cars

alphabetical grading system

bringing up a family

the smog problem

are relatively easy to define. The relationships between the operative words in each sentence are expressed by the following verbs or verb phrases:

may be on the way out

replace

dominates

bring up

doomed

keeping out

These too are relatively easy to explain and specify.

But sentence length alone may be deceptive. Some short sentences express ideas that are too broad to serve as the proposition of a short essay. Some operative words refer to too many different kinds of things or to things that are too hard to define, or the relationships they express among these words are too vague or complex. The following sentence is an example:

People should think primarily of themselves in trying to adjust to society.

This sentence would be very hard to defend adequately in a short essay. The key words, *people* and *society,* are all-encompassing. The sentence distinguishes neither which people the writer is talking about nor which society. It states neither the time nor the place in which these people and their society exist. The word *primarily* is ambiguous. Does it mean first in time or first in priority? The principal action referred to in the phrase *trying to adjust to society* has for many years been the subject of complex and inconclusive debate among professionals in the fields of psychology, sociology, anthropology, and political science. It would be impossible to define briefly the main verb in the phrase *think of themselves.* And the word *should* makes it unclear whether the writer is merely asserting a prejudice or is implying instead some tested method or proven way of life.

It is easy to sympathize with writers who try to explore, explain, or defend such a proposition. They want to say something important. That is an understandable motive. Furthermore, writers may be afraid that if they take a position that is limited or simple, readers will think that they have limited or simple minds.

But simple positions do not necessarily represent simple minds. $E = mc^2$ is after all a statement that is simply expressed. So is "All men are created equal." But neither the author of the first (Albert Einstein) nor the author of the second (Thomas Jefferson) had a simple mind. As you become more experienced as a writer, you will understand that in most cases the best way to say something important is to say it as briefly, clearly, and simply as you can.

In any case, that rule applies to the essays in this book. You cannot solve the problems of the world in five hundred words. So for these essays, take a position that you can develop thoroughly in the limits of time and space set by the assignment. (There is more about making succinct and readable sentences in Style, p. 137, and in Paragraph Development, p. 111.)

HOW TO TEST A PROPOSITION

One way to tell if a proposition is limited enough for the time and space you have at your disposal is to **look for the operative words in it and the central relationship among those words** expressed by the main verb of the sentence.

Suppose, for example, that you were trying to decide whether or not to use the following sentence as a proposition:

> Although Caesar dies in the first scene of Act III, his character dominates the whole play.

This sentence is about Shakespeare's play *Julius Caesar*. At sixteen words, it is a fairly long sentence. It is almost twice as long as several other examples listed previously. The question is, is it too long and complicated to use as the proposition of an essay?

You can answer this question by taking the sentence apart. It has two sections, a subordinate clause

> Although Caesar dies in the first scene of Act III

and a main clause.

> his character dominates the whole play.

For the purposes of the short essay you have been assigned to write (five hundred words, three paragraphs), the subordinate clause (Caesar dies in the first scene of Act III) doesn't count. It states one of the sentence's basic assumptions. You could establish that assumption by telling the story that the play dramatizes in your essay's introductory paragraph.

So the sentence is actually a lot shorter than it seems. Its working, or operative, part is the second half of the sentence, the main clause, six words long:

[Caesar's] character dominates the whole play.

That would be the real proposition of the essay you would write, the position you would be taking. The operative words in it are the subject of the sentence, *character*, and the verb, *dominates*. Your main task in exploring, explaining, or defending this sentence would be to define and explain the word *character* and define and explain the word *dominates*.

That seems like a reasonable thing to try to do in a short essay. But before you decide finally, you should take a closer look at those two operative words to see what issues arise when you try to define them.

The subject of the sentence, *character*, raises a number of general issues, such as what human character is and how it is dramatized in a play. The word also raises some issues that are specific to this particular play: What is the nature of Caesar's character in the play? What evidence is there in the play for deciding that his character is of one sort rather than another, and how are we to interpret that evidence? What limits our understanding of Caesar's character in this play? How could we overcome these limits?

The main verb in the sentence, *dominates*, also raises several issues, both general and specific. Two general issues that the verb raises are how characters may be said to "dominate" any literary work, and whether dominating other characters in the work physically or psychologically (or politically) is one of these ways. Issues specific to this play are related to these general issues: How exactly does Caesar dominate this play? Does he do so only by dominating other characters? If so, in what way does he dominate them? Is it psychologically, or physically, or politically? And finally, how does Caesar dominate parts of the play in which he does not appear, especially the scenes that occur after his death?

Several other words are also operative in this sentence, but they are less important than the subject and verb. These words set the conditions within which the operative words you have already looked at have significance. The name *Caesar* may raise a question about the differences between the historical figure and the character in Shakespeare's play. The way Caesar *dies* in the play, or rather the way the historical facts surrounding his death are dramatized in the play, may have something to do with your understanding of the way Caesar affects the characters who surround him. And certainly how you understand what happens in the *whole* play has something to do with your understanding of the difference between action that occurs before Caesar dies and action that occurs afterward.

Furthermore, *dominates*, the main verb in the sentence, expresses the main relationship in the sentence. As a result, if you used the sentence as a proposition, the definition and explanation of that word would be a major part of the essay.

But there is still another relationship implied in the sentence that would affect what you said. This is an implied relationship between the main clause ("his character dominates the play") and an unstated opposing view implied by the subordinate clause that introduces the sentence: that it is nonsense to think that a character who disappears from the action halfway through a play could actually dominate the play. This relationship is expressed by the transition word *although*. The sentence is written so that you would be setting out with an obstacle to overcome. Overcoming that obstacle might have to play some part in exploring, explaining, or defending the proposition.

This test of the proposition has brought to light most of the issues raised by the position you think you might take in your essay about *Julius Caesar*. Now it's time to decide whether or not to go ahead with it. Should you use the sentence as the proposition of your essay? Probably yes. The final criterion is not just how many issues a proposition raises, it is how easily you could deal with most of those issues. If you judge that your readers are likely to agree without argument to your assumptions on most of the minor issues, then you can refer to these issues in passing, or not at all. You can safely concentrate on the central issue in the sentence, expressed in the main clause: How come Caesar seems to dominate the whole play?

(There is another example analysis of operative terms in What an Essay *Says*, p. 154. See also Paragraph Development, p. 111, Some Ways to Question and Generalize, p. 31, and Assumptions, p. 132.)

PROPOSITION PITFALLS

Learning to analyze propositions in this way can help you avoid one of the most common pitfalls in writing propositions, namely, trying to say too much. It may also help you avoid some of the other difficulties writers sometimes have in writing a good proposition.

Wordiness

A *wordy* proposition (or any other sentence) is imprecise and vague. Here's an example.

78

Security has meant varying pursuits and differing goals for diverse periods of history.

This sentence means something like, "Security means different things to different people at different times."

(There is more about making sentences more succinct and readable in Style, p. 137, and in Some Ways to Question and Generalize, p. 31.)

Bifurcation

A *bifurcated* proposition is really two propositions in one:

These proposals are unreasonable and implementing them could make midair collision more frequent.

Each clause in this sentence says something quite different about "these proposals," and each could be explored, explained, and defended in a position paper of its own. To explain why "the proposals are unreasonable," we would have to explore the reasoning that lies behind them. To explain why "implementing the proposals would make midair collisions more frequent," we would have to discuss cause-and-effect relationships.

The sentence could be made into a nonbifurcated proposition by changing *and* to *because:*

These proposals are unreasonable *because* implementation could make midair collision more frequent.

Because indicates a cause-and-effect relationship between the dangers resulting from implementing the proposals and the writer's position that the proposals are unreasonable. The rest of the essay would explain this causal relationship, answering the question, "*Why* could these proposals make midair collision more frequent?"

A bifurcated proposition can limit an essay in three ways. First, it can give away the defense prematurely. It tips your hand, revealing subordinate points in the argument along with the main one. In the following bifurcated proposition:

Solid construction and a wide median make I-45 a very safe road.

the main point is "I-45 is a very safe road." This would be the proposition of a unified essay on this topic. In the unified essay, solid construction and a wide median would be subordinate points that the essay makes in order to support that main point. Part of the descriptive outline for such a unified essay would read something like this:

PROPOSITION   I-45 is a very safe road.

PARAGRAPH 2   *says:* One reason I-45 is safe is that the road surface is very well constructed.

PARAGRAPH 3   *says:* Another reason I-45 is safe is that it has a wide median.

But an essay with the proposition in its bifurcated form, "Solid construction and a wide median make I-45 a very safe road," would reveal these reasons ahead of time. There may of course be times when it is advisable to do just that. For example, if you are just learning how to state a clear position and explore, explain, or defend it, you may find it easier to state the major reasons in the proposition in this way. But you should work toward writing propositions that generalize the argument you are making in the essay without summarizing your argument or stating reasons in support of it. You should not summarize your argument or supporting reasons in the proposition, generally speaking, because readers are likely to lose interest in following you through the rest of the essay. Why read on when the whole argument has been succinctly summarized already?

The second way a bifurcated proposition can limit an essay is by changing its focus. It makes readers shift their attention from the position taken in the proposition to less important issues. The sentence about I-45 is an important statement because the writer has made a judgment (that the road is very safe) and takes responsibility for that judgment by supporting it. If, for example, the writer was a consultant to the Traffic Safety Commission, that expert judgment is what the commission would be paying for. The commission already knows what every commuter who drives along the road knows, that the road surface is unblemished by broken seams and potholes and that the median is wide. The commission doesn't have to pay an expert to find that out. The issue (and what the commission is paying the consultant to decide) is whether or not those two conditions mean that the road is really safe.

Therefore, what the essay says in paragraphs 2 and 3 about the road surface and the wide median is not important in itself. It is important because **it encourages readers to consider carefully the position that the writer has stated in the essay's proposition.** The writer should not let the supporting observations in paragraphs 2 and 3 deflect readers' attention from that most important issue.

The third and most important way a bifurcated proposition can limit an essay is related to the second way: It can limit an essay by disunifying it. Bifurcation tends to produce two two-paragraph essays with the same introduction instead of one three-paragraph essay. In this case, para-

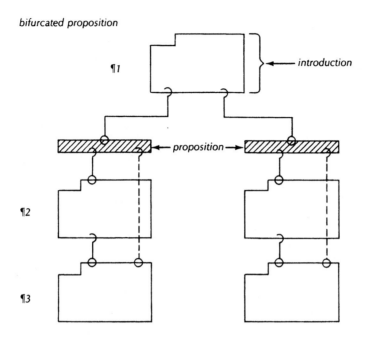

bifurcated proposition

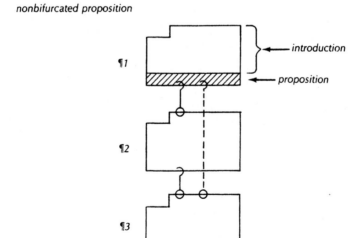

nonbifurcated proposition

graph 2 defends one-half of the proposition, that the road is well constructed. Then paragraph 3 defends the other half, that the median is wide.

Describing the Argument

The following example describes the argument instead of stating it:

> The purpose of this essay is not to defend the president, but to present an argument for a strong presidency.

This sentence describes the strategy of the paper. It states what the essay *does*, not what it *says*. To make a defensible proposition on this subject, the writer would have to say something like

> What the United States needs now is a strong presidency.

Weak Verbs

The final pitfall to avoid in writing propositions is using weak verbs. Weak verbs understate or misstate the point you want to make. The weakest verb to use in a proposition is one that merely sets up an equation. Take for example the following tentative proposition:

> In Whitman's poetry, the sea is solitude.
> In Whitman's poetry, the sea = solitude.

It's hard to say what this sentence really means. But there are many alternatives to *is* that would make the sentence more precise and easier to explore, explain, or defend. One possibility is

> In Whitman's poetry, the sea *represents* solitude.

Here are some others.

In Whitman's poetry, the sea
{
might represent
usually represents
never represents
in part represents
symbolizes
suggests
negates
deprives the speaker of
challenges
}
solitude.

The reason for taking care in choosing the verb in a proposition sentence is that the verb is almost always an operative word. It establishes the central relationship among the other operative words in the sentence.

In the following example, the word *dog* expresses a concept. So does the word *man*. These concepts have some meaning standing alone. But their meaning increases when you relate them with a verb that is active, vivid, and exact:

> The dog bit the man.
> The man bit back.
> Thereby hangs a tale.

(There is more about effective propositions in Descriptive Outlines, p. 152.)

COLLABORATIVE LEARNING

Follow the instructions for working in consensus groups on p. 20.

Task 1   Testing Propositions

Write out the proposition sentence from several example essays in this book. Then make the following decisions collaboratively:

1. Underline the operative words in each proposition.
2. List the issues raised by the operative words that you have underlined.
3. State the kind of relationship or action each proposition expresses. For example, the sentence "Children are cruel sometimes because they are selfish" expresses a cause-and-effect relationship. The sentence "Cars are on the way out" expresses change or decline. Other kinds of relationships that a proposition can express are change for the better, juxtaposition (one thing next to the other), one thing following another (narration or process), one thing the same as or similar to another (classification or comparison), and so on.
4. Are there any relationships or assumptions implied but unstated in any of the propositions you have tested? (For help on this question, see Assumptions, p. 132.)
5. Read the whole essay that explores, explains, or defends each proposition you have tested. Does the essay address all the issues implied in the proposition? If not, which issues does it leave out? Which does it emphasize? Why do you suppose the writer left out some of the issues implied in the proposition and emphasized others?

6. Are all the propositions you chose to test succinct and readable? What makes them so? Try revising some of these propositions to make them more succinct and readable without changing the position they are taking. (See Assumptions, p. 132.)

Task 2   *Questions That Sentences Raise*

List as many questions as you can that are generated by each of the following sentences:

We could solve the smog problem by keeping cars out of the city.

The purpose of this book is to provide a new method for teaching expository writing.

Ask not what your country can do for you; ask what you can do for your country.

I don't care what you say, I'm leaving.

If the TV doesn't work this time, I'm going to buy a new one.

REASONS

The essay exercises in Parts Two, Four, and Six ask you to give reasons that explore, explain, or defend your position. That is, they ask you to apply the principle of explanatory subordination by making a statement and then subordinating to it other statements, or reasons, that explain it. The example essays throughout this book show that these reasons can be made up of many things: judgments, examples, statistical data, things people have said or written, a law or directive, a way of going about doing something, and so on.

And yet, as this book uses the word, even though it can be many possible things, a reason is clearly one sort of thing. A *reason* is a statement that does not stand alone as the most comprehensive or important statement made in the essay. **A reason is an ingredient in the essay, one that helps readers understand or agree with some other statement that is more comprehensive and important than itself.** A statement is comprehensive when it covers many instances, not just one, and important when we value it highly. The most comprehensive and important statement in any essay is the proposition.

This book calls *reasons* what you construct to support the proposition in a position paper. One way to construct reasons—possibly the easiest way—is to use examples. The purpose of this note is to explain how to develop examples in order to support a proposition in an increasingly effective and complex way.

EXAMPLES AS REASONS

Suppose you are looking for a topic to write an essay on. You remember a talk you had with a friend of yours the other day that went like this:

YOU: You know that long Sixth Street underpass with the curve in it? I almost broke an axle there this morning on a pothole. I bet there's a pothole every fifty feet.

YOUR FRIEND: Do I know it? The lighting in that underpass was so bad last week I almost drove over into the left lane at the turn.

Obviously, you and your friend don't much like the Sixth Street underpass. That feeling is what your similar stories about similar experiences add up to when you tell them to each other in a spontaneous chat like this. You and your friend *synthesize* and make sense of some of your experiences by discovering common attitudes that have similar origins: both of you drive through the underpass to get home; both of you hate it. The considerable interest, utility, value, and personal satisfaction of your talk with your friend derives almost entirely from the common origin of the stories you have told each other and from the commonality that you feel in telling them.

The next day, as you think the conversation over, though, those two stories begin to add up to something else too, and you begin to think that what has happened to you and your friend should matter to other people as well—others who drive through the underpass and maybe even some who have never driven through it.

So you make a decision. You decide that between the potholes and the bad lighting, that underpass is really dangerous. That is, you now *infer* from the similar stories you and your friend have told each other, not the feeling you had yesterday that the two of you have something in common, but the generalization that certain characteristics of the underpass have something in common. This inference changes the way you talk about your experiences in the underpass in an important way and changes the sense you make of them. Before, you talked about the underpass as something the two of you dislike. Now you talk about it as something that's dangerous and, as a result, threatens other people as well as yourselves.

This decision is a crucial step. It opens the way for you to take a position in your essay on the dangers of the Sixth Street underpass that you can explore, explain, or defend with two reasons. Examples are the simplest kind of reason, and you just happen to have two terrific ones that you can use straight out of the can:

The Sixth Street underpass is dangerous.

For example, there is a pothole in the road surface every fifty feet. I almost broke an axle there this morning on a pothole.

And the lighting in the underpass is so bad that in some places you can't see your way. Last week a friend of mine almost swerved over into the left lane at the turn driving through there at night.

These examples fill the main requirement for reasons. Neither one stands alone as the most comprehensive and important thing you want to say, because each one is about only one aspect of the underpass. And synthesized as reasons instead of as personal anecdotes, the examples become ingredients that enhance another statement in the essay that *is* comprehensive and important: that the Sixth Street underpass is dangerous. This statement is comprehensive because danger is usually a product of several factors, not just one. It is important because danger can be a matter of life and death.

The following hook-and-box diagrams show your examples in both of the situations you have now used them in. Diagram 1 shows the examples in relation to your chat with your friend, before you converted them into reasons. We can call this relationship *narrative conversation*. Diagram 2 shows the examples in relation to the inference you drew from them after you converted them. We can call this relationship *reasoning conversation*.

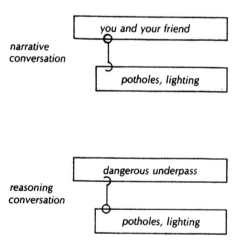

At first glance these diagrams seem to show that the two pairs of elements occupy the same position in a series of events. First, you meet your friend, then you tell the stories. First you state your inference, then you tell the stories. Because they follow in each case, the stories seem dependent on what precedes them: the second occurs because the first occurred. But the diagrams are actually somewhat ambiguous on this point. The hooks connecting the boxes are drawn to suggest that, for its own interest, utility, and value, one of the two elements in each case *reaches out and hooks on to* the other element. This reaching out suggests that one element needs the other element in some nonreciprocal way. That is, whatever its apparent place in the order of events, first or second, leading or following, the element that reaches out and hooks on to the other is subordinate to or dependent upon the element it hooks on to.

So the relationships between the boxes in the diagrams could be spelled out this way:

> *diagram 1:* Narrative conversation *synthesizes stories that people tell each other **in order to establish or confirm friendship.***

> *diagram 2:* Reasoning conversation *synthesizes stories that people tell each other **in order to draw inferences from the stories and then use them to explain or defend those inferences.***

That is, although the two diagrams look very much alike, they are actually quite different. To understand this difference and to understand reasoning conversation better it helps to look more closely at the nature of narrative conversation.

NARRATIVE CONVERSATION: WHAT IT IS, WHAT IT'S FOR

In narrative conversation, as in every kind of conversation, we interpret in language what we believe we have experienced, in order to establish or maintain our membership in communities that are important to us. What distinguishes narrative conversation is that we construct what we believe we have experienced in story form: novels, tales, anecdotes, movies, plays, poems, myths, and so on.

In telling each other these stories, we connect experiences in a chain-like way that is both associative (one thing makes you think of another) and temporal (things happen as time passes, one thing causes another). Sentences in narrative conversation may answer questions raised by the preceding sentence or sentences, whether we say them or someone else does ("And then what happened?" or, "What does that remind you of?"). Or sentences may answer questions that neither person in the conversation seems to have raised before ("It just struck me that . . ."). In short, narrative conversation is driven, sometimes rather mysteriously, by feelings as deep as the intimacy among community members that the conversation establishes or maintains.

What makes narrative conversation lively and intrinsically worth taking part in is that we get to hear people telling some good stories in this

87

easy-to-take, chainlike, sometimes unpredictable way, and we also get to tell some stories ourselves. Experiences interpreted as stories are exactly what give most narrative conversations their interest, utility, value, and satisfaction. That is why the hooks connecting the boxes in diagram 1 reach from the people engaged in dialogue down to the examples, the stories people tell. The diagram suggests that narrative conversation reaches out for what it needs, what it depends on, and what it is subordinate to: people's experiences interpreted and constructed as stories.

Narrative conversation depends on these origins—experiences told as stories and the people who tell them—more than it depends on any product, effect, or result of telling the stories. The possible products, effects, or results of narrative conversation are the ends to which people may put the stories they tell, such as, for example, telling the truth. But anyone who reads novels, goes to the movies, or even watches the evening news knows that telling the truth, whatever lip service people may give it, is not at the top of many storytellers' list of priorities. What is at the very top of every storyteller's list of priorities is making people feel as if they are members of a community based on mutual understanding.

We are all engaged in narrative conversation a good deal of the time. So we all know what narrative conversation usually sounds like. It sounds a bit disjointed, stringy, and unresolved: a lot like the following example paragraph. This paragraph is interesting, sort of fun to read, and maybe even instructive because the experiences that it constructs as stories and links together with the passage of time and by association have a common origin, namely the implied beliefs of the friendly, perceptive, but slightly scatterbrained speaker.

> I really enjoyed Gail's party. It was the best one I went to all year. In fact it was the first party I had gone to since my birthday party last August. That was a terrible party. We were at Ocean Beach that month, and the place was jammed with tourists. There were so many tourists in the stores it was even hard to get through the supermarket to buy hamburger and corn flakes, let alone get what you needed for a party. And the tourists in the stores there are so *rude*. Two summers ago a man carrying a big beach ball ran into me in the supermarket and almost knocked me over. Then he shouted it was all my fault. I got so mad I nearly ran his beach ball over with my shopping basket. I've got a terrible temper. It runs in the family.

The section on Unity and Coherence implies, of course, that there is something wrong with this paragraph. But from the point of view of narrative conversation, there's nothing wrong with it at all. The kind of conversation it represents, the kind of synthesis that produces it, and the kind of sense that it makes can be interesting, delightful, and useful on their own terms. Because narrative conversation is so inherently appealing, it is probably as close to a universal kind of conversation as there is. Almost everyone, almost everywhere, has almost always told stories in order to bring people together and cement commonality. We learn narrative conversation early in life. For most people, its satisfactions and intrinsic merit are sufficient unto themselves.

REASONING CONVERSATION: WHAT IT IS, WHAT IT'S FOR

There are some communities, however—typically, in the Western cultural tradition—that sometimes, in some situations, do something else with narrative conversation than enjoy the sense of commonality it provides. They recycle it by converting it into another kind of conversation, the kind we have called *reasoning conversation*.

Reasoning conversation in almost every case develops out of narrative conversation. We construct it by converting the narrative way of synthesizing experience into another, quite different way of synthesizing experience. Reasoning conversation is neither better nor worse than narrative conversation. It is just different. Both narrative and reasoning conversation are valued highly by some conversational communities and not valued much at all by others. And both are also valued by the same communities at different times, under different conditions, for different purposes.

But the differences between reasoning and narrative conversation mean that some of what is acceptable in one of them isn't always acceptable in the other. For example, although there is nothing at all wrong with the paragraph about Gail's Party from the point of view of narrative conversation, from the point of view of reasoning conversation—taking a position and exploring, explaining, and defending it—there is a lot wrong with it. What's wrong is that the paragraph is coherent but not unified. There are no reasons in it.

Reasoning conversation converts stories that make up narrative conversation by subordinating them all to a single generalization—the proposition of the essay, the position taken in it. In the paragraph about Gail's party, that hasn't happened. The kind of conversation that the paragraph represents is dependent upon and subordinate to experiences told as stories. There are of course inferences drawn from stories in the paragraph ("I've got a terrible temper"), but clearly, stories reign supreme.

In reasoning conversation, the reverse would be the case. Reasoning conversation does not depend on experience interpreted as stories—examples—for its interest, utility, value, and satisfaction. Examples depend on the conversation. Nor does reasoning conversation depend much on the origins of its examples. Reasoning conversation may certainly honor its sources through source evaluation and citation (see Part Five: Research and Research Writing, p. 245), but it is not subordinate to those sources.

What reasoning conversation does depend heavily on and is almost totally subordinate to are the inferences that it converts its examples into. The hooks in diagram 2 are drawn reaching upward to the inference instead of down to the examples because reasoning conversation depends for its interest, utility, value, and satisfaction on its products, the ends to which reasoning conversation puts them—such as, for example, a position paper on the dangers of the Sixth Street underpass.

Reasoning conversation is similar to narrative conversation in at least two ways: in both we construct something new—some kind of story—by reconstructing and interpreting in language what we believe we have experienced, and in both we do that in order to establish or maintain membership in communities that are important to us. Narrative conversation and reasoning conversation differ in the kind of stories we construct and what we do with them. In narrative conversation, we use stories to establish or maintain a sense of personal, immediate, spontaneous emotional contact and intimacy with other members of a conversational community. In reasoning conversation we establish or maintain membership in a conversational community by using stories to develop and support generalizations that we infer from them.

That is what is distinctive about reasoning conversation. In reasoning conversation, the ends to which we put stories that interpret experience matter more than the experience that produced them. In reasoning conversation stories don't reign supreme. The inferences we draw from them reign supreme.

In synthesizing experience in the reasoning way instead of the narrative way there is of course a trade-off. When we convert experience as stories into inferences, we may lose much of the significance of the stories. The significance of stories in narrative conversation is immediately emotional, personal, spontaneous, and intimate, but it is limited in most cases to a very small group—in the case of you and your friend talking about the underpass, it was limited to a group of only two. This loss of emotional, intimate significance is less likely to occur in narrative conversation, but it does happen. For example, in the paragraph about Gail's party, the inference, "I have a terrible temper," suggests a lot less of the speaker's quirky personality than the story the speaker draws it from, "I got so mad I nearly ran his beach ball over with my shopping basket."

But in return for this loss of spontaneity and intimacy in reasoning conversation, we do gain something else. What we gain is another kind of significance, one that is less personal, more studied and mediated, but shareable with a larger, more diverse community of people. Converting personal anecdotes into somewhat impersonal observations gives stories a role to play in another, more comprehensive kind of story, a reasoning story. The reasoning story implied in the position you are taking in your paper about the underpass is something like, "Many hazards add up to danger."

That's the bottom line. That is how reasons are constructed. In diagram 2 you have converted your examples and made the necessary trade-off by recycling your examples about potholes and lighting. That is, you have converted them by using them to illustrate the inference you have drawn: the inference that the underpass is dangerous. Instead of emphasizing where and how you found your examples, as you did when you were chatting with your friend, you emphasize the use you are putting them to.

PUTTING EXAMPLES IN CONTEXT

Converting examples into reasons straight out of the can in this way is the first step in learning explanatory subordination: using reasons to explain inferences. But examples used in this way are simple reasons. You are assuming that, without further explanation, readers will understand the relationship between your examples and the more important statement that you have related them to. So supporting a proposition without explaining that relationship is a weak defense. Most readers will not doubt that there must be some relationship between potholes, bad lighting, and the dangerous underpass. But some readers could probably think of several different kinds of relationships that might pertain. The essay does not yet make clear the particular nature of the relationship that you intend.

The next step is to explain how the examples, or any concrete experiences you use, enhance the position you are taking. By going on to make the nature of the relationship clear, you lengthen the reach of your controlling inference—you make its influence broader and more inclusive. And in that way you also make your inference more complex and informative.

Explaining your examples in this way makes the relationship between the essay's proposition and the examples a little like the relationship between the casserole you were planning to have for supper and the ingredients in it. You've got the mushroom soup, the tuna, the noodles, and the frozen peas, so you've got supper, right? Not by a long shot. If all you did was take the cans of soup and tuna, the box of noodles, and the frozen peas out of the cabinet and the fridge and put them on the table, you'd face a family rebellion. They'd say they can't eat raw ingredients. And they'd be right. There's a lot more to making a casserole than that. You have to open the cans and boxes, use the right amount of each ingredient, combine them in the right way, and put them in the oven long enough to cook, but not long enough to burn.

Whenever you construct reasons to support the position you are taking in an essay, you have to choose, combine, and cook the ingredients up in a similar way. The essay has to synthesize what you know so that it supports your position. Until now, you have assumed that both you and your readers know how your own experience and your friend's led you to the conclusion that the underpass is dangerous. But maybe your readers haven't been through that underpass lately. Maybe some of them have never even been through it at all. Even more important, most of them probably haven't been thinking about the issue for a week or so as you have.

So you have to help them catch up with you. Just as the casserole needs a cook who effectively subordinates mushroom soup, tuna, macaroni, and peas, your position needs a writer to construct and relate reasons so that they effectively synthesize and subordinate your concrete experience. Reasons show readers how you think concrete experience, such as examples or data, is related to your position. They help your readers catch up with the thinking you've been doing on the topic so that they can follow you more easily.

Maybe you haven't quite caught up with your own thinking. Trying to show your readers how you think concrete experience is related to your position may also help you explore and think through your position. What exactly is the relationship between your experience and the inference you have drawn from it?

When your readers see your statement that the underpass is dangerous, some questions are likely to come to mind:

What conditions in the underpass are dangerous?

Why, in your opinion, are those conditions dangerous?

How did those dangerous conditions come about?

The same questions might come to your own mind too, as you explore your thinking further. What would you come up with if you constructed answers to each of those questions? What you would come up with are reasons to support your inference in increasingly effective and complex ways.

Each question would of course have a different answer. That is, each question would subordinate your examples to the proposition in a different way. Each answer would generate a different kind of reason. Each answer would explore a different aspect of your position.

To answer the first question, "What conditions in the underpass are dangerous?", you would explain what is wrong with the underpass.

This kind of reason is closest to using examples straight out of the can. It is still a weak defense.

> The Sixth Street underpass is dangerous.
>
> One reason it's dangerous is that the road surface is riddled with potholes.
>
> Another reason the underpass is dangerous is that it is poorly lit.

But to answer the second question, "Why do you think those conditions are dangerous?", you would have to go beyond evidence of dangerous conditions. You would have to explain what makes those particular conditions dangerous, and that would involve explaining what exactly you mean by *dangerous*. In doing that you would be strengthening your defense.

> The Sixth Street underpass is dangerous.
>
> The underpass is dangerous because everyone who goes through it is forced to drive dangerously. I drive through it twice a day to and from work. I have to zigzag all the way through the underpass in order to avoid dozens of potholes. If I didn't, I'd break an axle. And people who have to drive there at night are in even greater danger. My friend almost swerved into the left lane last week because the underpass is so poorly lit.

You strengthen your defense with this explanation by going beyond the examples themselves to tell your readers more of what you know about the situation in the underpass, how you have been thinking about it, and what your assumptions are (what you mean by *dangerous*). Inserting people's perception of danger between the examples and the proposition places the examples farther away from your inference by synthesizing them under a subheading. It therefore lengthens the reach of your controlling inference, making its influence broader and more inclusive. The paragraph now subordinates potholes and lighting to your position indirectly rather than directly. First, it subordinates potholes and lighting to dangerous driving; then it subordinates dangerous driving to the dangerous underpass.

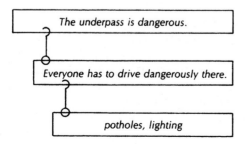

CONSTRUCTING A STRONG DEFENSE

Notice also that when you subordinate examples in this way, under a subheading of the proposition rather than under the proposition directly, that subheading may be the transitional generalization that controls the organization of a single paragraph. There are two kinds of transitional generalizations. One of them is the paragraph 2 kind of transition. It relates a paragraph directly to the essay's proposition, which is at the end of the previous paragraph.

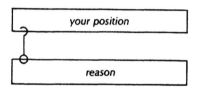

The other is the paragraph 3 kind of transition. It relates the paragraph to the proposition indirectly, around an intervening paragraph (or, in a longer essay, around several intervening paragraphs), and it also relates the paragraph directly to the immediately preceding paragraph.

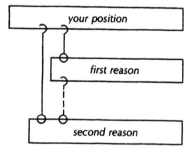

Using these two different kinds of transitional generalizations allows you to subordinate your reasons under more than one heading. Now your examples contribute to only one of these subdivisions (paragraph 2 of your essay) because you have subordinated them to only one sub-inference ("The underpass is dangerous because everyone who goes through it is forced to drive dangerously."). In order to develop a second subdivision (paragraph 3) you will have to make a second supporting subinference from other kinds of experiences you have had, such as,

94

for example, things you have read. And then you will have to use that experience to support that second subinference. Once again, you will be telling your readers more of what you know about the situation in the underpass, how you have been thinking about it, and what your assumptions are.

That is why this book asks you to write three-paragraph essays. They help you learn to synthesize more than one major element, or reason, in your writing. It is important to know how to synthesize more than one reason in support of your position because in order to make your readers willing to consider your position, you have to show them that the inference you have drawn generalizes from more than one experience, more than one example, more than one piece of evidence. Three-paragraph essays make you a smarter writer than you may think you are by requiring you to develop your ideas more fully than you may have been in the habit of developing them, and by requiring you to make connections among your ideas that you might not otherwise have made.

To put it another way, subordinating examples to more than one reason supporting your position helps you go beyond the material you have at hand, the material that may have set you off writing on this topic in the first place. So it helps you explore your position more thoroughly. That's what you would be doing if you answered the second question that might have come to mind about why certain conditions in the underpass are dangerous. In this case, let's say you have noticed that the local newspaper has run some articles lately on the Sixth Street underpass.

The Sixth Street underpass is dangerous.

Everyone knows that the underpass is dangerous because everyone who goes through it is forced to drive dangerously. I drive through it twice a day to and from work. I have to zigzag all the way in order to avoid dozens of potholes. If I didn't, I'd break an axle. And people who have to drive there at night are in even greater danger. My friend almost swerved into the left lane last week because the underpass is so poorly lit.

An article in the newspaper last week confirmed this danger by listing its effects. The article said that in the past two years one fatal accident and three near-fatalities have occurred in the Sixth Street underpass. Wreckers have to pull cars out of there on the average of two or three a month.

As strong as this defense is, however, it is possible to make it still stronger. That is, it is possible to tell your readers more of what you know about the situation in the underpass, how you have been thinking about it, and what your assumptions are. One way to construct an even stronger defense of your position would be to answer the third question

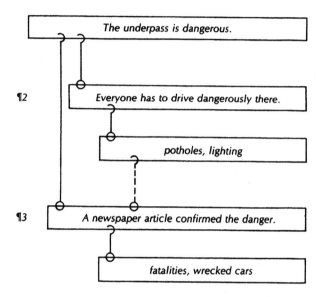

that might have come to mind, "How did those dangerous conditions come about?" In this case, you would explore your position more thoroughly still by including other relevant elements and in that way place your examples still further away from the controlling inference, the position you are taking in the essay as a whole.

The Sixth Street Underpass Is Dangerous.

One reason the underpass is dangerous is that the city's Thoroughfare Commission, which is responsible for maintaining the underpass, has been in a state of political turmoil for the past five years. As a result of this poor leadership, the commission's staff has failed to carry out many of its responsibilities. One of these responsibilities is to keep the city's roads, bridges, and underpasses in good repair. Clearly this has not happened in the case of the Sixth Street underpass, where the road surface is riddled with potholes and most of the overhead lights are burned out or broken.

Another reason that the underpass is dangerous is that the state has been holding up funds to repair it until the Thoroughfare Commission turns in its biannual report on the accidents that have occurred there. Last week an article in the newspaper did the job for them. It said that in the past two years one fatal accident and three near-fatalities have occurred in the Sixth Street underpass. Wreckers have to pull cars out of there on the average of two or three a month. As a result of that article, the governor says that the state will appropriate new funds to pay for repairs and will watch carefully to see that the commission uses the money wisely.

Although the examples are now a lot further away from the controlling influence of your inference, you have increased their value to the essay

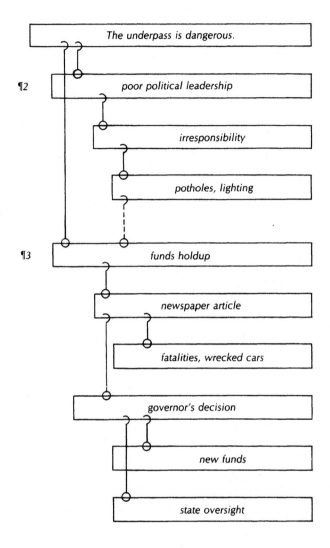

as a whole by increasing the significance of the context in which you have placed them. In that way you have lengthened the reach of your controlling inference, the essay's proposition, a great deal, making its influence still broader and more inclusive. You have increased the leverage, the weight, that your examples can bear.

When you began, engaged in narrative conversation with your friend, your examples were experiences that annoyed two people. Now they are experiences that represent the similar experiences of lots of people and that help indict an irresponsible government agency. You now know a lot more now than you did before about the position you took, and you have explained what you know a lot more thoroughly and convincingly to your readers. The strong defense you have constructed is likely to lead readers to take your position a lot more seriously.

COLLABORATIVE LEARNING

Task 1 A Hook-and-Box Diagram of a Descriptive Outline

Working in a group of two or three, diagram with hooks and boxes the *does* sections of the descriptive outline of "What Should Patients Be Told?" (p. 220) or "Going Back to School" (p. 323). Use the hook-and-box diagram on p. 109 as a model.

Join another group of two or three and compare the diagrams drawn by the two groups. Account for the differences in the diagrams.

Task 2 A Hook-and-Box Diagram of an Essay

Working in a group of two or three, diagram with hooks and boxes "McKay, Trepp, Inc.," p. 242, or "Stock Options," p. 327, or some other example essay that your group would like to work on. Use the hook-and-box diagram on p. 109 as a model.

Join another group of two or three and compare the diagrams drawn by the two groups. Account for the differences in the diagrams.

Task 3 Constructing Reasons

Working in a group of two or three, decide first on a movie that all of you have seen recently and liked (or particularly disliked), an episode of a TV show you have all seen and liked (or disliked), or an exciting ball game or other public event that you all watched. Or you could choose instead a problem that you have in common, a teacher or course you are taking, a place you like to go, an improvement or repair you think should be made, a person you like or dislike, or a task you like or dislike doing.

Working independently, each one write a few sentences that tell a story illustrating what is appealing, repulsive, interesting, or difficult about the subject you have chosen.

Read your stories to each other and then, working together, write a single short sentence that seems to synthesize your common experience. That is, take a position on the subject that you can all agree on and that you think your stories illustrate.

Then, working together,

1. Use your stories as examples to construct a weak defense of that position in which each example constitutes a paragraph (see pp. 97–98).

2. Decide on some subordinate generalizations or subinferences that would support the position; then write a paragraph that explores, explains, or defends your position using your examples indirectly by relating them to the proposition through the subordinate generalizations you have chosen (see pp. 103–105).

3. Write a second paragraph that strengthens your argument by referring to other aspects of the subject, and write another subordinate generalization expressing that synthesis (see pp. 106–110).

PARAGRAPH DEVELOPMENT

Some writers have trouble developing their ideas. They tend to write a series of related propositions without explaining or illustrating them or without exploring the implications of the operative words. For example, suppose a writer drafted an essay that looked something like this:

¶1   The smog in this city is terrible. We could solve the smog problem by keeping cars out of the city.

¶2   For one thing, cars produce all the worst kinds of air pollution.

¶3   Another reason is that cars produce a greater volume of pollutants than any other source.

This essay fits the form required by exercise 5. In fact, the writer shows that he has learned most of the principles that exercise 5 has to teach. The essay introduces a defensible proposition, states it succinctly and readably, and explains it, making appropriate transitions among the parts of the explanation.

But the essay is far from five hundred words long. Obviously it needs development. Every paragraph lacks development. The essay assumes that every reader will know which city the writer is talking about. In fact, it seems to assume that every reader lives in the city that the author of the essay lives in. It assumes that every reader would agree without further explanation that there is no other source of smog in that city.

HOW TO DEVELOP A PARAGRAPH

To *develop an essay* means to explain these assumptions rather than assume that every reader knows what you know and assumes what you assume. You can learn paragraph development by analyzing the sentences you write according to the following principle:

Every sentence raises questions in readers' minds.

To develop a sentence, find the questions it raises and answer them.

Some of the questions that any sentence may raise in readers' minds are "What do you mean by that?", "Why?", "How come?", "Who says?", and "So what?"

Take yourself, for example. When you first read the sentence "Every sentence raises questions in readers' minds," you may have wondered, "What does that mean?", "What kinds of questions does every sentence raise?", and "So what? What should I do about it?" To develop that sentence I had to imagine these questions, and then I had to answer them. You have to do that as a writer, too. In order to develop your paragraphs, you have to try to imagine the questions that the sentences you write may raise in your readers' minds and then answer them.

In the example essay about smog, the first sentence, "The smog in this city is terrible," raises at least the following questions:

What is smog?

Where does the word *smog* come from?

How can you tell that we have smog in this city?

Which city?

Is this the only city that has smog?

If so, why?

If not, why not?

What makes smog so terrible?

The essay's first paragraph, its introduction, could be developed by answering some of these questions. It could answer them directly by explaining or defining the operative word, *smog*. Or it could answer them indirectly, by describing a scene or telling a story. (There is more about writing introductions in Introductions, p. 81, and in What an Introduction Does, p. 201.)

The second sentence in the undeveloped example essay, "We could solve the smog problem by keeping cars out of the city," is the essay's proposition. The proposition is developed in paragraphs 2 and 3. (There is more about what makes a good proposition and how to develop one in Propositions, p. 85.)

To develop paragraph 2, we repeat what we did to develop paragraph 1. We try to imagine the questions that the sentence that now constitutes paragraph 2, "For one thing, cars produce all the worst kinds of air pollution," might raise in readers' minds. It looks as if that sentence might raise these questions:

What are the worst kinds of air pollution?

What makes them so bad?

How do we know cars produce all the worst kinds?

And the fourth sentence, which now constitutes paragraph 3, "Another reason is that cars produce a greater volume of pollutants than any other source," is likely to raise the following questions in readers' minds:

How do you measure the volume of air pollution?

How can cars, which are relatively small machines (compared to trucks and power generators), produce so much pollution?

How much pollution do other sources produce, and what kind?

If we were going to develop paragraphs 2 and 3 of this essay, we would have to answer some or all of these questions by explaining operative words, by logical argument, by reference to authoritative sources, or, as in the first paragraph, by description or narration.

READING WELL-DEVELOPED PARAGRAPHS

Understanding paragraph development in this way can help you write better. It can also help you read more constructively. If you are aware that every sentence has operative words and that every sentence raises questions in the reader's mind, you can look ahead as you read to what is coming. You can anticipate what is likely to follow (or what should follow) in whatever you are reading simply by asking yourself what questions each sentence raises in your mind. You will also be able to keep track of what's going on in whatever you read, because you will be aware of how writers organize (or should organize) paragraphs, and how writers relate paragraphs (or should relate them) to the main point of an essay.

For example, let's read the third paragraph of Frederic Garsson's essay, "Family and School," p. 319:

Another way families can give their children emotional support in college is through rituals, acts performed on a regular basis that a person can depend on to occur. Rituals tend to put order into a person's life and provide a sense of self-assurance and security. A common ritual is Sunday dinner. No matter what the children in the family are doing, even studying for exams, family rules may require them to eat dinner with the family. In this case the whole family can anticipate this one time of the week, knowing that no matter what, they will be together. It is an event that the whole family, and most important, the children, can rely on and find comfort in. My family first learned about this use of Sunday dinner as a family ritual through a friend of mine. On several occasions, he turned down an invitation to have dinner at my house, explaining to my parents that his father insisted that his whole family eat dinner together on Sunday evenings. My parents thought that this mandatory attendance at Sunday dinner was something that would work well at our house too. At the time I did not understand the psychology behind the plan. But now I think I do. Furthermore, I feel that it has succeeded in achieving its desired effect. It gave my sister and myself a feeling of security that we not only experience every Sunday, but that we also carry with us into the world beyond our family.

In reading this paragraph, to make use of the principle that every sentence raises questions in the reader's mind, we would ask ourselves as we read what questions each sentence raises in our mind, and then look to see how those questions are answered, or if they're answered.

The first sentence in the paragraph, which is likely to be the most important sentence in the paragraph, generates several questions based mainly on the sentence's operative words, *families, emotional support,* and *rituals.* The sentence itself answers one question it raises, "What are rituals?" They are "acts performed on a regular basis that a person can depend on to occur."

Here are some of the other questions that the sentence raises.

> What do family rituals do for people?
>
> Can you give me an example of a family ritual?
>
> What happens in one?
>
> What does that particular ritual do for people?
>
> How did you find out about family rituals?

The paragraph answers all these questions:

> *What are rituals?*
> Rituals are acts performed on a regular basis that a person can depend on to occur.
> *What do family rituals do for people?*
> Rituals tend to put order into a person's life and provide a sense of self-assurance and security.
>
> *Can you give me an example of a family ritual?*
> A common ritual is Sunday dinner.
>
> *What happens in a family ritual?*
> No matter what the children in the family are doing, even studying

for exams, family rules may require them to eat dinner with the family. In this case the whole family can anticipate this one time of the week, knowing that no matter what, they will be together.

What does it do for people?
It is an event that the whole family, and most important, the children, can rely on and find comfort in. . . . It gave my sister and myself a feeling of security that we not only experience every Sunday, but that we also carry with us into the world beyond our family.

How did you find out about family rituals?
My family first learned about this use of Sunday dinner as a family ritual through a friend of mine. On several occasions, he turned down an invitation to have dinner at my house, explaining to my parents that his father insisted that his whole family eat dinner together on Sunday evenings. My parents thought that this mandatory attendance at Sunday dinner was something that would work well at our house too.

The first sentence in the paragraph raises some other questions too, of course, questions such as

What is emotional support?

Why do people in college need it?

What are some other ways that families can support their children in college?

The paragraph we have read does not answer these questions. But other paragraphs in the essay do answer them. Take a look at the whole essay "Family and School," on p. 319. The first paragraph explains why college students (in particular, commuting students) need emotional support. It says that they tend to feel insecure because they find it hard at first to replace their high school friends, and because in college they have more freedom than they're used to. The second paragraph explains some of the other ways that families can provide emotional support for their children in college. It says that families can be sympathetic people to talk to and they can reassure their children that everything will work out.

But the essay never does explicitly define *emotional support*. Instead, it gives an example of it: a family ritual that helps people "put order into their lives and provide a sense of self-assurance and security."

(There is more about paragraph development in Introductions, p. 81, Propositions, p. 85, Reasons, p. 96, Descriptive Outlines, p. 152, Unity and Coherence, p. 116, and Assumptions, p. 132. Essay exercises 7 and

8 can help you learn to develop paragraphs, because they ask you to discover opposing arguments and refute them. Invention exercises 1 through 4 can help you discover what you have to say and help you produce material that you can use to develop paragraphs. There is more about reading constructively in Part Three: Constructive Reading.

COLLABORATIVE LEARNING

Follow the instructions for working in consensus groups on p. 20.

Task 1 Developing a Paragraph (Developing Operative Words)

Identify the operative words in the following sentences. Then explain what you think a writer would have to say to develop each of them fully.

> This school should revise its grading system.
>
> Project Head Start has become a necessary part of our present-day system of education.
>
> Yet it is also clear that Haitians can unite effectively.
>
> Our investigation has shown that although some personnel problems exist, a complicated mix of internal and external factors was the main cause of the slowdown.
>
> By being so long in the lowest form, I gained an immense advantage over the cleverer boys.

Task 2 Reading a Well-Developed Essay

Choose a sample essay in this book and write out the proposition sentence and the first sentence of paragraph 2 and paragraph 3.

Mark the operative words in each sentence.

List the questions that you think the sentences generate.

Which of these questions do paragraphs 2 and 3 of the essay answer? How do they answer them?

That is, what does the essay *say* and *do* to answer the questions? (See What an Essay *Says*, p. 154, and What an Essay *Does*, p. 158.)

UNITY AND COHERENCE

Unity and coherence refer to the structure of an essay. *Unity* means oneness. *Coherence* means stick-togetherness. Good essays need both. If your essay lacks coherence, its parts don't stick together. Readers won't be able to follow you. That is, they'll miss the point you want to make, the position you're taking. If an essay lacks unity, your readers won't get any point at all, because the essay hasn't a point for them to get, or maybe it has too many points, all of them undeveloped.

Unity and coherence do not come easily. Nobody's mind works naturally with the kind of unity and coherence that a well-planned, well-developed essay requires. That kind of unity and coherence is a convention—an agreement among readers and writers about how they expect writing normally to be organized. To achieve unity and coherence of that kind, most of us have to work consciously to shape the parts of an essay and make them fit together, just as a cabinetmaker shapes the parts of a table or chair so that they fit together. To gain unity you have to work consciously to focus the essay on one topic alone. And to gain coherence you have to work consciously to make sure that all the parts of the essay are explicitly related to one another.

The key to both is the essay's proposition. Anything that contributes to exploring, explaining, or defending the proposition is relevant to the essay and therefore helps gain unity. Anything that does not contribute to exploring, explaining, or defending the proposition is not relevant to the essay, disunifies it, and therefore does not belong to it. To unify an essay, include only what is related to the proposition. Cut out everything that isn't related to the proposition. If you like, save what you cut out for another essay.

The proposition not only creates unity, it also helps create coherence. For unity, it is enough that everything in an essay is relevant to the essay's proposition. For coherence, relevance is not enough. For coherence, the essay has to make clear how everything is relevant to the proposition. Throughout the essay, readers should be able to say what the relationship of what they are reading is to the proposition. An essay should make explicit the relationships both among the parts of the essay and between the parts and the whole. These relationships are important because they construct the idea of the essay. An *idea* is not an isolated concept or a loose collection of facts. An idea is an explicit relationship between facts and concepts. In this sense, then, an incoherent essay simply has no idea in it.

COHERENCE BETWEEN PARAGRAPHS

Writing a transitional generalization or transition sentence at the beginning of every paragraph is one way to create coherence in an essay. Transition sentences relate the paragraph to preceding paragraphs and to the proposition. They guide readers so that they will be able to follow the writer's thought. They are necessary at the beginning of every paragraph, because at the end of every paragraph readers reach a corner. Having gotten to that corner, their minds are willing to go in any number of directions. As the writer, at just that point you have to take readers by the hand and lead them in the direction you want them to go. That is the purpose of transition sentences: to reach back to something the writer has already said and at the same time point ahead to what you are about to say next.

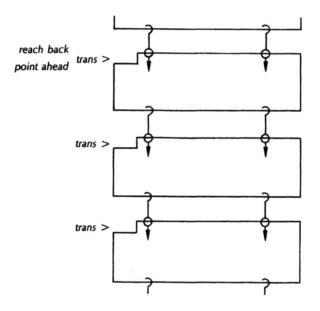

If you do not reach back and guide readers in this way, they won't understand. They won't follow. They'll get lost. (There is more about transitional generalizations in Constructing a Strong Defense, p. 106.)

UNITY AND COHERENCE WITHIN PARAGRAPHS

Readers can get lost within paragraphs as well as between them. Just as the end of every paragraph is a corner, the end of every sentence is a corner too. At the end of every sentence, you have to take the lead and direct your readers' attention where you want it to go. If you don't lead, readers won't follow. The paragraph will lose coherence and won't make sense.

There is another way to describe unity and coherence within paragraphs. It uses the principle explained in the section on developing paragraphs:

Every sentence raises questions in the reader's mind.

To develop a sentence, find the questions it raises and answer them.

A paragraph is *unified* when all its sentences answer questions raised by the paragraph's first sentence and when none of its sentences answer questions that are not raised by the paragraph's first sentence. And a paragraph is *coherent* when every sentence answers a question raised by the sentence (or sentences) that precede it. This paragraph, for example (the paragraph you are reading), is unified because the sentences that begin "A· paragraph is unified . . ." and "And a paragraph is coherent . . ." answer the question raised by the paragraph's first sentence, "There is another way to describe unity and coherence within paragraphs" (*What* is another way to describe unity and coherence?). The second half of the paragraph (beginning "This paragraph, for example . . .") also helps answer that question by giving concrete examples.

The paragraph you have just read is also coherent. Each sentence in it answers a question raised by a sentence that precedes it. The paragraph begins with a sentence that raises the question: What is another way to describe unity and coherence? The second and third sentences in the paragraph answer that question with generalizations ("A paragraph is unified when . . ."; "And a paragraph is coherent when . . ."). These sentences in turn raise the question that every generalization raises: Can you give me an example? The last two sentences in the paragraph answer that question by giving examples drawn from the paragraph itself.

EXAMPLES OF DISUNITY AND INCOHERENCE

The following paragraph is *disunified*. Even though everything in it pertains in some way to the writer's trip home, nothing in it answers the question raised by the first sentence: Why was your trip home a disaster? The paragraph is also *incoherent*. No sentence in it answers a question raised by the sentence or sentences that precede it.

[1]My trip home was a complete disaster. [2]The weather was fine all the way. [3]It took me eleven hours to drive a little over a hundred miles. [4]And I have never seen such beautiful fall foliage as I saw that day along the road. [5]The sky was clear until almost three in the afternoon, with the sun shining brightly. [6]Once I saw two rabbits playing in a field beside the road, chasing each other through the grass back and forth across a stream that ran along the edge of some woods. [7]The bright sun brought out the color in the leaves so that I could distinguish a dozen shades of red and orange. [8]You can't spend all that time traveling without noticing a lot of scenery as you go along.

If you were rewriting this paragraph, you would have to decide first of all what exactly you want to say most. Is the point really that the trip was a disaster, or is the point that the trip was fun even though it took so long? If you decided that you really do want to say how awful the trip was, you would have to discard most of the paragraph as it is now written and save that material for another paragraph in the same essay or put it aside for another essay altogether. In its place, you would write some new material that really does answer the question raised by the first sentence.

> [1]My trip home was a complete disaster.
> *Why was it so bad?*

If this was the question you decided to answer, you might keep the third sentence.

> [3]It took me eleven hours to drive a little over a hundred miles.

You would then develop that sentence by describing all the things that slowed you down: a flat tire, a bridge washed out, the muffler that fell off at seventy miles an hour and then the ticket you got for speeding and not having a muffler, two ten-mile traffic jams, dropping your only quarter under the car in the toll booth correct-change line, and a spontaneous nosebleed.

If you decided instead that what you wanted to say was that in spite of the long, slow drive you had a pretty good time, then you could keep most of what is in the paragraph now. But you would have to change the first sentence so that it raises a question that the rest of the paragraph answers. And you would have to rearrange some of the sentences that follow:

> [1]My trip home wasn't a complete disaster.
> *What went wrong and what made up for it?*
> [3]Of course, it did take me eleven hours to drive a little over a hundred miles. [2]But the weather was fine all the way.

So far, you would have answered in general terms the question raised by the first sentence. Now you would have to develop that answer. To do that, you would have three alternatives. You could give details of what was good about the trip, you could give details about what was bad about it, or both. The most economical choice would be to make better use of the sentences you have already written that explain what was good about the trip.

But those sentences are not coherent as they stand. They're out of order. To make them cohere, you would have to rearrange them by asking, at the end of each sentence, "What should follow here?" The result might look something like this (the superscript numbers refer to the order of the sentences in the first version):

¹My trip home wasn't a complete disaster. ²The weather was fine all the way. ⁵The sky was clear until almost three in the afternoon, with the sun shining brightly. ⁸And you can't spend all that time traveling without noticing a lot of scenery as you go along. ⁴I have never seen such beautiful fall foliage as I saw that day along the road. ⁷The bright sun brought out the color in the leaves so that I could distinguish a dozen shades of red and orange. ⁶Once I saw two rabbits playing in a field beside the road, chasing each other through the grass back and forth across a stream that ran along the edge of some woods.

In rearranging these sentences, you would of course have to change the direction signals at the beginning of some of them. For example, sentence 4 would lose its introductory *And,* because it doesn't need it any more. But sentence 8 would get a new introductory *And,* because it now introduces the third item in a series (fine weather, clear sky, time spent traveling).

The following example is coherent because every sentence answers some question raised by the sentence that precedes it. But the paragraph is disunified because nothing after the third sentence has anything to do with the topic announced in the first sentence.

¹I really enjoyed Gail's party. ²It was the best one I went to all year. ³In fact it was the first party I had gone to since my birthday party last August. ⁴That was a terrible party. ⁵We were at Ocean Beach that month, and the place was jammed with tourists. ⁶There were so many tourists in the stores it was even hard to get through the supermarket to buy hamburger and corn flakes, let alone get what you needed for a party. ⁷And the tourists in the stores there are so *rude.* ⁸Two summers ago a man carrying a big beach ball ran into me in the supermarket and almost knocked me over. ⁹Then he shouted it was all my fault. ¹⁰I got so mad I nearly ran his beach ball over with my shopping basket. ¹¹I've got a terrible temper. ¹²It runs in the family.

Readers can follow this paragraph's chain of association fairly easily, mostly because the paragraph repeats several key words (*I, we, party, tourists*) throughout. These words give it coherence. But the paragraph begins with a party and ends with a peculiarity of family temperament. In between, it wends its way amusingly through an anecdote about an argument in a supermarket. But when we get to the end of the paragraph, we don't know quite how we got there. And we don't know any more about what happened at Gail's party than we did when we began.

In short, the paragraph is coherent but disunified because every sentence answers a question raised by a sentence that precedes it, but after sentence 3, none of the questions that the paragraph answers are related to the first sentence in the paragraph. Just conceivably the second, third, and fourth sentences could be said to answer questions raised by the first sentence, but only if you stretch the point, since the fourth sentence qualifies the answer given by the third.

> [1]I really enjoyed Gail's party.
>
> *Why did you enjoy it?*
>
> [2]It was the best one I went to all year. [3]In fact it was the first party I had gone to since my birthday party last August. [4]That was a terrible party.

But sentence 4 also represents an important corner in the paragraph. At this point, if you were rewriting this paragraph you would have to take a firm hand in order to lead readers where you want them to go. To do that, you would have to choose between the two questions that sentence 4 raises. One of these questions "remembers" the sentence's context: the three sentences preceding it that refer to Gail's party.

> [1]I really enjoyed Gail's party.[2]It was the best one I went to all year. [3]In fact it was the first party I had gone to since my birthday party last August. [4]That was a terrible party.
>
> *What made your birthday party worse than Gail's party?*

The second question raised by sentence 4 "forgets" the sentence's context, the preceding sentences about Gail's party. Instead, it treats the sentence as if it stood alone. That is, it treats sentence 4 as if it were itself the main point of the paragraph.

> [4]That was a terrible party.
>
> *Why was your birthday party such a terrible party?*

To make the paragraph unified, you would have to answer the first of these two alternative questions, the one that remembers why the birthday party came up at all (because it contrasted so unfavorably in the writer's mind with Gail's party) and *also* remembers the direction that the first sentence in the paragraph seemed to be going (to tell us why Gail's party was so great). As it was originally written, the paragraph chooses instead to answer the second alternative question, the one that forgets its context. So it leads readers way off the track.

We can analyze any paragraph to discover whether it is unified and coherent by discovering the questions generated by each sentence in it. If the paragraph is unified, discounting allowable assumptions, it will answer only the questions raised by the first sentence, or first few sentences, in the paragraph (see Assumptions, p. 132). If the paragraph is coherent, every sentence will also answer questions raised by preceding sentences that are also relevant to the first sentence or first few sentences in the paragraph.

To put it another way, when you set out to discover the questions raised by sentences in a paragraph, you are really looking for the *expectations* that those sentences imply. We ask each sentence: **What does this sentence make me *expect* the paragraph will say next and then say later on?** Then we look to see if the paragraph fulfills our expectations. If you anticipate the questions that your sentences are likely to raise in the reader's mind and answer them, then you will probably satisfy the reader's expectations. As your skill as a writer increases, you will not only be able to answer the questions that your sentences raise, but you will be able to do so in ways that truly inform, enlighten, surprise, or entertain your readers.

ORGANIZING FOR COHERENCE

Even if a paragraph answers all the questions its initial sentences raise (and does not answer any questions that they do not raise), it will be coherent only if its sentences proceed in a fairly clear and simple overall order or sequence. Essay exercises 5 through 9 will help you learn a few basic ways to organize paragraphs so that they will follow each other in an orderly sequence. You can, and should, use these same organizational forms within paragraphs as well.

For example, essay exercise 6, Nestorian Order, p. 59, asks you to put several less important reasons in paragraph 2, and put the single most important reason in paragraph 3. You can also use this climactic order within a single paragraph. Nestorian order is an appropriate organization to use whenever you have to arrange a list containing a number of items—evidence, reasons, proposals, books, rivers, string quartets, whatever. Put an important item first, collect less important things next, and save the best for last.

Here are some more ways to organize material that you can use for relating the parts of a paragraph:

- **enumeration** (first, second, third)
- **spatial relation** (left to right, top to bottom, here to there, from the inside out)
- **time** (Then . . . now; at 5:30 . . . and then at 7:15; two summers ago . . . last August . . . today)
- **association** (bird, wing, feather, down, pillow, sleep)
- **logical sequences**
  deductive (from the general to the particular: from carnivores to

mammals to dogs to Spaniels to Rex. Novels . . . Conrad's novels . . . *Lord Jim*)

inductive (from the particular to the general: there are ten dogs in
every room of that building . . . so it must be a dog pound)

progressive (a series of rhetorical syllogisms—or, more correctly,
incremental associations that sound logical but may or may not
be: today is Wednesday; I go to work on Wednesday; I hate
work because what I do at work bores me; so on Wednesdays
I'm always bored; that's why I feel so bad today)

dialectical (a series of questions and answers in which every answer
generates the next question)

- **structure**
  simple climax (he carries tens, twenties, even hundred-dollar bills
  in his pocket all the time)

  Nestorian (a cross between simple climax and simple enumerative;
  see essay exercise 6, p. 59)

- **parallel syntax** (with dogs on the porch, mice in the cellar, and cats
  in the boys' room, this place is a zoo)

- **hypothetical** (if one thing, then another: if the TV doesn't work this
  time, I'm going to buy a new one; if both Keats and Byron are
  romantic poets, then *romantic* does not mean what most of us think
  it means)

DIRECTION SIGNALS: TRANSITIONAL WORDS AND PHRASES

If the ends of sentences and paragraphs are corners where you have to
direct your readers' attention, one of the best ways to do that is with
direction signals, both at the beginning of every paragraph and at crucial
points within them. Direction signals help readers remember the context
of what they are reading—what has gone before. We include these
direction signals in an essay for the same reason that we signal left or
right when we drive a car, so that other people will know which way
we are turning.

You may sometimes be tempted to leave direction signals out of your
writing because you feel that you would be insulting the reader's intelligence with them. They're too obvious. This is misguided humility.
What is obvious to you may not be obvious to your readers. Even the
best professional writers feel lucky if they can get 50 percent of what
they have to say across to their readers. It is part of your job as a writer
to command the reader's attention and keep it.

Often you can keep your reader's attention with the simplest kinds
of transitions. In climactic or Nestorian order (exercise 6), for example,
the transitional phrases are almost automatic: "One reason is. . . . There
are also several other reasons. . . . But the most important reason is. . . ."

The main kinds of transition among sentences within a paragraph are

- **conjunctions** (*and, but, however, therefore,* etc.)
- **referential pronouns** (*this, these, it, she, he,* etc.)
- **key words repeated**
- **parallel constructions**

In the following paragraph from *My Early Life,* Winston Churchill uses all these. He connects the sentences to each other with conjunctions such as *however, but,* and *thus;* with referential pronouns such as *they* and *it;* with key words, such as *English, I,* and *he* repeated throughout the paragraph; and with parallel construction ("Each had its color and its bracket. It was a kind of drill. We did it almost daily." "Latin as an honor, and Greek as a treat.").

I continued in **this** unpretentious situation for nearly a year. **However,** by being so long in the lowest form I gained an immense advantage over the cleverer boys. **They** all went on to learn **Latin** and **Greek** and splendid things like that. But I was taught **English. We** were considered such dunces that **we** could learn only **English. Mr. Somervell**—a most delightful man, to whom my debt is great—was charged with the duty of teaching the **stupidest boys** the most disregarded thing—namely, to write mere **English. He** knew how to do **it. He taught it** as no one else has ever **taught it.** Not only did **we** learn **English** parsing thoroughly, but **we** also practiced continually **English** analysis. **Mr. Somervell** had a system of **his** own. **He** took a fairly long sentence and broke it up into its components by means of black, red, blue, and green inks. Subject, verb, object: Relative Clauses, Conditional Clauses, Conjunctive and Disjunctive Clauses! **Each** had its color and its bracket. **It** was a kind of drill. **We** did **it** almost daily. As I remained in the Third Form (B) three times as long as anyone else, I had three times as much of **it. I** learned **it** thoroughly. Thus I got into my bones the essential structure of the ordinary British **sentence**—which is a noble thing. **And** when in after years **my schoolfellows** who had won prizes and distinction for writing such beautiful **Latin** poetry and pithy **Greek** epigrams had to come down again to common **English,** to earn their living or make their way, I did not feel **myself** at any disadvantage. Naturally I am biased in favor of boys learning **English. I** would make them all learn **English,** and then I would let the clever ones learn **Latin** as an honor, and **Greek** as a treat. But the only thing I would whip them for is not knowing **English. I** would whip them hard for **that.**

This conscious transitional process that joins sentences within paragraphs and paragraphs within essays strengthens your work and makes your essays capable of standing up of their own accord. It's good carpentry.

TESTING FOR UNITY AND COHERENCE

One way to check to see if an essay is unified is to write a detailed descriptive outline of it and then compare the *says* statements for paragraphs 2 and 3 with the proposition given in the essay. *Says* statements should paraphrase in a single sentence the main point of each paragraph. Check them by looking to see if they support the proposition as written. If they do, and you have paraphrased the paragraphs accurately, then the essay is probably unified.

One way to check to see if an essay is coherent is to write a descriptive outline and then compare the *does* statements for paragraphs 2 and 3 with the essay's overall plan. Check them by looking to see if paragraphs 2 and 3 do what the plan says they should be doing. There is more about writing descriptive outlines in Part Three: Constructive Reading.

Another way to check for coherence is to reread the transition sentences of paragraphs 2 and 3 and compare them with the essay's proposition. Does each transition sentence deal explicitly with one or more of the proposition's operative words? If so, then go on to reread the whole paragraph. Do all the sentences in each paragraph deal with the generalization made in the transition sentence? If the essay passes both of these tests, it is probably coherent.

COLLABORATIVE LEARNING

Follow the instructions for working in consensus groups on p. 20.

Task 1 Testing for Unity

Someone in the group read the following passage aloud. Then answer the questions and follow the instructions collaboratively.

> [1]Writing on a computer isn't like writing on a typewriter. [2]The typewriter I worked on for years is an old upright standard Underwood that must weigh fifty pounds. [3]When a burglar broke into my home fifteen years ago, he stole my TV, but he didn't steal my typewriter. [4]I don't think he could lift it, much less carry it out of the house. [5]It is taking me almost as long to learn to work on my computer as it took me to learn to type in the first place. [6]I feel forever confused by RAM, DOC, and DOS. [7]That bewildering array of F keys makes me nervous. [8]To do word processing, even though I can already type, I've had to learn a lot. [9]When the monitor says "Bad command," I feel like a puppy that's made a mess on the carpet. [10]I want to whine and creep off into a corner with my tail between my legs. [11]But today my old typewriter is an antique gathering dust in a closet. [12]My brand new computer weighs a lot more than fifty pounds, and it takes up a lot more space than my old typewriter.

1. What question does the first sentence in the paragraph generate?
2. How is the question answered?
3. What question does most of the paragraph seem to be answering?
4. Is there a sentence anywhere in the paragraph that seems to imply that question?
5. Which sentences seem out of order?
6. Rewrite the paragraph. Begin your revision with the first sentence as given, but rearrange the rest of the sentences, adding or deleting material to make the paragraph more unified and coherent.

Task 2   *Testing for Unity and Coherence*

Someone read the following passage aloud. Then answer the questions and follow the instructions collaboratively.

¹There are two reasons I like thunderstorms. ²One of them is that I just like strange things. ³I have strange tastes in just about everything. ⁴Not that I'd eat chocolate-covered ants. ⁵But I know someone who'll even do that. ⁶He spent three years in Africa where they have ants like you wouldn't believe. ⁷Once he got caught in the path of some army ants and they began to crawl up his legs, so he had to be broomed down or the ants would have eaten *him*. ⁸People who live in that part of Africa have to be on guard against that sort of thing all the time. ⁹The heat gets to you there too. ¹⁰That's one thing I can't stand. ¹¹Last summer the sidewalk in front of our house was so hot I bet my buddy I could fry an egg on it and, you know what, I did. ¹²Not that I wanted to eat the egg after I fried it. ¹³Dirt bothers me a lot. ¹⁴I spend a lot of time cleaning house.

1. What question does the first sentence in this paragraph generate? Does the second sentence help answer that question?
2. List by number all the sentences in the paragraph that *do not* answer a question raised by the sentence that precedes it. (That is, does sentence 3 answer a question raised by sentence 2? Does sentence 4 answer a question raised by sentence 3?
3. Write a general principle of paragraph coherence based on this analysis.
4. Write a question that most of the paragraph seems to be answering.
5. Is there a sentence anywhere in the paragraph that seems to raise that question?
6. List by number all the sentences in the paragraph that help answer the question that the first sentence generates.
7. Write a general principle based on this analysis that distinguishes between paragraph unity and paragraph coherence.

8. If a friend of yours wrote this paragraph in an essay and asked you to help her with it, what would you tell her is well done? What suggestions would you give her to improve the paragraph?

Task 3   Direction Signals

Someone in the group read aloud the following paragraph from John Fischer's "Substitutes for Violence." Then answer the questions and follow the instructions collaboratively.

[1]As civilization began to dawn, fighting became more organized—a community enterprise rather than a family one. [2]In addition to their daily skirmishes with wolves, cattle thieves, and passing strangers, the able-bodied men of the village (or polis, kingdom, or pueblo) normally banded together at least once a year for a joint killing venture. [3]The covenient time for settled farming people was early fall, after the harvest was in; then they had both enough leisure and enough surplus food to mount an expedition. [4]So it was about September when the Assyrians swept down like a wolf on the fold, when Gideon smote the Philistines, when Vikings ravaged the Kentish coast, when the Greeks shoved off for Troy, when the Dorians swept into the Argive plain, irresistibly armed with that first mass weapon, the iron sword. [5](Because iron ore was much more plentiful than copper, it could be used—once the secret of smelting was learned—to equip every man in the ranks. [6]The victims of the Dorians, still lingering in the Bronze Age, normally armed only their officers with metal blades; the rest carried flint-tipped spears and arrows.) [7]Tribes in the preagricultural stage sometimes found other seasons more suitable for rapine. [8]The War Moon of the Great Plains Indians, for example, came in May—since the spring grass was then just high enough to graze the horses of a raiding party, and the full moon made it easy to travel fast at night. [9]Regardless of timing, however, warfare was for centuries the main social enterprise, absorbing virtually all of the community's surplus time, energy, and resources. [10]"History," as William James put it, "is a bath of blood . . . war for war's sake, all the citizens being warriors . . . [11]To hunt a neighboring tribe, kill the males, loot the village, and possess the females was the most profitable, as well as the most exciting, way of living."

1. Map the paragraph (mapping is explained in Getting Ready to Write a Detailed *Does* Statement, p. 165).
2. Mark the words and phrases in each sentence that refer backward to something said in an earlier sentence and those that refer ahead to something said later. Draw an arrow under each of these words showing the direction of their connection, backward or forward.
3. List the types of transitional elements that occur in the paragraph.

Task 4 Paragraph Organization Game

The following sentences are the scrambled second paragraph of an essay. The essay's proposition is "Reform must take place within the reservation system."

Read the sentences aloud in the order that they appear here. Then number them in an order that seems to make the paragraph coherent. Read them aloud again in that order to check your results.

1. _____   a. They offered $24 in glass beads to take it off the hands of the white man.

2. _____   b. They want government's role reduced to hired experts living outside the reservation and some financial aid—

3. _____   not total control.

   c. In a dramatic demonstration of this dissatisfaction, four-

4. _____   teen Indian college students invaded Alcatraz, claiming ownership "by right of discovery."

5. _____   d. In 1961, they published the *Declaration of Indian Purpose*, advocating the development of their own program and

6. _____   asking for assistance from a local decentralized staff.

   e. In addition, they formed the "Bureau of Caucasian

7. _____   Affairs," the counterpart of the white Bureau of Indian Affairs.

8. _____   f. The Indians themselves do not favor ending the system, although they are greatly dissatisfied with the reserva-

9. _____   tion as it stands.

   g. The Indians may want to continue living on the reservation, but with their own tribal councils.

   h. The island, they asserted, had all the features of a reservation: dangerously uninhabitable buildings, no fresh water, inadequate sanitation, and the certainty of total unemployment.

   i. Despite the implications of this demonstration, however, the Indians do not want to do away with the reservation.

Task 5 Paragraph Organization Game

The following sentences are the scrambled third paragraph of an example essay in this book. The essay's proposition is "The best way tutors can help struggling students is by maintaining a relaxed and warm relationship with them."

Read the sentences aloud in the order that they appear here. Then number them in an order that seems to make the paragraph coherent. Read them aloud again in that order to check your results.

1. ___   a. Again, I speak from experience.

2. ___   b. In these cases, I have found that once the tutor breaks through that feeling of tension and discouragement by chatting informally, students are able to loosen up and

3. ___   their thoughts flow more freely.

c. On the contrary, tutors begin to serve as faithful friends

4. ___   or as relaxing-agents whom struggling students know they can rely on in time of need.

5. ___   d. The tutor may then find it unnecessary to offer so many suggestions.

6. ___   e. This attitude can become an enormous obstacle to progress.

7. ___   f. In this case, I was the one who profited from working in a relaxed and warm atmosphere.

8. ___   g. Students become so obsessed with the idea that they are incapable of writing.

9. ___   h. But tutors are not the only people who benefit.

i. This is not to say that tutors come to play an unimpor-

10. ___   tant role.

j. In the two months I have spent as a tutor I have met

11. ___   many students who have begun to believe that they will never be able to write a passing paper without help.

k. They begin to realize that they know more about writing than they thought they did, and many times they can find their own mistakes.

Task 6   *Reorganizing a Paragraph*

Read the following passage aloud. Then rewrite it. Begin the revision with the first sentence of the paragraph as given. Make that sentence the topic sentence of your revision. In analyzing the paragraph, use these questions as a guide:

1. What belongs in the paragraph and what does not?
2. What, if anything, should be added?
3. How should the sentences be rearranged to make the paragraph more unified and coherent?

¹In Israel today, one cause of the difference between the way European-American people and Afro-Asian people raise their children is the great difference in the family structures of these two groups. ²As a general rule, Afro-Asian families tend to be closer than European-American families. ³The Afro-Asian woman marries at a very young age. ⁴She usually has an average of five or six live births during her lifetime. ⁵The European-American woman has an average of two or three live births. ⁶A great many women of European-American descent put their children in nursery schools and go out and work to supplement their family incomes. ⁷Afro-Asian families tend to be very religious and old-fashioned. ⁸Very few of their women work outside the home. ⁹Because their families are so large, Afro-Asian people make up the poorer segment of the Israeli population. ¹⁰They live in far-off villages, farm areas, or the slum areas of the major cities. ¹¹Statistics have shown that there is a higher divorce rate among European-American couples, even though they tend to marry at an older age compared to Afro-Asian couples. ¹²Until recently there was very little intermarriage among these two groups. ¹³In fact, these two groups rarely mix socially.

"BUT WHY CAN'T I WRITE A 'CONCLUSION'?"

Of course you can write a "conclusion"—that is, put an ending on your essay—eventually. But please, not right now.

There are three reasons you should avoid "conclusions" in the early stages of learning about formal organization in writing.

One reason is that you may have been misled into thinking that a "conclusion" is just a summary of your argument. You may have been taught the venerable principle: Tell them what you're going to say, say it, then tell them what you've said. A summary that tells them what you said can sometimes be useful at the end of a very long essay. But a summary tacked onto the end of a short essay is the least useful way to end it.

Another reason to avoid writing a "conclusion" at first is that writing an effective ending for an essay is a unique problem in itself. An effective ending is not part of the explanation or defense of the paper's proposition, although it may extend the paper's exploration of the implications of that proposition. An effective ending is part of the way the essay packages its proposition. Paragraphs of explanation or defense refer inward to the position taken in the paper's proposition. An ending refers outward to the readers' interests, just as introductions do.

The third reason to avoid writing a "conclusion" at first is the danger that what you "save for the conclusion" might be the whole point of the essay. The formal exercises in this book ask you to make that point not at the end of the essay but toward the beginning: in the last sentence of the first paragraph.

You may find the temptation to write at least a "concluding sentence" overwhelming at first. That is a good sign. It shows that you have already gained a kind of innate formal sense. You feel the need to wrap things up. So, if not writing a "conclusion" is too painful at first, by all means go ahead and write one. Then just leave it off the final version of the paper. This is a kind of ruse, but it may ease the withdrawal process some, and it won't do any harm.

The only thing to make sure of in doing the essay exercises in this book is not to put a formal ending on the final version of the essay. At the end of the explanation or defense, just stop. No "conclusion."

(There is more about how to package an essay effectively in Part Four: Reaching Out to Members of Other Communities, p. 189.)

Assumptions

Assumptions are beliefs, facts, or opinions that you take for granted. You usually do not discuss them, explore them, explain them, defend them, or subject them to analysis. You often aren't even aware of many of your assumptions, although every statement you make is based on many of them. They are the premises or biases that you tend not to bring up or mention in conversation with your friends, because you assume (another assumption) that your friends assume what you assume.

As a writer and reader, though, it is important to try to become as aware of your assumptions as you can. As a writer, you cannot assume that all your readers asusme what you assume. If they don't, they may well misunderstand you. As a reader, you may misunderstand what you are reading if you are not aware of the assumptions that underlie it. So when you analyze something to discover its assumptions, you may find out something you may not know about yourself while you are finding out something about your readers or the writer of something you have read.

Sometimes writers come clean and tell us their assumptions. Sometimes they do not. If writers do not tell us what their assumptions are, they are not necessarily being dishonest or devious. They may only be assuming (as we tend to do with our friends) that all their readers share their assumptions. So it is often a good idea to try to discover the assumptions that underlie what you read, the unstated assumptions, just to be absolutely sure that you understand what the essay is getting at and to make sure that it isn't trying to pull the wool over your eyes.

Discovering Assumptions

One way to discover a writer's unstated assumptions is to analyze key sentences in the essay to discover the questions that they raise. For example, the undeveloped essay on smog, p. 112, makes several unstated assumptions. Some of these the writer may be aware of, some of them he may not.

¶1   The smog in this city is terrible. We could solve the smog problem by keeping cars out of the city.

¶2   For one thing, cars produce all the worst kinds of air pollution.

¶3   Another reason is that cars produce a greater volume of pollutants than any other source.

The writer could develop the proposition in this example by developing paragraphs 2 and 3. But the proposition cannot be developed completely in this way. The paragraph raises a number of questions. A coherent essay could answer only one of them: "Why will keeping cars out of the city solve the smog problem?" The essay as it is sketched out now cannot answer at least three more questions that the proposition raises. The answers to these questions are among the essay's unstated assumptions.

We could solve the smog problem by keeping cars out of the city.

Who is "we"?

"Who are we? . . ."

How *can* cars be kept out of the city?

Who is "we"? The *we* in this example essay is a rhetorical, or editorial, *we*. By talking about what "we" can do, the essay tries (whether consciously or not) to enlist our sympathy on behalf of the position taken in it. Because the essay's *we* includes us without asking our permission, using the word may be a subtle form of intimidation. The essay assumes the reader's agreement with its position before it has legitimately gained that agreement by exploring, explaining, or defending its position.

"Who are we? . . ." The *we* in the example essay is also a device for suggesting—without stating it explicitly—that engaged, active members of the public have power to effect important changes in the quality of life everyone shares. That is, the essay assumes that "we" have power that some timid or reserved readers might not actually feel. They might say to themselves, "Sure pollution is bad, but who are we to say what ought to be done about it?" The essay tries to enlist our sympathy by assuming that, on the contrary, "we" know what's good for us, "we" have a right to say what we think, and "we" have a right to take action to make things better.

How *can* cars be kept out of the city? Finally, the essay assumes that keeping cars out of the city is technically and politically feasible. Or perhaps, on the other hand, it assumes that how cars are to be kept out is not a matter of immediate concern: it's a problem we can solve when we get around to it. That is, the essay is apparently willing to leave until later the problem of how to put into effect the change it proposes. Maybe the writer will take a position on that in the next essay.

Another example of a proposition that makes unstated assumptions is the proposition of the paper on cars in exercise 5: "Cars may be on the way out as our major means of transportation." This proposition leaves unspecified exactly what it means by "cars" and exactly what it means by the phrase "on the way out." Readers might also want to raise issues such as how long the process of phasing out cars as a means of transportation has been going on, why it began, and how one might be expected to measure such a trend.

Every issue but the central one ("Are cars on the way out?") reveals unstated assumptions that the proposition rests on, assumptions about causes, definition of terms, criteria of measurement, and criteria of judgment. Even the in-out metaphor in which the position is expressed (cars may be "on the way out") may reveal something about the writer's values that is not made explicit anywhere in the essay. For example, we often refer to something being in or out of fashion (jeans are in, saddle shoes are out). So the proposition implies something about our choice of transportation that the essay doesn't really think about, since it doesn't focus on taste but on utility.

ALLOWABLE ASSUMPTIONS

Because every statement you make contains implicit assumptions, it would be redundant and exhausting to explore all the assumptions that writers make. For this reason, every essay's proposition expects readers to accept something on faith for the sake of argument.

Assumptions that readers are willing to accept on faith are allowable assumptions. Writers have to judge which aspects of their subject and which of their assumptions they can leave unexplained, in the belief that readers share and will not question them. Conscientious writers make their more dubious and arguable assumptions explicit, because they want readers to be aware that they are making them.

In this book, for example, the first two paragraphs of the Introduction explain some of the book's assumptions but leave others unexplained in the hope that readers will allow them:

> The purpose of this short course in writing is to help students learn to read and write better through collaborative learning. Collaborative learning assumes that reading and writing are not solitary, individual activities, but social and collaborative ones. When we read and write we are never alone, although

we may seem to be. We are always in the company of communities of other readers and writers whose language and interests we share.

Collaborative learning places this social, collaborative nature of reading and writing at the center of college and university education. This book, based on collaborative learning principles, turns writing classrooms into collaborative classrooms by making them active, constructive communities of readers and writers and by making students' own writing the most important text in the course.

Most of the assumptions in these two paragraphs are about the nature of collaborative learning and its place and function in college and university education. The paragraphs make one of these assumptions explicit:

Collaborative learning assumes that reading and writing are not solitary, individual activities, but social and collaborative ones.

The paragraphs also assume, less explicitly, that teachers who make their classrooms into "active, constructive communities of readers and writers" in which the "students' own writing" is "the most important text in the course" are actually teaching. Some readers might allow both these assumptions. Others might allow the first but not the second. Still others might regard both of them as nonsense.

To defend these assumptions would go beyond the scope of a writing textbook. So the writer leaves unexplained how readers might arrive at the assumptions he has arrived at. He also leaves unexplored the assumptions that underlie some of the metaphors he uses such as *company, share, center,* even *collaborate.* He assumes, without explanation, that most readers' reflections upon their own experiences as writers and teachers will verify what he assumes. He hopes in any case that, after this reflection, most readers will allow his assumptions, because they are the assumptions on which the rest of the book is based.

When readers refuse to allow a writer's assumptions, or when readers and writers are unaware that their assumptions differ, the inevitable result is misunderstanding. This is what happens when people use the same words to describe different things, or use different words to describe the same thing. When economists talk about *full employment,* for example, they may mean a situation in which only 3 or 4 percent of the labor force is unemployed. To a person who cannot find a job, and is therefore a member of that 3 or 4 percent, an economist's idea of full employment is little better than a bad joke. To unemployed people, full employment occurs when they themselves have jobs and can support their families.

The same sort of difference, which sometimes leads to misunderstanding, occurs between academic disciplines. For example, ask a mathematician, a biologist, an economist, and a historian what they mean by the word *description* and you will get quite a different answer in every case. A mathematician means a graphic action or a kind of equation (as in "describe an arc"). A biologist means a systematic and schematic diagram of a living creature or organ. An economist means a nonchronological generalization based in most cases on accumulated individual decisions, that is, statistical evidence. A historian means a narrative— the story of an event—usually chronological in nature, cut across with analytical discussion that relates one moment with some other moment. Students who face exam questions in different courses in which the word *description* appears have to be aware of the different ways the word is used and the different assumptions underlying its use, or else they risk failing their exams.

DANGER: UNALLOWABLE ASSUMPTIONS

This discussion of unstated or unacknowledged assumptions reveals some startling aspects of writing. Most writers leave assumptions unstated because they take it for granted that their readers agree with them and know as much about the subject as the writer knows. Most writers assume that they and their readers share important values and preconceptions as well as relevant background information. If this agreement is all we discover when we look for writers' assumptions, then we can probably feel relatively safe in their hands.

But some writers may leave their assumptions unstated for less honest reasons. They may not state their assumptions because they are sure (or are willing to bet) that their readers do *not* share their knowledge and values. They hide their assumptions in order to delude or misinform their readers. These writers sense that if they stated their assumptions clearly, readers would reject what they have to say. They leave their assumptions unstated in order to try to con readers into accepting ideas that otherwise, with full knowledge, they would not accept. When you discover writers doing this, you have to read cautiously.

COLLABORATIVE LEARNING

Follow the instructions for working in consensus groups on p. 20.

Task   Discovering Assumptions

Write out the proposition sentence and the first sentence in paragraphs 2 and 3 of an example essay in this book.

1. List the operative words in each sentence. (There is more about finding operative terms in Propositions, p. 85, and What an Essay *Says*, p. 154).

2. Write out as many questions as you can that each of these sentences may raise in the reader's mind. (There is more about the questions that sentences raise in Paragraph Development, p. 111.)

3. Which questions raised by the proposition sentence do paragraphs 2 and 3 of each relevant essay *not* answer? What do you suppose the writer's reasons were in each case for not answering them? Has the writer made only allowable assumptions?

STYLE

Suppose you are reading an essay that defends the proposition, "It is time to abolish capital punishment." The essay begins with these two sentences:

> The most serious method of punishment in human society is the death penalty, the exacting of the life of offenders for their offense. In making use of such means of punishment, society incurs a grave responsibility.

Now suppose that the writer tells you that she's not satisfied with these sentences and asks for our help. If you respond only that you think the sentences are bad or awkward and need to be rewritten, she will be offended as well as justifiably confused. The sentences are rather awkward, although they are perfectly grammatical, and they do need to be rewritten. But if you condemn them out of hand you will not help this writer improve them.

TALKING CONSTRUCTIVELY ABOUT STYLE

You could help her improve them in two ways. One is to show her that in some respects she had done exactly what she should have done. The other is to help her see how she can do those things better. (See Learning to Write Peer Reviews, p. 173.)

There is a lot to praise in the passage. For one thing, it deals with an important topic. Some people, of course, may think that as a topic to write an essay on, the death penalty is old hat, whereas in fact it continues to be a legal and moral issue throughout the Western world. For another thing, the passage approaches that topic in a serious way. Of course, some people may not agree with what the writer seems to be saying about it. But to her, these views on capital punishment may be a real discovery. It may be the first time she has worked out her ideas on the subject and the first time she has realized why she feels as she does about it. In approaching the topic, she has made a decisive value judgment (the death penalty involves human responsibility) and she has accurately defined the key term in the passage, *the death penalty.*

Furthermore, the main clause in the second sentence, "society incurs a grave responsibility," is succinct, readable, and appropriate in tone to the idea expressed. The intent of the opening phrase of the second sentence, "In making use of such means," indicates that the writer is aware of the need to make transitions, in this case linking the definition of the key term to the major value judgment stated in the passage "society incurs a grave responsibility," a statement that will probably lead to the proposition of the paper. Even the serious pun (the death penalty is a "grave responsibility") enforces the point of the passage. These virtues, as well as the rhythm and sound of some parts of the passage, suggest that the writer may have a good native ear for the language.

You could also point out that the writer probably intentionally avoided at least two ways in which she could have improved the passage. The two ways to improve the passage are to make use of rhetorical repetition and break the passage up into shorter sentences. She may have avoided both because she has been told that to repeat words and write short sentences will make her writing repetitious and choppy— that is, they would make her writing seem childish: Dick and Jane writing.

HOW TO IMPROVE AWKWARD STYLE

So one thing you could say to this writer is that in trying hard to avoid childish style, she has obscured the real potential of these sentences. She has tried to make the first sentence say more than any single sentence should be asked to say, or at least more than she is yet able to make a single sentence say:

> The most serious method of punishment in human society is the death penalty, the exacting of the life of offenders for their offense.

The first suggestion you could give her about this sentence is to make it into two sentences, not one:

> The most serious method of punishment in human society is the death penalty. [This is] the exacting of the life of offenders for their offense.

Once she divides the sentence in half, she will probably see right away that she can improve the first of these two new sentences by the simple process of cutting out some words:

> The most serious ~~method of~~ punishment in human society is ~~the~~ death ~~penalty~~.
> The most serious punishment in human society is death.

Also, although it is not necessary and would only provide other ways of saying the same thing, she could rearrange the parts of the sentence:

> Human society's most serious punishment is death.
> Death is human society's most serious punishment.

There are of course other ways she could state the idea just as simply and effectively.

The second sentence, created by cutting the original first sentence in half, became a sentence by giving the unattached phrase a subject and a verb:

> **This is** the exacting of the life of offenders for their offense.

In this form, however, the most important aspects of the idea are unrelated to the most important parts of the sentence. The most important parts of most sentences are the subject and verb. To help the writer make the important aspects of the idea and the important parts of the sentence coincide, you could ask her two questions:

> What is doing something in this sentence? A: **Society.**
> What does it do? A: **It exacts.**

Then you could suggest that she turn the answer to question 1 into the subject of the sentence and turn the answer to question 2 into the verb.

> **This is** the exacting of the life of offenders for their offense.
> **Society exacts** the life of offenders for their offense.

In this way, the first sentence of the original passage

> The most serious method of punishment in human society is the death penalty, the exacting of the life of offenders for their offense.

has become by stages two new sentences:

> The most serious punishment in human society is death.
> Society exacts the life of offenders for their offense.

You could also show the writer at this point that she could state the idea expressed in the second sentence allusively, if she wanted to. She could give the idea extra force by referring to a commonly known phrase drawn from the Bible.

Society exacts the life of offenders for their offense.
Society demands an eye for an eye and a tooth for a tooth.

So much for the first sentence in the original passage. Now you could show the writer that the second sentence shows in a different way that she does know what she wants to do but does not know yet quite how to do it:

> In making use of such means of punishment, society incurs a grave responsibility.

In the introductory phrase of this sentence

> In making use of such means of punishment . . .

she quite properly links the first thing she says in the essay with the second:

> Society exacts the life of offenders for their offense. In making use of **such means of punishment** . . .

But in doing so, she confuses two idioms. We usually do not say that we *make use of* means. We usually say that we *adopt* means. We say that we *make use of methods*. But even with this change, the phrase is not entirely satisfactory:

> In making use of such methods of punishment . . .

The phrase is euphemistic. It avoids saying something directly and in the way we are most likely to say it when we are talking to each other. It beats around the bush, and it takes too many words to say a fairly simple thing. Other ways to say it are

> In punishing people in that way . . .

or

> In taking that life . . .

If the writer substituted one of these phrases for the one she began with, the opening of her essay, in thirty-seven words,

> The most serious method of punishment in human society is the death penalty, the exacting of the life of offenders for their offense. In making use of such means of punishment, society incurs a grave responsibility.

128

would finally become the following, in twenty-eight words:

> The most serious punishment in human society is death. Society exacts the life of offenders for their offense. In taking that life, society incurs a grave responsibility.

Now the passage fulfills its original potential. It is succinct and readable. The sentences are a little shorter—at nine, ten, and nine words respectively—than the professional average, which is about fifteen words. But they are varied in form, their structure is uncomplicated, they are well articulated, and they contain no words or phrases used merely to dress up the writing. The passage repeats the key word *society* twice, but this in itself does not make the passage repetitious. On the contrary, it helps make the passage cohere.

The result is simple but in no sense simpleminded. You would have helped this writer toward the kind of unpretentious, economical writing from which her own personal style can grow as she grows.

COLLABORATIVE LEARNING

Follow the instructions for working in consensus groups on p. 20.

Task 1   Simplifying Sentences

Rewrite the following sentences to make them less pretentious and more succinct and readable.

1. Prior to the acquisition of my college diploma, I formulated my goals on the assumption that I would have little difficulty obtaining a remunerative and satisfying position.
2. Upon receiving an aural impression of the detonation, the somewhat overweight officer of the law emerged from the edifice at a rapid pace and apprehended the perpetrator of the disturbance.
3. Security has meant varying pursuits and differing goals for diverse periods of history.
4. His verbal accomplishments notwithstanding, how could the author of *Pilgrim's Progress* hope to find a receptive reader in the present epoch: small the hope indeed if Bunyan were merely one of the many polemicists of the day in whom the spirit of the artist had not fused with the soul of the reformer.
5. The answer to your inquiry is the positive one, Virginia, that the existence of Santa Claus is certain.

Task 2 *Muddling Sentences*

Rewrite the following sentences to make them as wordy, pretentious, uneconomical, and muddled as you can.

1. Last Saturday I got a terrific bargain on a boat.
2. A farm is a great place to bring up children.
3. If you can't stand the heat, stay out of the kitchen.
4. We could solve the smog problem by keeping cars out of the city.
5. As the sun rose, he kissed her and told her he would never leave her, and then he left.

Task 3 *Testing Sentence Length*

Here again is the paragraph from Winston Churchill's *My Early Life*. Test the length of Churchill's sentences.

First, guess what you think the average length of Churchill's sentences is, and write down your guess.

Then count the words in each sentence and group the sentences by number in order of length, beginning with the shortest.

Write out the six shortest sentences in order of length.

Figure out the average length of sentences in the paragraph, leaving the longest sentence in the paragraph out of your calculations (because it is extreme and therefore abnormal).

How close did your guess come to the actual average? What does the difference tell you about how long you think your own sentences should normally be?

[1]I continued in this unpretentious situation for nearly a year. [2]However, by being so long in the lowest form I gained an immense advantage over the cleverer boys. [3]They all went on to learn Latin and Greek and splendid things like that. [4]But I was taught English. [5]We were considered such dunces that we could learn only English. [6]Mr. Somervell—a most delightful man, to whom my debt is great—was charged with the duty of teaching the stupidest boys the most disregarded thing—namely, to write mere English. [7]He knew how to do it. [8]He taught it as no one else has ever taught it. [9]Not only did we learn English parsing thoroughly, but we also practiced continually English analysis. [10]Mr. Somervell had a system of his own. [11]He took a fairly long sentence and broke it up into its components by means of black, red, blue, and green inks. [12]Subject, verb, object: Relative Clauses, Conditional Clauses, Conjunctive and Disjunctive Clauses! [13]Each had its color and its bracket. [14]It was a kind of drill. [15]We did it almost daily. [16]As I remained in the Third Form (B) three times as long as anyone else, I had three times as much of it. [17]I learned it thoroughly. [18]Thus I got into my bones the essential structure of the ordinary British sentence—which is a noble thing. [19]And when in after

years my schoolfellows who had won prizes and distinction for writing such beautiful Latin poetry and pithy Greek epigrams had to come down again to common English, to earn their living or make their way, I did not feel myself at any disadvantage. [20]Naturally I am biased in favor of boys learning English. [21]I would make them all learn English, and then I would let the clever ones learn Latin as an honor, and Greek as a treat. [22]But the only thing I would whip them for is not knowing English. [23]I would whip them hard for that.

LEARNING FORMAL ORGANIZATION: THE CRUNCH

Before you have completed the first nine exercises in this book, you may begin to feel impatient and irritable. You may feel that doing these five-hundred word, three-paragraph exercises is futile, perhaps even destructive of your identity and creativity. If you found it easy at first to repeat the three-paragraph form mechanically, you may now discover that you can't do that any longer. And if you found the form hard at first, you may now begin to find it utterly impossible. You may begin feeling that you can't find subjects to write about that seem to fit the form. You may want to tear the book up, drop the course, and forget the whole thing.

This is the writing course crunch. No writing course should be without one.

The writing course crunch is the moment when you face the question, "Am I going to control my words and my ideas, or am I going to go on letting my words and ideas control me?" To choose to control your words and ideas, you may have to undergo a disturbing change. This change involves a change in the way you think about yourself. You may have to become less passive, dependent, and self-deprecating, and instead become more autonomous, self-possessed, and self-controlled.

A change of this sort is necessary because of the deep and complex relationship between language and identity. When you write you tend to feel exposed. Everyone does, because we do expose aspects of ourselves when we write. You began learning language very early in your life, so language is strongly tied into your identity. When you write, your language reveals your thoughts and feelings, some deeply buried in the core of your self, as saplings are buried at the core of mature trees. Your first words, and the feelings you expressed with them, don't go away. They get buried within you. They become part of who you are. As a result, when you write you may feel you are inadvertently revealing aspects of your identity that you are not wholly aware of and that may not be entirely under your control.

That is why criticism of your writing may feel like criticism of your self. In a limited sense, it is. You construct a lot of what you call your *self* with the language you learn in early life. So when someone criticizes the language you use, they are criticizing something that feels as close to you as your self.

It is hard to escape that feeling entirely, but you can at least control how strongly you feel it. You can control your feelings about criticism of your writing by shaping what you write, by giving it form, and in that way distancing it from yourself. Formal control in writing is an act of social adaptation. When you control what you say with formal conventions of the sort that you learn in this book, you adapt your inner thoughts and feelings, derived from the language of communities that you belonged to earlier in life, to the new communities of people that you now address when you write.

Because your inner thoughts and feelings are compounded of the languages of the many communities you have belonged to and that you belong to now, they have a logic of their own. That logic may be so complex that it is hard for other people to understand. Trying to make some of your own particular mix of many languages understandable and accessible to other people when you write can therefore make you feel a little bit apprehensive. Will you be able to get through to them? You can allay some of that apprehension by shaping your ideas in conventional, formal ways.

But allaying your anxiety by shaping your ideas in conventional ways is not always an easy task. The random, associative logic of your inner thoughts is so complex that it sometimes feels like a hodgepodge that is peculiarly and hopelessly your own. You cannot possibly present yourself in that way in writing. No one would understand you. And yet to untangle the knot so that other people can grasp the thread and follow it requires, as one of my students once put it, much mental sweat.

In order to control your thoughts and feelings by giving them some kind of form, furthermore, you have to know what other people's expectations are. You have to know the form that people in the community you are addressing are used to and agree on in order to communicate with each other. The form that this book teaches is one of the forms that the community of educated people agrees on.

But you change your thoughts and feelings when you give them form. So you also change yourself to some extent. While you are making that change, you may feel somewhat unsure of yourself and about the outcome. This uncertainty adds a new element of anxiety to the fear of exposure when you write. When you write, you volunteer to reveal your thoughts and feelings, and by revealing them, change them. At that moment, you are in a sort of no-man's-land between your old self and some unknown new self in the making. Your anxiety in writing results from the fact that you are vulnerable. You are courting exposure during a process of change, a process that would make you feel insecure even if you underwent it entirely in private.

132

This condition of writing never changes. Writing anxiety is never likely to disappear entirely for anyone. I feel a little nervous even revising this book. Fortunately, however, most of us can reduce that anxiety to the point where it no longer paralyzes us but prods us to do better work.

The best way I know of to reduce writing anxiety is, as Eleanor Gaffney explains in her essay (p. 325), to join a community of fellow writers. To be able to share anxiety often helps allay it. This is one reason that collaborative learning is valuable in learning to write. During the period of change that is involved, you give your student peers sympathy, encouragement, and support, and you expect your student peers to give you sympathy, encouragement, and support as well. It may help if you spend an hour or so in a group gripe session once in a while, talking about how hard writing is, why anyone bothers to write, why essays are sometimes such a pain to write, and what the benefits of writing in a controlled way may be. It often helps to talk about why, as Mark Twain put it, we often hate to write but love having written.

Your teachers can help by reminding you of the practical payoff of controlled writing. The payoff is that you will be able to write clearer, more substantial, and, therefore, more successful examinations and papers in academic courses. Later on you will be able to write clearer, more substantial, and more successful letters, reports, and memos at work. You will be able to discover and formulate an opinion about any subject— academic, political, aesthetic, or whatever, just as Mr. Metzger can in William Perry's essay (p. 343), but more knowledgeably and honestly. In doing that, you also stand to gain more self-knowledge. It is valuable to feel strongly about something, it is more valuable to be able to generalize and formulate what you feel so that you know why you feel that way, and it is even more valuable still to be able to explain what you feel to other people in hopes of leading them to feel the same way.

This is why it is important to remain firm during the writing course crunch. Keep on practicing writing essays in the form the book asks for. You can always write extra essays, if you want to, in any other form you choose.

If you let up on yourself at this crucial moment, and if your peers and your teacher let up on you, you will lose the opportunity that the form offers to confront yourself, your ideas, and your language. To grow as a writer and gain new confidence in your ability to write well and the value of your own ideas, you have to endure the writing course crunch.

PART THREE

Constructive Reading

To be a good writer, you have to be a good reader. The better you can read, the better you can write. Good readers are constructive readers. *Constructive readers* read in order to understand how something they are reading is constructed—how it is put together—as well as what it means.

That is, many good readers are in effect writing something like a descriptive outline in their heads all the while they are reading. They are continuously aware of what something they are reading *does* in relation to the whole essay, as well as what it *says*. That is why you have to be a good reader in order to be a good writer. To control what you write, you have to know what your writing *does* and *says*. You have to read what you write in the same way that you read what anyone else has written: constructively.

There are several reasons to read constructively when you write. One reason is that your first reader is always yourself. You read what you write while you're writing it. When you write something and then read and revise it, you make sense to yourself and other people. **Making sense is constructing sense.** So to make sense you have to be a constructive writer as well as a constructive reader.

The second reason to read constructively when you write is that no one writes in a vacuum. Every time you write you join a conversation already in progress. Other writers write, and sooner or later you write back. You write, and sooner or later someone else writes back. Whenever you feel that you have something to say, you are responding to what other people have already written and said. What you write keeps the conversation going. You read constructively because you want to know whether you are keeping the conversation going in the direction it was already headed or sending it off in an entirely new direction.

Because writing is part of a conversation with other readers and writers, you have to be able to understand what other writers have written. So the third reason to read constructively is that when you are using professional writing as a source, such as textbooks and scholarly articles, you can feel more confident that you understand what they are saying and doing.

Finally, reading constructively helps you find out *how* other writers write, so that you can do the same sort of thing yourself sometime, maybe even better, or at least you can avoid their mistakes. After a lot of practice reading constructively, you may even find yourself reading your own writing more objectively, almost as if someone else had written it. Constructive reading helps you control your writing by making you one of your own peer reviewers.

The purpose of Part Three is to help you read more constructively in all these ways. It explains how reading aloud gets you involved in a community of writers. It explains using descriptive outlines to show how writers construct their essays to make sense. And it explains how peer reviews help you and your classmates improve your writing.

(There is more about communities of writers in Part Four, Reaching Out to Members of Other Communities, p. 189.)

READING ALOUD

Reading is a constructive activity because it is a social activity, just as speaking and writing are social activities. All three are social activities because all three involve language. Language is a social construct. This means that human beings continually make and remake language and learn and relearn language in conversation with each other.

Because language is a social construct, even reading alone is a social process. When you read, you are engaged in conversation with the person who wrote what you are reading. And you are also engaged in conversation with the other people who have read what you are reading, who are now reading it, or who are going to read it. Some of these people are alive. Some of them have been dead for centuries. Some have yet to be born. Dead, alive, or unborn, they are all engaged in conversation with you through what they have written, are writing, and have yet to write; and you are engaged with them in turn through what you write.

WHY READ ALOUD?

Reading aloud is actually a form of publication, like getting your essay printed in a journal or a magazine. In fact, reading aloud is the oldest, easiest, friendliest, and most economical form of publication. Writers have been reading their work aloud for thousands of years. What happens among writers when they read their work aloud is that, right from the start, they begin to get interested in each other and begin to trust each other. They become a community of writers engaged in constructive conversation about writing.

Constructive conversation about writing takes two forms. It can be direct talk, face-to-face. Or it can be indirect talk, talk displaced into writing. Reading aloud is an important part of learning to read and write constructively because it instantaneously transforms one sort of thing (written conversation) into another (face-to-face conversation). Reading aloud puts the ball into play.

Writers sometimes read aloud in order to transform written conversation into face-to-face conversation for the same reason that composers and playwrights perform their work publicly and painters and sculptors display their work in museums and galleries. Knowing how writing sounds when you read your work aloud and hear other writers read their work aloud helps you control language instead of letting language control you. When you hear yourself read what you have written aloud, and when you hear others read aloud, you begin to feel more responsible for what you write.

You begin to acquire this new responsibility when you get the immediate response of a community of sympathetic peers. Sympathetic peers don't necessarily agree with what you write, or even know much about it, but they know how hard it is to write anything at all, and they are willing to listen to you and to talk with you about what you've written. If you know that other people are going to listen to what you are writing and are going to talk about it with you, you will be a lot more careful about what you write and how you write it. Response from other writers diminishes the solitude of writing that encourages carelessness and that makes writing sometimes feel futile and obsessively self-involved.

With time and practice, reading your own work aloud and hearing other writers read their work aloud can also help you become more aware of what is actually down there on the page. You will discover that people can hear relationships, some of which you weren't quite aware of yourself, among the parts of your essays. You will discover that they can respond to what you have written in ways that are really helpful. You will begin to trust those responses and discover that your fellow students respect the helpful responses you are making to their writing. And you will discover that people can even find ideas in what you have written that you hadn't been aware of.

You may also discover that reading aloud gives you new courage by making you more willing to risk writing what you really have on your mind. You will find that other writers really are interested in what you have to say. They will want to talk to you about it and write back. You will find yourself getting interested in what they have to say, too. You will want to talk to them about that and write back. You will collect more topics to write about than you would have time for in a dozen writing courses. And you will discover differences you never knew about between your own interests, ideas, and background and other people's interests, ideas, and backgrounds: between your likes and dislikes and other people's.

Finally, when you read your work aloud and hear other writers read their work aloud, sooner or later you will begin to write "by ear." When you read aloud, you can't help but hear what you have written. So by reading aloud you will eventually learn to hear what you write as you write it, before you read it aloud. That will help you write better, because a lot of awkward, incoherent, pretentious writing results from only seeing writing on the page instead of hearing it there. The more you read aloud and listen to your classmates read aloud, the more likely your own writing will become succinct and readable.

WHEN AND HOW TO READ ALOUD

You can read your work aloud in different ways for different purposes. First, read your work aloud to yourself often while you are writing and revising. That will help you hear your work as you write. It will also get you ready to read clearly and effectively to your classmates.

All the writers in a writing class should read their essays aloud, even if it takes more than one class hour to do it. Every writer should be heard so that every writer gets to publish and every writer gets an idea of what every other writer is doing and thinking about. The class might let someone who is shy off the hook the first time around. But not the second time. Sooner or later, everyone has to read their work aloud. You, your fellow writers, and your teacher can give everyone, even the shyest members of the class, the encouragement they need to be willing to read their work aloud. Say, "I want to hear what you have to say," and mean it.

When you read aloud, both to yourself and to your classmates, read slowly and clearly. Make the major corners in the essay clear too. When you begin a new paragraph, announce it ("paragraph 2 . . .", "paragraph 3 . . ."). When you have finished reading, nobody has to comment, except maybe to say a reassuring thank-you.

After everyone in the class is more or less used to reading aloud, the group can hear fewer papers at one time and learn to analyze by ear and take notes. To do this, writers may have to read an essay more than once and should certainly repeat the proposition and the first sentence of each paragraph, so that people have time to write them down. Sooner or later everyone in the class will be able to tell writers, on the hoof, what each paragraph *says* and *does* and what its relation is to the proposition. (See Descriptive Outlines, p. 152.)

Then writers can compare their own descriptive outlines with what their classmates heard. This comparison can lead to an even more detailed analysis of what each paragraph *says* and *does* to see who understands better how each paragraph is constructed, the writer or the class. It may help to write out the class's descriptive outline on the blackboard. During this discussion the class's most frequent and helpful remark may simply be, "Can we hear it again, please?"

One reason you may have to ask writers to read a passage aloud again, or as a reader you may have to reread it, is that the passage creates expectations that it does not fulfill. It points you in one direction and then goes off in another. This happens when your understanding of the conventions of written language and the writer's understanding of them don't yet match. For the moment, the conversation between you breaks down.

For the conversation to continue, there can of course be a lot of disagreement among people on the issues. If everyone agreed on the issues, there would be no discussion. But everyone does have to agree on one thing: how they will discuss those issues. Community members agree on what they expect, and they agree on how writers ought to fulfill their readers' expectations. The ways in which most readers and writers agree to say and do things are the conventions of written language. You make sense when you organize what you write according to these conventions. You and your readers can follow what you say and understand it. The conventions of well-planned, well-developed position papers are the conventions of unity and coherence. (See Unity and Coherence, p. 116.)

Reading passages aloud repeatedly does not diminish the value of reading aloud as a form of publication. On the contrary, by calling attention to expectations that have not been fulfilled, repetition increases everyone's awareness of the importance of the conventions of written language.

ANONYMITY

Despite these advantages of reading aloud, you may still object to it because it feels like a breach of confidence. You may feel that you write your essays for your teacher, and your teacher is the only person you can trust with your faults and limitations. You may feel that they will embarrass you if you read your essay aloud.

But the whole point of writing is to make your private thoughts available to the people you care about in the form you would most like them to be known. Writing makes your private thoughts public. It is public–ation—the act of entering a conversation with other people. Conversely, your thinking is internalized conversation. When you write, you make public again what was public in the first place, or at least what was originally shared familiarly within a community of people speaking or writing to each other.

So if you are a member of an understanding community of writers, it may turn out that you will not feel embarrassed by your mistakes at all when you read your work aloud. You will simply hear your own and other people's mistakes, talk them over, and learn not to make them again. (See "The Benefits of a Writing Community," p. 325, and "What Tutors Can Learn," p. 308.)

Because writing is a social act, furthermore, reading essays aloud anonymously inhibits collaboration. It makes writing less of a conversational exchange among student peers and instead more of a privileged exchange between you and your teacher, so it increases dependency rather than diminishing it. Anonymity also discourages you from talking about writing with your fellow students, so it inhibits trust among peers rather than fostering it.

In short, anonymity in writing is a form of censorship. Of course there may be some rare situations in which you may want to conceal your identity as the author of an essay because of the personal or controversial nature of its subject matter. But in most cases anonymity has no place in the healthy, coherent, working group that a writing class should be.

DESCRIPTIVE OUTLINES

Descriptive outlines help you become a constructive reader by making you more aware of what writers are doing when they write, as well as what they are saying. So descriptive outlines also help you become more aware of what you are doing when you write. They reveal the parts of an essay that have to work smoothly in relation to each other. Descriptive outlines may be time consuming, but in the long run they can save you a lot of time in writing a well-planned, well-developed essay.

It would be easy to become a self-aware writer if you always had plenty of time. You could put everything you write in a drawer for six months so that when you came back to it you would read it with new eyes. You can just hear what you'd say: "Did I write *this*?" But you don't usually have that kind of time. Most people don't. You have deadlines to meet. So in order to control your words instead of being controlled by them, you have to learn to be two persons at once: writer *and* constructive reader. Writing descriptive outlines can help you gain a measure of this valuable objectivity in writing.

Conventional topic or sentence outlines will not help gain this objectivity. Topic or sentence outlines are supposed to be written before you write the essay. They are plans you are supposed to follow when you write. If you find it hard to plan ahead that way, you are not alone. If you find that you have trouble following an outline even when you have planned ahead, you are not alone. And maybe, when you are supposed to write an outline first and then write the essay, you sometimes write the essay first and then write the outline. You're not alone in that either.

Descriptive outlines ask you to do just that. First you **write the essay.** Then you **write a descriptive outline of it.** And then you **rewrite the essay.**

READING AND REWRITING: DESCRIPTIVE OUTLINES AND HOW TO USE THEM

A descriptive outline is really a tool for constructive reading and for rewriting. It is the closest thing in reading and writing to what mathematicians call a *proof*. You can use it to test whether what you have read is what you think you have read and to test whether what you really have written is what you think you wrote. A descriptive outline sets up a workshop relationship between you and the writer of the essay you are reading, whether that writer is you or a fellow writer. A workshop relationship is one in which you consider an essay as something under construction.

That is, a descriptive outline sets up a workshop relationship between you and your essay's very first constructive reader—yourself. In a descriptive outline you declare what you think you have said and done in your essay. Reading your descriptive outline along with the essay, your readers can look over your shoulder as you work. Writing a descriptive outline of your own essay lets you look over your own shoulder as you work.

A descriptive outline is a kind of aside to constructive readers, a running commentary on what you intended to do as you did it. It calls their attention to parts of the essay that you had difficulty with but couldn't figure out why; to special effects you intended but didn't quite bring off; to special effects you brought off without being aware of it; to things you wanted to do but didn't know how. With this workshop tool you ask constructive readers for help, and they can help you, where you need it most.

Every descriptive outline has two elements. One element is made up of statements that explain what each part of an essay *says*. The other element is made up of statements that explain what each part of an essay *does*. The overall form of a descriptive outline looks like this:

PROPOSITION

    PLAN

PARAGRAPH 1   *says*

          does

PARAGRAPH 2   *says*

          does

PARAGRAPH 3   *says* ·

          does

A *says* statement restates or paraphrases a paragraph in one sentence.

A *does* statement describes a paragraph's relation to the essay's proposition and describes how the paragraph is organized.

The *Proposition* in a descriptive outline is exactly the same as the proposition in the essay. It is a *says* statement for the whole essay. It paraphrases the essay in one sentence.

Similarly, the *Plan* in a descriptive outline is a *does* statement for the whole essay. It explains how the essay as a whole is organized. In effect, it summarizes the *does* statements of all the essay's paragraphs by describing in general how the paragraphs are related to the proposition and to each other.

WHAT AN ESSAY SAYS

Says statements show that a constructive reader of your essay (including its first constructive reader, you) has understood the main point of each paragraph and has therefore read the essay accurately. If an essay's *says* statements are accurate, when you read them consecutively you are reading a concise paraphrase of the essay as a whole. So whenever you have to paraphrase an essay, an article, or even a book, writing a basic descriptive outline of it may be the best way to begin.

An Example

Here is a basic descriptive outline for the essay on cars in exercise 5, p. 44.

PROPOSITION   Cars may be on the way out as our major means of transportation.

    PLAN   To support the proposition with two reasons.

PARAGRAPH 1   *says:* Use of cars is at a peak, but there are signs of change.

142

does: Introduces the proposition by describing the present situation.

PARAGRAPH 2   *says:* Our diminishing oil supply is made worse by the way cars waste gas.

does: Develops the first reason by citing comparative statistics.

PARAGRAPH 3   *says:* Cars waste time and human energy.

does: Develops the second reason by telling an anecdote.

If you omit the *does* statements from this outline, you are left with the essay's proposition plus a *says* sentence that paraphrases each paragraph:

PROPOSITION   Cars may be on the way out as our major means of transportation.

PARAGRAPH 1   *says:* Use of cars is at a peak, but there are signs of change.

PARAGRAPH 2   *says:* Our diminishing oil supply is made worse by the way cars waste gas.

PARAGRAPH 3   *says:* Cars waste time and human energy.

If you rearrange this series by moving the proposition from its place in the outline to its place in the essay—at the end of the first paragraph—these *says* statements paraphrase the whole five-hundred word essay in fifty-one words:

The use of cars is at a peak, but there are signs of change. Cars may be on the way out as our major means of transportation. One reason is that our diminishing oil supply is made worse by the way cars waste gas. Second, cars waste time and human energy.

In some cases, the best *says* statement for a paragraph may be its topic sentence or transitional generalization: the sentence at the beginning of the paragraph that most clearly states the main point. If a paragraph does not have a topic sentence or transitional generalization, then make up a *says* statement that paraphrases the paragraph. Better still, if the essay is your own and you discover that one of its paragraphs doesn't have a transitional topic sentence, write one. Then include it in the descriptive outline as the paragraph's *says* statement. Doing that, you will already have used your descriptive outline for one of its intended purposes: it has helped you to spot a flaw in your essay and correct it.

Testing Says *Statements*

There are several ways to test your *says* statements to see if they are accurate. For example, here is paragraph 2 of the example essay "Kingsgate High School," p. 240.

> ¹The two most troublesome features of Jim's reality this fall seem to be geometry and football. ²The first month of Mr. Trager's plane geometry course has left Jim very much behind. ³He has a weekly quiz average of 68, and Trager says that Jim is inattentive in class, hands in his homework irregularly, and makes thoughtless errors in class recitation. ⁴His performance puzzles Trager because he taught Jim algebra last year and knows that the boy is potentially very good in math. ⁵On the surface, it seems that the cause of Jim's difficulty in geometry may be the fact that he is trying out this fall for quarterback on the football team. ⁶But Coach Tolland says that Jim spends more time joking with the other boys than he spends practicing passes and signals. ⁷Tolland thinks Jim will probably not make Junior Varsity quarterback, and he thinks Jim knows that Billy Fazio, who moved to Hobart just this summer, is the more likely choice.

If you read this paragraph quickly, you might think that its main point is Jim's relation with Mr. Trager and Coach Tolland. Or that Jim is doing poorly in football because he is having so much trouble with geometry. Or the reverse.

Suppose you decided to write a *says* statement based on one of those readings:

> PARAGRAPH 2   *says:* Jim had trouble coping with reality this fall because he has had to reevaluate his abilities.

One way to test this *says* statement would be to see if the paragraph develops the operative words in the *says* statement you have written and to compare those operative words with the essay's proposition. *Operative words* are working words: words that the paragraph or the essay as a whole keeps referring to, defining, and explaining. One or more of the operative words or their synonyms in most paragraphs— and therefore one or more of the operative words in the *says* statement for the paragraph—will be operative words in the essay's proposition too. Here is the proposition of the "Kingsgate High School" essay.

> PROPOSITION   Jim's major problem at the moment seems to be that he is having a little trouble coping with reality.

The operative words in that sentence are *problem, trouble, coping,* and *reality.* Another look at the second paragraph of the essay shows that

144

two of these terms, *trouble(some)* and *reality* do appear in the paragraph's transitional sentence.

> ¹The two most troublesome features of Jim's reality this fall seem to be geometry and football.

They also appear in our *says* statement for the paragraph.

> PARAGRAPH 2   *says:* Jim had trouble coping with reality this fall because he has had to reevaluate his abilities.

These and other operative words in the proposition keep turning up in the essay because they are central to the position the essay takes. (There is more about operative words in Propositions, p. 85.)

But in some cases the operative words test is inconclusive, so it is often worthwhile to test the accuracy of *says* statements in another way as well. One alternative is to look at the way the paragraph is organized. Understanding a paragraph's organization helps you write accurate *says* statements because it helps you avoid mistaking subordinate points for major ones. You examine paragraph organization when you write *does* statements. So you can test the accuracy of the *says* statement for each paragraph in a descriptive outline by comparing it with the *does* statement for that paragraph.

In the "Kingsgate High School" example, although the first sentence in paragraph 2 mentions the reality of geometry and football and tells you that they are both part of Jim's problem, it doesn't say explicitly what the nature of that reality is for Jim. So the first sentence in the paragraph does not state the main point of the paragraph. In fact, the paragraph never states its main point explicitly. It only implies that point.

You discover that implication only when you begin to write a *does* statement for the paragraph. Then you notice that the paragraph has two main parts, sentences 2 through 4 and 6 through 7. Each part is about a different activity (geometry and football) but both parts relate Jim to those activities in the same way: Jim's trouble with geometry and football is a result of another problem, a deeper one. He is disappointed in both cases, and in both cases his disappointment results from being forced by his difficulty with football and geometry to reevaluate his abilities. Jim is discovering that he is not quite as good as he thought he was going to be at everything he undertakes.

So, on the basis of this analysis of the paragraph's organization, if you wrote a *says* statement for the paragraph it might read like this:

> PARAGRAPH 2   *says:* Jim had trouble coping with reality this fall because he has had to reevaluate his abilities.

If you were writing this descriptive outline for another writer and you told him that this is what you think the main point of the paragraph really is, he might infer—correctly—that he ought to revise the paragraph. He would probably decide to make this point at the beginning of the paragraph. He would no longer begin the paragraph this way:

END OF   . . . Jim's major problem at the moment seems to be
PARAGRAPH 1   that he is having a little trouble coping with reality.

PARAGRAPH 2   ¹The two most troublesome features of Jim's reality this fall seem to be geometry and football. ²The first month of Mr. Trager's plane geometry course has left Jim very much behind. . . .

Instead, he would probably begin the paragraph something like this:

END OF   . . . Jim's major problem at the moment seems to be
PARAGRAPH 1   that he is having a little trouble coping with reality.

PARAGRAPH 2   ¹The most troublesome feature of Jim's reality this fall seems to be his discovery that he is not quite as good at sports and math as he thought he was. ²The first month of Mr. Trager's plane geometry course has left Jim very much behind. . . .

If you had written the essay yourself, checking the *says* statement you had written for the paragraph by comparing it with the detailed *does* statement that you had written for the paragraph could have tipped you off too. You too could have revised the paragraph accordingly.

Still another way you can check the accuracy of *says* statements is to examine the assumptions of each paragraph and of the essay as a whole. In this example, examining the assumptions of the essay would confirm the revised *says* statement you wrote. The introduction implies some of the writer's assumptions about people's attitudes toward themselves. Our attitudes do not derive so much from what we can or cannot do as from the way we feel about what we can or cannot do. The "Kingsgate High School" essay is not so much about Jim's abilities as it is about his feelings. (There is more about assumptions beginning on p. 132.)

WHAT AN ESSAY DOES

What you usually want as a reader, naturally enough, is to find out what an essay *says*. You read mainly to join conversations already in progress, find out what people are talking about, and talk about it with them. That is, if you are going to join any conversation actively, you have to be ready to talk back. Whenever you read, you are in some way getting ready to write, just as whenever you write you are getting ready to read what you write and then write more.

So you have read constructively in order to be sure that you understand what you are reading. To be sure that you understand an essay you are reading, you have to pay attention to how it is organized and how its parts fit together. To be able to follow what something you read *says*, it helps to be aware of what it *does*. Otherwise you are likely to get lost and misunderstand. So it turns out that you can learn something from writing descriptive outlines both as a constructive reader and as a constructive writer.

Since you normally read first for what an essay *says*, when you are first learning to write descriptive outlines, *says* statements seem easier to write than *does* statements. Yet in some respects *does* statements are the more important of the two. *Does* statements help make you aware as a reader and writer that words on a paper are always *doing* something as well as saying something.

This awareness gives you greater control when you write and gives you greater control over your response to what you read. Until you discover that language really does do something instead of just somehow existing passively in its own realm of meaning, you tend to read and write as if language is magic. You are writing magically when you hope your readers will be enthralled or mystified rather than interested, edified, or convinced. And you are reading magically when you are enthralled or mystified by what you are reading rather than interested, edified, or convinced.

In short, the *does* statements in a descriptive outline can help you control words instead of being controlled by them.

Descriptive outlines come in two flavors, **basic** and **detailed,** depending on how detailed and thorough their *does* sections are.

Does statements in both basic and detailed descriptive outlines

- state how each paragraph is related to the essay's proposition and
- describe briefly the unity and coherence of each paragraph as a whole.

In addition, *does* statements in detailed descriptive outlines also describe in detail

- the function each part of the paragraph serves in the paragraph and
- how each part of the paragraph is related to all the other parts and to the paragraph's topic sentence or transitional generalization.

In the short run, writing basic descriptive outlines is a step on your way to writing detailed ones. If you are just learning how to write descriptive outlines, begin by writing basic descriptive outlines. But make it your goal to learn also to write detailed descriptive outlines that capture every aspect of the organization of every paragraph.

The reason for learning to write both basic and detailed descriptive outlines is that in the long run they have different uses. You can use detailed descriptive outlines for examining the paragraph structure of shorter essays or a few crucial paragraphs in a long essay. You can use basic descriptive outlines for analyzing longer essays and books, where the details of paragraph organization would be cumbersome and distracting. To write a detailed descriptive outline of a book, you'd have to write another book.

Basic Does *Statements*

The descriptive outline for the example essay on cars in exercise 5, p. 44, is a basic descriptive outline. Its *does* statements describe each paragraph's relationship to the essay's proposition and its overall organization.

PROPOSITION	Cars may be on the way out as our major means of transportation.
PLAN	To support the proposition with two reasons.
PARAGRAPH 1	*says:* Use of cars is at a peak, but there are signs of change.
	does: Introduces the proposition by describing the present situation.
PARAGRAPH 2	*says:* Our oil supply is going, and this is made worse by the way car motors waste gas.
	does: Develops the first reason by citing comparative statistics.
PARAGRAPH 3	*says:* Cars waste time and human energy.
	does: Develops the second reason by telling an anecdote.

You could use a basic descriptive outline like this one to check the unity and coherence of the essay as a whole. For example, if you compare a basic descriptive outline with the essay it describes you might find out that the proposition stated in the essay is not the proposition that the essay actually explores, explains, or defends. Or, as in the case of the "Kingsgate High School" essay, it could reassure you that the proposition stated in the essay is the proposition that the essay actually does explore, explain, and defend.

It may seem odd that you could write a proposition in a descriptive outline that differs from the one you wrote in the essay. But that often happens, because writing descriptive outlines is one way of reading and writing constructively. When you write an essay and then write a descriptive outline of it, you are not doing two different things. You are doing the same thing in different ways. When you write a descriptive outline of an essay, you are still writing the essay.

As a result, sometimes you may not discover what you really want to say until after you have finished the first draft of the essay and are working on the descriptive outline. If that does happen, great! It means that writing a descriptive outline has done one thing it is supposed to do. Just decide which proposition you like better, the one you put in the essay or the one you put in the descriptive outline. Then, if necessary, revise the essay.

Comparing a basic descriptive outline with its essay could also tell you that there is no transitional generalization at the beginning of a paragraph to be explored, explained, or defended, or that a paragraph in the essay doesn't actually explain or defend the transitional generalization that appears at the beginning of that paragraph (as in the case of the paragraph from the "Kingsgate High School" essay). Or the comparison could tell you that the way you have described the organization of a paragraph isn't quite the way the paragraph is actually organized. It might even suggest a better way to support the proposition than the way the essay actually supports it.

When your comparison of an essay with the basic descriptive outline you have written turns up discrepancies like these, if the essay was one you had written yourself you could improve it by changing it to agree with the descriptive outline. If the essay was one a fellow student had written, you might be able to suggest some ways to improve it. And if the essay was a professional article in a journal or a textbook, you might be justified in wondering if the writer is really not a very good writer after all, or else was trying to pull the wool over your eyes (see Danger: Unallowable Assumptions, p. 136).

So a basic descriptive outline can help you understand and improve the unity and coherence among paragraphs. But it isn't much help in understanding and improving the unity and coherence within paragraphs. For that, you have to learn to write detailed descriptive outlines.

Detailed Does Statements

The *does* sections of a **detailed** descriptive outline identify the parts or subdivisions of each paragraph and explain their relation to each other and to the paragraph's transitional generalization. You may find it easier to understand what goes on in detailed *does* statements if you think of them dramatically. Imagine you are a teenager who wants to use the family car this weekend.* What do you *do*? Naturally, you ask. To ask, you have to *say* something. What do you say? You say, "Dad, may I use the car this weekend?"

WHAT EACH OF YOU *DOES*	WHAT EACH OF YOU *SAYS*
You **ask**.	"Dad, may I use the car this weekend?"
He **refuses**.	"No."
You **beg**.	"Aw, Dad, please let me use the car."
He **refuses** again, but he **shows signs of weakening**.	"Well . . . no."
You **offer to do something in return**. (That is, you **offer to negotiate**.)	"If you let me use the car, Dad, I'll clean out the garage."
Finally, he **agrees**.	"Well, ok."
You **thank** him.	"Gee, thanks, Dad."
But he **expresses concern**.	"But you've got to drive carefully."
You **reassure** him.	"Sure, Dad, I'll be careful."

Notice that the highlighted words in the left column of this analysis have nothing to do with cars, fathers, or garages. They are all about language: the kind of language that people are using in the dialogue in the right column, and the way they are using it. That is, the terms in the left column describe the kind of "work" that the remarks in the right column do in the conversation between a father and his teenage offspring. They describe what each remark *does*. So a *does* statement for the teenager's part in that conversation would run something like this:

First, the speaker asks someone for something and intensifies the request by begging for it. Then the speaker begins to negotiate, offering to do something in return if the negotiation is successful. Finally, after reaching agreement, the speaker thanks the person the speaker has been negotiating with and reassures him.

*I am indebted to David Liss for this example.

In a detailed descriptive outline, the *does* statement for each paragraph talks about the language of the paragraph in this way. It does not talk about the subject matter of the paragraph. Specifically, the *does* statement explains in detail how the paragraph is organized. For example, here again is the second paragraph of the "Kingsgate High School" essay, this time with the new first sentence that you wrote for it earlier in this section, p. 158:

. . . Jim's major problem at the moment seems to be that he is having a little trouble coping with reality.

¹The most troublesome feature of Jim's reality this fall seems to be his discovery that he is not quite as good at sports and math as he thought he was. ²The first month of Mr. Trager's plane geometry course has left Jim very much behind. ³He has a weekly quiz average of 68, and Trager says that Jim is inattentive in class, hands in his homework irregularly, and makes thoughtless errors in class recitation. ⁴His performance puzzles Trager because he taught Jim algebra last year and knows that the boy is potentially very good in math. ⁵On the surface, it ssems that the cause of Jim's difficulty in geometry may be the fact that he is trying out this fall for quarterback on the football team. ⁶But Coach Tolland says that Jim spends more time joking with the other boys than he spends practicing passes and signals. ⁷Tolland thinks Jim will probably not make junior varsity quarterback, and he thinks Jim knows that Billy Fazio, who moved to Hobart just this summer, is the more likely choice.

The paragraph's *says* statement would remain the same whether you wrote a basic or detailed *does* section:

PARAGRAPH 2   *says:* Jim had trouble coping with reality this fall because he has had to reevaluate his abilities.

If you wrote a **basic** *does* statement for the paragraph it might read like this:

PARAGRAPH 2   *does:* Supports the proposition by analyzing two causes of the problem stated in the proposition.

If you wrote a **detailed** *does* statement for the same paragraph it might turn out something like this:

PARAGRAPH 2   *does:* Supports the proposition by analyzing two causes of the problem stated in the proposition. Sentence 1 makes a transition from the first paragraph of the essay

151

by repeating two key words, *trouble* (as in *troublesome*) and *reality*, and it introduces the paragraph by stating a probable cause of the problem. The rest of the paragraph is divided into two parts, each of which relates the probable cause stated in the proposition to a specific activity. Sentences 2, 3, and 4 explain the relationship of the probable cause to the first activity by citing an authority, by giving details of a person's character traits and performance, and by making a historical comparison. Sentence 5 makes a transition to the next part of the paragraph by comparing two aspects of the situation. Sentence 6 refutes that comparison by citing another authority. And sentence 7 explains the relationship of the probable cause of the problem to the second activity by giving evidence to support a prediction of future events.

This detailed analysis of paragraph organization explains how the first sentence in the paragraph, the transitional generalization, connects the paragraph to the proposition of the essay (by repeating key words), and how that sentence also sets up the terms of the paragraph's argument (by listing a probable cause of a problem). Then it outlines how the rest of the paragraph is organized (it is divided into two parts). The rest of the *does* statement describes in detail how each of these two parts is organized.

It is worth pointing out again that neither the basic nor the detailed *does* statement for this paragraph mentions anything about what the paragraph *says*. In neither *does* statement do Jim, geometry, or football ever appear. *Does* statements describe organization and coherence, how paragraphs are constructed, as much as possible without reference to content. This distinction between form and content is artificial, but it is a useful analytical tool.

Because the distinction between form and content is artificial, some *does* statements cannot entirely avoid referring to content. When they do have to refer to content, however, they **generalize** it or refer to it as **a type**. For example, in this detailed *does* statement, Jim's lack of attention in class, his failure to turn in homework regularly, and his 68 average are generalized to the type of observations that these are: "details of a person's character traits and performance." Mr. Trager's comparison of Jim's work this year in geometry with his work last year in algebra becomes "a historical comparison." And Coach Tolland's belief that Billy Fazio, not Jim, will become junior varsity quarterback becomes "a prediction of future events."

GETTING READY TO WRITE A DETAILED DOES STATEMENT

In order to write a detailed *does* statement, you have to find out how the paragraph is organized. The best way to find out how a paragraph is organized is to "map" it.

To map a paragraph, first **number the sentences** by marking them lightly in pencil in front of the first word of each sentence. Then **read the whole paragraph** to yourself, preferably aloud.

Second, **subdivide the paragraph.** The first time through, just guess or follow your intuition. If sentences 1 through 4 seem to hang together, call them part 1. If sentences 5 through 8 seem to hang together, call them part 2. Continue in this way. Each subdivision will be a series of sentences that seem to be more strongly related to each other than to the sentences that precede or follow. Sometimes a single sentence can constitute a part.

Third, test your intuitive division of the paragraph by asking the following questions about each part of the paragraph and about the paragraph as a whole:

- **Who or what** are the sentences in each part about?
- At **what level of generality** do the sentences in each part talk about the subject? (For example, some parts may talk generally about the traits of canines—dogs, foxes, wolves—whereas other parts may talk concretely about the traits of Rover and Spot.)
- Is there any kind of sequence or "story" involved in the paragraph? (For example, are things arranged in **numerical order:** one, two, three? **temporal order:** now as opposed to then? **causal order:** this resulted from that? **problem-posing order:** problem plus solution? **inductive order:** evidence leading to an inference? **deductive order:** a principle applied to experience, leading to a conclusion?) If there is such a sequence in the paragraph, what role does each part of the paragraph play in this sequence?

Fourth, think of an appropriate name or label for each part of the paragraph. The terms you use should describe or explain succinctly the purpose or function of each part. In thinking up names for the parts, you might find some of the following questions helpful:

- How do the parts differ from each other?
- How are the parts connected or related to each other?
- How is each part related to the main point of the paragraph?
- What role does each part play in the paragraph?

If necessary, based on your answers to these questions, adjust the boundaries that you drew intuitively.

Fifth, write a *does* statement based on your division of the paragraph into parts and the terms you devised for labeling them. The statement should name the relation of the paragraph as a whole to the essay's proposition. Then it should describe in as much detail as possible how the paragraph is organized and how it works.

Here are some of the many things a paragraph *does*.

- **tells a story** (See "Homer's Use of the Gods in the *Iliad*," paragraph 2, p. 340, and "Going Back to School," paragraph 2, p. 324.)
- **lists** (catalogue, itemize, enumerate; See *The Sea Gull:* A Great Play Makes a Bad Movie," paragraph 2, p. 63.)
- **shows how something is done** (See "Family and School," paragraph 2, p. 319.)
- **reasons** (syllogistic, inductive, dialectical; See "To Number or Not To Number," paragraph 2, p. 56.)
- **describes** (See "The Role of Planning in Making Films," paragraph 2, p. 27.)
- **explains** (See "Stock Options," paragraph 1, p. 327, and "Mitosis," paragraphs 2 and 3, p. 334.)
- **compares** (See *The Sea Gull:* A Great Play Makes a Bad Movie," paragraph 3, p. 63.)
- **defines a term** (See "Family and School," paragraph 3, p. 320.)
- **gives examples** (See "Stock Options," paragraphs 2 and 3, p. 328, "Project Head Start," paragraph 3, p. 76, and "The Pluralist Model of Power and Modern Society," paragraph 2, p. 333.)
- **analyzes** (takes something apart; See "The Role of Planning in Making Films," paragraph 3, p. 27, and "What Should Patients Be Told?", paragraph 2, p. 220.)
- **synthesizes** (puts two or more ideas together showing the relationship between them; See "Homer's Use of the Gods in the *Iliad*," paragraph 2, p. 340.)
- **cites** (refers to an authority; See "Drug Testing in Sports," paragraph 2, p. 331, "Gene Manipulation and Huxley's *Brave New World*," paragraphs 2 and 3, p. 337, and "No One Knows Anything," paragraphs 2 and 3, p. 338.)
- **evaluates** (explains how good something is or what it's good for)
- **offers a hypothesis** (makes an educated guess)
- **gives a history**
- **projects the future**

(There is more about what a paragraph *does* in Organizing for Coherence, p. 123. If you would like to compare another pair of basic and detailed descriptive outlines, the example essay "Project Head Start" on p. 75 has both. Other example essays have basic descriptive outlines, and still others have detailed descriptive outlines. And some have no descriptive outline at all. You can use the essays with no descriptive outline to practice writing descriptive outlines.)

COLLABORATIVE LEARNING

Task 1   Practice Descriptive Outline: Short Essays

Follow the instructions for working in consensus groups on p. 20.

Complete the detailed descriptive outline for "Kingsgate High School," p. 240, begun on p. 163 by writing *says* and **detailed** *does* statements for paragraphs 1 and 3.

Task 2   Practice Descriptive Outline of a Paragraph

Follow the instructions for working in consensus groups given on p. 20.

Read aloud to the group this paragraph from Robert C. Chanaud's "Aerodynamic Whistles." Then write a *says* statement for it and two *does* statements, one **basic**, the other **detailed.**

[1]Class I whistles are the most widely encountered, perhaps because so many of them occur naturally. [2]This category includes telephone wires, tree limbs, and aeolian harps singing in the wind. [3](The aeolian harp is an ancient Greek instrument consisting of a set of strings stretched over a sounding box and set in motion by the wind or the breath.) [4]This kind of Class I whistle, called an aeolian-tone generator, basically consists of a long, thin cylinder in a stream of air or some other kind of fluid. [5]Above a certain speed there will develop behind the cylinder two symmetrically placed vortexes that are stable and steady. [6]If the speed of flow increases above a second threshold and one of the vortexes is disturbed by a sound pressure wave, the vortex will oscillate around its stable position and ultimately break away from the cylinder and move downstream. [7]The breaking away of this vortex causes the opposite vortex to become unstable, and it too breaks away. [8]Another vortex forms in the place of the first one and it in turn becomes unstable. [9]The feedback appears to be entirely hydrodynamic: each vortex gives rise to instability in the other directly, without any intervening agent such as a sound wave. [10]As a result of the influence of one vortex on the other a chain of alternating vortexes soon stretches downstream from the cylinder. [11]As the vortexes develop they generate a sound field with a maximum at right angles to their path.

Task 3 *Writing Descriptive Outlines by Ear*

For this task work with a small group or with the whole class. One person choose an example essay from the book and read it aloud once slowly, then again, pausing to repeat the proposition and the first sentence of each paragraph so that people have time to write them down.

Work toward a consensus on what each paragraph *says* and a detailed statement of what each paragraph *does*. (See Descriptive Outlines, p. 152.)

One person in each group keep a record of how the group describes the essay. In doing this task with the class as a whole, the recorder can work at the blackboard.

Read passages aloud as often as necessary until the description is complete.

Task 4 *Practice Descriptive Outline: Long Essays*

Work in pairs or groups of three. First, each person write a descriptive outline independently. Then confer. Compare the descriptive outlines you have written, discuss the differences between them, and try to decide on a single descriptive outline that you agree on.

Write a basic descriptive outline of John Fischer's "Substitutes for Violence," p. 367, or Walter Lippmann's "The Indispensable Opposition," p. 353; or choose another article from a magazine, journal, or essay anthology.

For convenience, number the paragraphs of the essay lightly in pencil before you begin. If the essay you choose is longer than seven or eight pages, treat clusters of related paragraphs as units, describing in your outline how each cluster of paragraphs fits into the essay as a whole.

Then confer.

Use the following guide:

1. **What is the central point or proposition of the essay?** What position does it take? Using your words or the essay's, state the essay's proposition in one sentence.

(If you are not sure at first what the essay's main point or proposition is, write down two or three possibilities and complete parts 2 through 5 of this task. Then decide, after working out what each part of the essay *does* and *says*, which possible proposition you wrote down seems correct.)

2. **Describe the essay's introduction.** Where does it end? How many paragraphs are in it? What does it *do* to introduce the essay? What does it *say*?

156

3. **Describe the essay's ending.** Where does it begin? How many paragraphs are in it? What does it *do* to end the essay? What does it *say?*

4. **Describe the essay's explanation or defense of its position.** What does it *do* to explain or defend that position? What does it *say?*

5. What is the essay's overall plan?

6. Revise your original statement of the essay's proposition.

Task 5   *Descriptive Outline Conference*

Work in pairs (groups of three are also possible, but may be logistically more difficult).

Exchange essays with a classmate. Number the sentences in the essays lightly in pencil, but do not otherwise mark it up.

Write a **detailed** descriptive outline of each other's essays. Do not evaluate the essay.

Then confer. Compare descriptive outlines of each other's essays. Ask each other if what you said each paragraph *does* is what you intended to do. Ask each other if what you said each paragraph *says* is what you intended to say.

After the conference if you would like to revise your essay go right ahead.

(This task is the first step in peer review.)

PEER REVIEW

One purpose of reading aloud is to make both writing and learning to write more actively collaborative. That is also one purpose of writing descriptive outlines. In writing descriptive outlines and conferring about them, you learn the language that is most useful when, as a reader and writer, you talk constructively about reading and writing.

Peer review combines these two activities. It is a social relationship in which you read each other's writing constructively and write and talk to each other constructively about it. Learning peer review introduces you to the *constructive conversation* that goes on all the time among writers, among readers, and between writers and readers. As peer reviewers of each other's writing, you join that constructive conversation indirectly by corresponding with each other, writing descriptive outlines and written evaluations. And you join it directly when you confer with each other about your essays.

Both kinds of constructive conversation, corresponding and conferring, have advantages. **Corresponding**—writing to each other about reading and writing—is more exacting and rigorous than conferring. **Conferring**—talking with each other about reading and writing—is more immediately responsive to a writer's needs than corresponding. The most helpful kind of constructive conversation combines the two, conference and correspondence. So in peer review you write to each other about your essays first, and then you talk about them.

WHAT PEER REVIEW IS NOT: GRADING VERSUS EVALUATION

Evaluative judgment of some sort is always involved in peer review. Sometimes peers explicitly evaluate each other's essays during peer review, telling each other what is done well in the essay and what needs improvement. Other times peers do not evaluate explicitly. Instead, they evaluate each other's essays only implicitly, by describing them in detail. Learning to make sound evaluative judgments about each other's writing and explain them effectively is what peer review is all about.

People tend to understand the term *evaluation* in different ways. As a result, people tend to understand the purpose of peer review in different ways as well. But understanding what peer review is not is just as important as understanding what it really is. For peers working together, **evaluating** each other's writing **does not mean grading** each other's writing.

Grading is of course related to evaluation. Grades are an administrative convenience used to simplify record keeping in schools, colleges, and universities. Teachers have to reduce complex evaluative judgments to a single quantity, a grade (A, B, C, 92, 81, 75), so that keeping a record of the evaluation of many people taking many courses can be done efficiently. Grading, an institutional function, is part of a teacher's job as long as the teacher is employed by an educational institution that requires grades, as most do, and as long as students need a record of their work in the simplified form that employers and professional schools ask for.

When your teachers give grades, they think about many factors other than the details of the work itself. For example, they consider your level of development, your progress, the type of institution you are at, and the level of the course you are taking. Because as a student you are not in a position to consider all of these factors, you cannot grade each other's work accurately and responsibly.

But as a student you can evaluate each other's work. You can learn to evaluate skillfully, responsibly, and helpfully. And being in a position to evaluate without grading actually increases your usefulness to each other as peer reviewers.

Evaluation is something you do every day. You make evaluative judgments as consumers, citizens, workers, professionals—even at play. Which new dress or suit should you buy? Why? Which candidate should you vote for? Why? Which stock option should you choose, how good a job have you done, which concert or movie should you go to, which first baseman is good enough to make the all-stars, should you sell Boardwalk or hang on to it for a while? And why?

It may be, in fact, that the most important lesson you can learn from a college or university education is the ability to make evaluative judgments like these in a way that makes your own life and each other's lives better, safer, and more responsible.

WHAT IS PEER REVIEW?

Writing peer reviews of writing is one way to learn to make effective, responsible evaluative judgments. Through peer review, you learn how to help other students become better writers by describing and evaluating their writing and then by writing and talking helpfully about it. You do that in order to learn how to become a better writer yourself by describing and evaluating your own writing and by writing and talking about it.

Peer review does not of course make your teachers' evaluative judgment any less useful to you. Teachers represent the community of mature writers and readers that you are trying to join. Part of their job is to tell you how far you have gone toward gaining full membership in that community. That's what teachers do when they evaluate your work and grade it.

Peer review is an additional kind of evaluation that can sometimes be even more helpful to you and your classmates than evaluation by a teacher. If teachers tell you that they can't understand what you have written, you may feel . . . well . . . you know how teachers are. They never quite understand what you're trying to say. But if other students tell you that *they* can't understand, the criticism sticks. And naturally you sometimes feel safer knowing that your mistakes have been noticed first by a sympathetic peer who doesn't wield the power to grade what you have written.

To be a helpful peer reviewer, you have to suspend judgment about what an essay *says* while you are trying to understand what it *does*. You have to find language to describe writing accurately. You have to learn to evaluate tactfully so that other writers can accept what you say and make changes accordingly, emphasizing what is well done as well as what needs improvement. You have to explain your evaluative generalizations and support them with details. You have to learn to trust each other's judgment.

That trust comes hard. No one reviews someone else's writing well the first time. And since every essay you read is different from the last one, every peer review you undertake is in some way a new beginning. At first you may feel a little afraid of evaluating another student's work.

It may feel as if you are ratting on a friend. And you may feel a little afraid at first of having your own work evaluated by other students. Will the teacher take advantage of something negative they say about your essay and lower the grade?

You may also feel wary at first about how other students will treat you. You may think that they will be harder on you than the teacher would be. You can usually count on teachers to be kinder to you than your peers, to tell you only part of the truth and tell it tactfully. Only a mean or vindictive teacher is likely to tell you everything that is wrong with your work all at once. Your student peers may not exercise that kind of professional restraint. They may let you know it straight between the eyes.

Finally, and most importantly, you may find it hard to believe in your authority to evaluate another student's work and in another student's authority to evaluate yours. When you read another student's essay you may feel like saying, "What right do *I* have to tell you what's good or bad about your work?" And when another student reads your essay, you may feel like saying, "What right do *you* have to tell me what's good or bad about my work?"

Sometimes this fear of peer review is realistic. You have learned in traditional, competitive classrooms that everyone knocks the competition given half a chance. You also learned on the playground to fear peer review. Kids know what they'll hear from other kids if they bobble an easy grounder to third, because kids know what to say when another kid bobbles one.

But you can overcome these competitive gut responses. The way to overcome them is by learning how to work together collaboratively and by learning a systematic, constructive approach to evaluating each other's writing. Constructive reading establishes constructive relationships among student peers. You will learn to respect each other's evaluative judgment of each other as you learn to read and write constructively. And as you learn to read and write constructively you will also learn to respect your own evaluative judgment and assume some responsibility for other students' improvement as writers, a self-respect and responsibility that you may never have felt before.

This new collaborative relationship with your peers involves learning a new kind of language, the language that people use to converse constructively about reading and writing. Learning a new language is never easy. For a while you may find that corresponding and conferring with each other about writing is some of the hardest work you have ever done in school. It is such hard work because you have three immediate and demanding audiences. The first audience is yourself. Somehow, you have to tell the truth as you see it. The second audience is the teacher, who will evaluate your written peer review and grade it for its thoroughness, accuracy, insight, tact, and writing quality.

160

The third and most important audience is the writer of the essay you are reviewing. As a peer reviewer you have to be tactful, constructive, sympathetic, and firm all at once. You have to avoid alienating your peers. At the same time, you want your peers to respect you enough to want to write equally careful, helpful reviews of your essays in return. In short, peer review writing is some of the most *real* writing you will ever do in school. That's why you can learn so much from writing peer reviews.

(I am indebted to a Brooklyn College peer tutor, Christopher Guardo, for this analysis of the peer reviewer's three audiences. See p. 305.)

LEARNING TO WRITE PEER REVIEWS

Peer reviewing requires three different kinds of constructive reading: descriptive, evaluative, and substantive. You don't normally separate these ways of reading in your mind. But as peer reviewers (and as writers as well) you will have to learn to separate them so that you can read constructively one way at a time.

The first kind of reading you will learn to do as a peer reviewer is descriptive. To **describe what you're reading**—that is, to write a descriptive outline of it—you set aside explicit evaluation for the moment. You avoid pointing out what you think is well done in the essay and what you think needs to be improved. And you also set aside whether or not you agree with the position the essay takes. You avoid taking issue with the essay.

Second, as a peer reviewer you will learn to read descriptively and evaluatively. You will describe the essay—write a descriptive outline of it—**and explain what you think is well done and what needs improvement.** But you will still set aside whether or not you agree with the position the essay takes. You will still avoid taking issue with the essay.

And third, you can also learn to read descriptively, evaluatively, and substantively all at once if you are in a course that lends itself to learning all three. A course lends itself to substantive peer review if everyone in the class can write on the same topic or has a working knowledge of the topics that everyone else is writing on. In that case, **you will describe the essay, explain what you think is well done and what needs improvement,** *and* **comment on the topic of the essay and on the position it takes on that topic.**

COLLABORATIVE LEARNING

You can approach learning peer review in three phases that correspond to the three kinds of constructive reading. Begin each phase by writing an essay and a descriptive outline of the essay. Read your essay aloud to other students and exchange essays, keeping the descriptive outline

161

you wrote for your own essay. If you can, exchange essays with different people each assignment, so that you get different opinions about your work.

For each task, answer the peer review questions carefully and accurately. Write a draft of your peer review and revise it. Treat other writers' work with the respect you want from them when they read your work.

Task 1   *Practice Descriptive Peer Review*

Write a detailed descriptive outline of the following essay. Check your descriptive outline twice against the essay, and revise the outline until you are confident that it represents the essay accurately. (Detailed descriptive outlines are explained on p. 153.)

In groups of two or three, compare descriptive outlines. Where they don't match, try to find out why. Negotiate a description of the essay that all of you can agree on.

☐ Example Essay

Acting Is Believing

Joyce Bresnick Slevin

[1]One of the first assignments in my Introduction to Acting course was to make believe I was an animal of my choice. [2]So I went home and watched my cat Isis for an hour. [3]When I returned to class, I simply imitated all her actions. [4]I licked my chops, cleaned my paws, and chased my tail. [5]Obviously, seeing a woman as a cat required some imagination from myself and the audience. [6]Yet the class was convinced that I was a cat, because I did exactly what the assignment called for: I *made believe* I was a cat. [7]That is, I did not just *pretend* to be a cat. [8]I made myself actually *believe* that I was a cat and did what I would do if I were one. [9]This technique will work for any type of character portrayal, not only that of an animal. [10]As a rule, actors have to believe what they are doing in order to be successful in a role.

[1]The best way for actors to believe in a role is to concentrate on simple physical actions. [2]In *The Actor Prepares* Stanislavsky, the famous Russian actor and director, frequently emphasized that "small physical actions, small physical truths and the moments of belief in them . . . acquire a great significance on the stage." [3]In fact, he developed a practical technique called "making a score of the

role," in which an actor makes a sequential list of the specific physical actions he will perform in a scene. [4]For example, for a scene in which an actor must wait nervously for an appointment he could list the following actions: (1) enter room carrying a newspaper, (2) sit down and read newspaper, (3) stop reading and place newspaper on table, (4) cross legs, (5) uncross legs, (6) look at watch. These actions are tangible, controllable, and repeatable. [5]They give the performer something to fall back on in order to sustain belief. [6]While an actor may not be able to "be nervous" on cue, he can perform the actions that a nervous person would perform.

[1]Besides physical actions, actors can use "verbal actions" to help them believe the role they are playing. [2]A verbal action is not the actual line an actor delivers. Rather, it is the intention behind the words. [3]For example, when Hamlet says, "To be, or not to be," his verbal action is to decide whether or not to kill himself. [4]Actors must have a verbal action for every line they utter in order to make themselves believe their own role. [5]This requires a full understanding of characters and their intention. [6]As with physical actions, a verbal action is more *doing* than *being*. [7]When actors write down verbal actions in the margins of a script, they use verbs of action rather than states of being. [8]The actor playing Hamlet would use the verbal action "to decide" instead of "to be confused." [9]A state of being is not acceptable, because it provides nothing specific to do and leaves the actor stuck with a general emotion. General emotions are elusive and unpredictable. [10]If an actor begins by thinking about emotions and tries to squeeze them out, the result will be distorted and forced. [11]If an actor begins with verbal actions, emotions will come as a result of the actor's own belief in the role. □

Task 2   Essay Exchange and Descriptive Peer Review

Exchange essays with a classmate (preferably not one you have exchanged with before). Writing lightly in pencil, number the sentences in the essay you have received in exchange for your own. Don't write anything else on the paper. On a separate sheet write a detailed descriptive outline of the essay. Check your descriptive outline twice against the essay, and revise the outline until you are confident that it represents the essay accurately. (Detailed descriptive outlines are explained in this section, on p. 153.)

Confer with the writer whose essay you have read and who read your essay. Compare descriptive outlines. Where they don't match, try to find out why. Negotiate a description of both essays—yours and your partner's—that the two of you can agree on.

The purpose of this first collaborative peer review task is to help you treat an essay as something someone has constructed, like a chair—

something designed, organized, and put together to serve a purpose. The purpose of a chair is to hold people up when they sit on it. To do that well, the chair has to be well constructed. A poorly constructed chair won't serve that purpose. It will collapse when someone sits on it. The essays written for the exercises in this book have a purpose too. It is to state a position and then explore, explain, or defend it. To do that well an essay has to be well constructed, just like a chair. An essay that is poorly constructed won't serve its purpose. Its position won't hold up any better than a poorly constructed chair.

If you describe an essay accurately, you may not be able to avoid implying that the essay does (or does not do) what the writer intended it to do, or whether or not it says what the writer intended it to say. If that happens, so be it. Implicit evaluation of this kind can sometimes be more effective than explicit evaluation. **But for this peer review task, don't evaluate the essay explicitly.** Let your descriptive outline speak for itself. **And do not take issue with any of the opinions expressed in the essay.**

Task 3   *Accepting Authority in Evaluative Peer Review*

Follow the instructions for working in consensus groups on p. 20.

1. A student wrote the following notes in a process log when the first descriptive and evaluative peer review was assigned. Her entries raise at least two issues: **authority among peers** and **social relations among peers.** Explain the writer's attitudes toward each issue.

Log Entries

4/8 I don't feel right judging someone else's work.

4/15 I don't feel adequate trying to gauge anyone else's work. Who am I to tell other students what's wrong with their writing? Grammar and spelling are one thing. Sentence structure, paragraph structure, arrangement of ideas, even the ideas themselves—they're something else entirely.

I don't take well to criticism myself. And I don't know how to review someone else's work effectively without hurting their feelings by being obviously critical.

4/17 I asked Fran to look at a draft of my essay, because she knows how to criticize, and I trust her judgment. But I simply do not want to criticize anyone else's work. It takes more time than I've got. And anyway, I'm very critical of myself. I don't think it's fair to apply the standards I apply to myself to anyone else.

2. In light of your discussion of the previous log entries, explain the attitudes toward the same issues, authority among peers and social

relations among peers, in the following remarks from another student's log.

Log Entry

4/19 I really appreciate the way Steven explained to me how to revise my second paragraph. I didn't want to ask him, because in high school everybody says you shouldn't ask another student anything. If you do, they'll think you're dumb. Or they'll think you're cheating and trying to make them cheat. That really stunk. This year, the teacher told us over and over again that we could ask other people in the class anything. So I did.

Task 4   Analysis of an Example Descriptive and Evaluative Peer Review

Have one person in your group read the essay and the descriptive outlines and evaluative peer review that follow it to the rest of the group. Then arrive at consensus answers to the following questions:

1. Notice that the descriptive outlines written by the writer and the peer reviewer do not exactly match. One of the issues that the two students involved would have to negotiate in a peer conference would be why their understanding of the essay's organization differs. Which parts of the two descriptive outlines (*says* and *does*) do you think most accurately represent the essay as written?

2. How would you rewrite the peer reviewer's evaluation to make it more complete, accurate, and acceptable to the writer?

3. How would you rewrite the essay to improve it?

EXAMPLE DESCRIPTIVE AND EVALUATIVE PEER REVIEW

☐ EXAMPLE ESSAY ————————————————

The Issues Surrounding Electronic Music

Kerri Weiss

In *Electronic Music*, Elliott Schwartz, traces some of the important musical developments that led historically to electronic music. He provides a basic introduction to the way various studio systems work using computers to generate sound. With computers, the composer "programs every facet of the sound by means of his instruction to the computer" (Schwartz 89). He controls his music by selecting the "instruments" and dictating, note by note, his entire composition. Since there are many advantages to this process, the number of active computer studios is steadily increasing. Therefore, the main issue that concerns most writers on electronic music is the impact of computer technology on the future of music.

Many writers agree that computers have opened doors to greater opportunities in the music industry. They have "unlocked a universe of musical sounds," ideally allowing composers to produce a very different kind of music (Grey 14). The computer offers composers "incredible power" and "options that never existed in a standard recording setup" (Van Gelder 43). For example, with the proper software, a musician can create new sounds, compose a piece with those sounds, and perform it, all while seated at a computer keyboard (Grey 16). Composers are able to maintain more control over the way their recordings sound than they ever have before, since they can work directly with their material in this way. The costs involved are also reduced, since inexpensive equipment is now readily available. Popular music today reflects these advances. Variations, repetitive rhythmic patterns, and built-in sounds have combined "to transform the very form and content" of pop music (Holden 22). This technology continues to increase the number of possibilities for even greater changes in music in the future.

Although many writers agree that computerization is purely beneficial, others argue that computer technology also has its downside. Purists and traditionalists insist that the "villain . . . is computer-driven tunes," and they "want to smash those dark, satanic music mills" (Pareles 28). They complain that "machines produce music of such plastic perfection that it could have been produced by R2-D2" (Van Gelder 44). Computer music, they say, lacks physical presence and seems cold, impersonal, and unnatural. It threatens the quality and character of music. It has also "thrown a wrench into musical careers" (Newton 19). This is because computers are taking over jobs once performed by live musicians. Officials from the American Foundation of Musicians note that computers have already replaced studio musicians on many movie sound tracks and in the advertising jingle business (Newton 19). This trend, many fear, is the beginning of a technological nightmare, "the final victory of the Machine over Man" (Schwartz 3).

WORKS CITED

Grey, Harold. "Computer Music: Unlocking a New Universe of Musical Sounds." *Brooklyn College Magazine* March 1989: 14–17.

Holden, Stephen. "Why the Melody Doesn't Linger On." *New York Times* 14 Feb. 1988, sec 2: H22.

Newton, James S. "What's New in Music Technology." *New York Times* 1 March 1987, sec 3: F19.

Pareles, Jon. "Just Give Me a Chip Off the Old Bach." *New York Times* 10 Jan. 1988, sec 2: H28.

Schwartz, Elliott. *Electronic Music.* New York: Praeger, 1973.

Van Gelder, Lindsy. "Enjoying the Brave New World of Computer Music." *Ms. Magazine* Oct. 1987: 42–45.

DESCRIPTIVE OUTLINE

PROPOSITION   The main issue that concerns most writers is the impact of computer technology on the future of music.

PLAN   To discuss an important issue that concerns most writers on the topic by summarizing two views. To explain how the book relates to the issue.

PARAGRAPH 1   *says:* The number of active computer studios is growing since the studio creates many advantages for composers.

does: Introduces the proposition by providing background information. The paragraph is divided into two main parts. The first section, sentences 1 through 4, can be subdivided into two more parts. Sentences 1 through 2 introduce the subject matter with a general overview of a book. Sentences 3 through 4 describe a specific aspect of the subject by explaining a process. The second section of the essay, sentences 5 through 6, has two functions. Sentence 5 makes a transition from the first part of the paragraph by showing the result of the process. The last sentence in the paragraph (6) is the proposition, which relates an important issue to these ideas.

PARAGRAPH 2   *says:* Computer technology increases the number of opportunities for positive changes in the music industry.

does: Supports the proposition by summarizing one point of view. The paragraph is divided into three main parts. Part One (sentence 1) makes a transition by expanding the issue presented in paragraph 1. The second part, sentences 2 through 6, can be subdivided into three subsections. Sentences

167

2 through 3 integrate quotations from magazines to support the point of view. Sentence 4 provides an example that explains the quotations. Sentences 5 through 6 show two additional benefits and the reasoning behind them. The third part (7 through 9) describes a new form that reflects the other ideas.

PARAGRAPH 3   *says:* The use of computers in the music industry has many negative consequences.

does: Supports the proposition by summarizing the alternative point of view. The paragraph is divided into four main parts. The first sentence makes a transition by developing opposition to the view stated in paragraph 2. The second part (sentences 2 through 5) presents some negative aspects of a new technology. This section can be subdivided into two more parts. Sentences 2 and 3 both integrate quotations that vividly describe faults of the new technology. Sentences 4 through 5 list additional problems. The third part (6 through 8) describes the conditions that a specific group of people is facing as a result of these problems. The last sentence (9) makes a general statement that reinforces the importance of the issue.

☐ EXAMPLE PEER REVIEW ————————————————

Reader: Eric Miller
Author: Kerri Weiss

DESCRIPTIVE OUTLINE

PROPOSITION   The main issue that concerns most writers is the impact of computer technology on the future of music.

PLAN   To support the proposition by summarizing the two main positions on the issue.

PARAGRAPH 1   *says:* Composers can now write music in an entirely new way, by using computers.

does: Introduces the proposition by giving background information about a book. The paragraph is divided into three parts, one that gives general background information about the book, one that states a specific topic discussed in the book, and one that relates the book to the proposition. Sentence 1 gives a general summary of the book. Sentences 2 through 4 explain a specific topic discussed in the book. Sentences 5 through 6 relate the book's content to the paper's proposition.

PARAGRAPH 2   *says:* Computers have opened the doors to greater opportunities in the music industry and changed the form and content of popular music.

does: Summarizes the first position on the issue as stated in the proposition. The paragraph is divided into three parts. Sentences 1 through 2 introduce the first position on the issue. Sentences 3 through 6 state and explain three benefits of using a system. Sentences 7 through 9 explain the effects of the system on a modern art form and state the possible future effects of the system.

PARAGRAPH 3   *says:* Some writers argue that computerization is not beneficial because computer music seems impersonal and because computers have taken jobs away from musicians.

does: Summarizes the second position on the issue. The paragraph is divided into four parts. Part 1 (sentence 1) introduces the second position on the issue. Part 2 (2 through 3) explains two complaints about the system made by two different groups of people. Part 3 (4 through 5) explains two more complaints. Part 4 (6 through 9) discusses an injustice caused by the system for a particular group of people.

EVALUATION

On the whole, your essay is a pleasure to read. You state your position clearly and simply. Everything in the essay explains and defends this main point. The essay is coherent. All the paragraphs, as well as the sentences within them, are in the right order. Most transitions, especially between paragraphs, are effective. The essay is well developed too. Everything you set out to say is fully and carefully explained. Your writing style is clear. The essay is intelligently written, and yet in talking about a difficult subject that most people don't know much about, you do not rely on obscure or technical words. Finally, the essay's mechanics are excellent. Your grammar, spelling, punctuation, and citation form are almost all very good.

It seems to me, though, that a few changes would make the essay more effective.

1. Although the proposition is clear and quite adequate as is, it could be a little more succinct and more firmly attached to the introduction. You make one transitional word, *therefore*, do more work than it may be able to bear. In place of it, you could pick up the idea of *increase* from the foregoing sentence, maybe something like

. . . the number of active computer studios is steadily increasing. This increase raises an important issue in the minds of many writers: the impact of computer technology on the future of music.

2. Some transitions between sentences within paragraphs can use some strengthening too. Right now, your second and third paragraphs seem a little like lists of benefits or faults of computer music. Instead of listing items, you might try grouping them into categories. On the other hand, it may just seem like you've just listed items instead of grouping them because your inter-sentence transitions are hard to locate. More effective sentence transitions would overcome this "listing" effect and create the groups of items I mentioned, so that the paragraphs would flow better.

3. The word *downside* in paragraph 3, sentence 1, seems to me to be an unfortunate choice. *Flaws* or *faults* might fit better.

4. I may be a punctuation nitpicker, but it seems to me that the comma after *Schwartz* in paragraph 1, sentence 1 is unnecessary.

All in all a very good job. I learned a lot. □

Task 5   *Practice Descriptive and Evaluative Peer Review*

Write an evaluation of the essay you wrote a descriptive outline for in task 1, "Industrialization and Modernization in Two Latin American Countries," p. 313. Follow this format:

- **Explain the essay's strengths.** What do you like about the essay? What do you think is well done?
- **Explain what you think could be done to improve the essay.** How exactly do you think the writer can go about doing that?

Plan your evaluation carefully using the following criteria. They are listed in order of importance, with the most important first.

Unity: Is the proposition of the essay clear? Is it stated as concisely as it could be stated? Does everything in the essay defend or explain that proposition, not some other? (See Unity and Coherence, p. 116, and Propositions, p. 85.)

Coherence: Are the paragraphs in the essay in the right order? Does each paragraph begin with an effective transitional generalization? Are the sentences within each paragraph in the right order? Are there transitional elements that relate the sentences? (See Unity and Coherence, p. 116.)

Development: Is everything the essay sets out to say fully explained? Does the essay tell you everything you feel you need to know to understand the main point of the essay? (See Paragraph Development, p. 111, and Introductions, p. 81.)

Style: Is the essay's position expressed and explained as clearly and simply as possible, with no apparent effort to impress by using big words, long sentences, or elaborate word order? (See Style, p. 137.)

Mechanics: Is the essay written in standard written English with generally accepted grammar, spelling, and punctuation? Is it presented neatly, with a good general appearance? (Refer to a standard writer's handbook.)

In evaluating the essay, respond as an honest, demanding, but sympathetic reader—as a constructive reader. Try to make your evaluative comments tactful, but also make them direct, detailed, and helpful.

To strike the right tone in your evaluative comments, keep in mind that you are writing to three audiences. One is the writer. **You want the writer to feel that you are trying to help, not hurt.** The second is your teacher, who will read your peer review to see how carefully, tactfully, and thoroughly you have written it. And the third audience is yourself. You want to say what you really think, as honestly as you can.

Tactfully expressed peer reviews are a sign that reviewers respect writers and understand their problems. Other writers respond positively, just as you do, to thorough, detailed, carefully and kindly worded reviews, both positive and negative. Tactfully worded reviews make writers feel that reviewers really care, have their best interests at heart, and want to help them improve.

If you withhold your comments, positive or negative, from other writers you may keep them from knowing something they need to know in order to improve. Your answer to the first evaluative question, "What is well done in the essay?", is just as important as your answer to the second, "What could be done to improve it?" So a complete and helpful review explains *both* evaluative questions fully. **Writers have to know what they are doing right** in order to keep doing it, just as much as **they have to know what to change in order to improve their work.**

Explaining carefully what is done well is not just an opportunity to be comforting and supportive. **Tell writers what you really do think is good about their work.** Don't be afraid to be obvious. What seems obviously good to you may not be so obvious to everyone, especially the person who wrote the essay. Besides, everyone likes a genuine compliment on something they've done well, even if they already know it's pretty good.

It is also important, of course, to explain fully and in detail what the writer can do to improve an essay. Notice that the question does not ask you to tell writers what you think is bad about their work. Instead, it asks you to tell them something else: what one thoughtful, constructive reader (you) thinks they could do to make reading easier. As you explain what to improve and how to improve it, help the writer set some priorities if you can. Some problems are more troublesome and harder to deal with than others. Try to suggest what you think the writer should work on first.

The *way* you explain what you think is well done, what could be improved, and how to do it, is as important as *what* you say. Pay careful attention to how you express your views. **Explain every generalization you make, and give examples.** If you say that the proposition is wordy, give some examples of what could be cut out. If you say the paragraph transitions are good, point out the words or phrases that make them effective.

In any case, don't worry about pushing other writers around with your peer review. No one has to do what you suggest. Writers can choose to do it or ignore it. But they cannot make that choice if you don't tell them what you think, if you say what you think tactlessly, or if you don't explain it carefully. Detailed explanation of the points you make in your peer review will help writers understand what you're getting at. Try to be as thorough, straightforward, practical, and helpful as you can.

Task 6   *Essay Exchange and Descriptive and Evaluative Peer Review*

Exchange essays with a classmate (preferably not one you have exchanged with before). Number the sentences in the essay you have received in exchange for your own. Write lightly in pencil. Don't write anything else on the paper.

Then, first, on a separate sheet write a detailed descriptive outline of the essay. Check your descriptive outline twice against the essay, and revise the outline until you are confident that it represents the essay accurately. (Detailed descriptive outlines are explained beginning on p. 153.)

Second, write an evaluation of the essay following the format used in task 5, p. 182.

This peer review exercise begins with a descriptive outline for two reasons. One is to reassure yourself that you understand how the essay is written and that your evaluation is accurate. The other reason is to reassure the writer that you have read the essay carefully.

While you are writing your descriptive outline, you may begin to notice some of the essay's strengths and some things you think the writer could do to improve it. Make a note of these responses, but don't include them in your descriptive outline. Save them for your evaluation. Then plan your evaluation carefully using the criteria given in task 5, p. 182.

In evaluating an essay, respond as a constructive reader. Make your evaluative comments tactful, practical, detailed, and helpful.

Task 7 *Essay Exchange and Descriptive, Evaluative, and Substantive Peer Review*

This advanced peer reviewing task involves three students in constructive conversation about each essay. It requires two exchanges, so that each essay has two different peer reviewers. The writer gets to respond twice: between the first and the second peer reviewer and at the end of the sequence.

The task can be done only in courses in which everyone can write on the same topic or in which everyone has a general knowledge of what other people are likely to write about, such as subject matter courses or peer tutoring courses (in assignments where the topic is peer tutoring and related subjects). Also, this task should be done only after everyone has practiced doing entirely descriptive and evaluative reviews.

In this task, peer review takes another step in developing your ability to read constructively. The first peer reviewing task asked you to describe but not evaluate or comment on substance. The second asked you to describe and evaluate but still not comment on substance. **This task asks you, as a peer reviewer, to describe, evaluate, *and* comment on substance.** It asks you to reply to the positions taken in the essays you read in a way that takes into account the assumptions made in those essays. As a writer, furthermore, this task asks you to help your classmates improve their work as peer reviewers by evaluating the peer reviews

173

they write. Make your evaluation of other students' peer reviews as helpful as you would like theirs to be of your own.

First peer reviewer
Write a descriptive and evaluative peer review of the essay as you did for tasks 5 and 6. Then add to it an evaluation of the issue raised in the essay, the position the essay takes on that issue, and the assumptions it makes.
    First, write a descriptive outline of the essay.
    Second, evaluate the essay's writing technique.

- What is effective and well done in the essay?
- What could be done to improve it?

    Third, evaluate the essay's content:

- Do you agree with the essay's main point?
- Do you accept the essay's assumptions? Explain why. (See Assumptions, p. 132.)
- If you do not agree with the essay's position, or if you do not accept one or more of its assumptions, what position would you take on the issue yourself? What assumptions would you make? How would you defend your position, and how would you refute the main point of the essay in question?
- If you do agree with the essay's position, do you think the essay makes the best possible argument supporting it? How would you strengthen that argument? What would you change, add, or omit? Why?

Writer's response
Evaluate the first peer reviewer's evaluation of your essay.

- You may defend your essay, if you like.
- More important, explain how each part of the review affects you as a writer.
- From the point of view of a writer, what is well done in the review? How could it be improved?

Second peer reviewer
    First, mediate between the writer and the first peer reviewer:

- In what respects is the first peer reviewer's evaluation of the essay tactful, thorough, detailed, and helpful? In what respects could it be improved?

- Is the writer's response to the first evaluation reasonable? Is it tactful, thorough, detailed, and helpful?

Second, evaluate the essay from your own point of view:

- Explain where you agree or disagree with the first peer reviewer.
- Add anything that you think would help the writer see what is well done in the essay and how to improve it.

Writer's second response
The writer gets the last word:

- **First, reevaluate your essay** in light of the peer review it has received.
- **Second, evaluate both peer reviews.** In what respect has this conversation about your essay been constructive? Has it helped you to improve the essay? If so, how? If not, what would have helped more?
- **Third, evaluate the whole peer review process** from the point of view of both a writer and a peer reviewer. What effect, if any, has the process had on your attitude toward writing and on the way you write? Add anything else you would like to say.

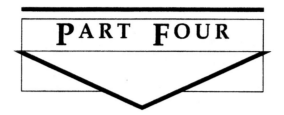

PART FOUR

Reaching Out to Members of Other Communities

Whatever you read, you want to feel it's worthwhile. Everyone feels that way. It's the most compelling reason to read. And whatever you write, you want your readers to feel that what you have written is worthwhile. You want them to understand your position. Everyone feels that way. It is the most compelling reason to write.

But readers sometimes reject what they read before they give it a chance. You may do that yourself sometimes. You know what it's like. You feel bored. You squirm and yawn. You have an irresistible urge to do something else—*anything else*—rather than keep on reading. You think "this writer doesn't speak my language." You say "baloney" or something worse, and you quit.

That may happen for two reasons. Sometimes you reject what you read because you haven't suspended judgment long enough to understand it. Sometimes you reject it because the writer hasn't worked hard enough to make you want to understand. Either way, you stand to lose. You are rejecting something that might be worth your while to know.

So the question is, what can you do about it? How can you be sure when you read that you are giving the writer a chance? And when you write, what can you do to interest readers so they don't reject what you're saying?

Just stating your position and exploring, explaining, or defending it won't do the trick. That is the insides of an essay. It will interest a few readers who already care about what you have to say, but it probably won't catch the interest of anyone else. In order to interest other readers, besides making parts of the insides relate to each other, you have to show how the insides are related to something outside. You have to make the insides of your essay accessible to readers beyond the boundaries of the community of like-minded people you belong to.

When we talk about ourselves as readers and writers it is helpful to call communities of like-minded people language communities or **discourse communities.** What distinguishes true language or discourse communities is that their members talk with each other about the same sorts of things in the same sorts of ways. Baseball fans talk with other baseball fans about batting averages, pitching techniques, and league standings. Surgeons talk with each other about successful procedures, anatomy, new equipment, and fees. Discourse communities are groups of people who are distinguished by the fact that they "speak the same language."

Discourse communities are also distinguished by the fact that the language they speak with each other is *not* the language that the members of *other* language communities speak. Baseball fans do not normally talk with each other about surgical procedures and surgeons do not normally talk with each other about batting averages. If two surgeons do talk about batting averages, they are not talking as members of the community of surgeons. They are confirming their common membership in another discourse community, the community of baseball fans.

Surgeons sometimes talk baseball with their patients, too, in order to explain to them the surgery they are going to perform or to put them at ease before surgery. If your surgeon talks with you about batting averages, striking out, and hitting home runs, it is true that he is confirming his common membership with you in the discourse community of baseball fans, but he is likely to be doing so for a particular purpose. What the two of you, a surgeon and a patient, are really talking about is surgery, not baseball. So your surgeon is using baseball language in an unusual way, at the boundary between the discourse community he normally belongs to, the community of surgeons, and the discourse community you belong to, the community of patients. He is trying to make it possible for you to accept and understand the experience that the two of you are going to be sharing in such different ways.

That is what people do at community boundaries. They try to make what they have to say accessible to members of other communities of like-minded people, other discourse communities, so that the members of those different communities can understand each other and get along. They do that by negotiating differences in language and by translating from one community language into another. Baseball talk between you and your surgeon is a negotiating gesture, a common language which he is using to help him translate between two languages, the language of his discourse community and the language of yours.

As a writer, that's what you have to do, too, in order to catch the interest of readers who are members of communities other than your own. To interest readers in other communities, you have to show them how the topic you are writing about and the position you are taking on it affect their opinions, involve their experiences, or touch their feelings. You have to find terms that are familiar to both of you and that you both understand in pretty much the same way. You have to show your readers that you can speak their language.

SPEAKING OTHER PEOPLE'S LANGUAGE

It is important to learn how to show your readers that you can speak their language, because most of the readers whose interest you would like to catch probably do not quite speak *your* language. On any topic you write about there is a lot of difference between the opinions, experience, and feelings of people like you and those of people who are different from you. What you talk about with your friends and the way you talk about it in the discourse communities that you belong to differ at least a little bit, and in some cases a great deal, from what members of other discourse communities talk about and the way they talk about it. Even some of the people you think you know pretty well may differ from you in ways that you are not aware of, because they belong to discourse communities that you are not aware they are members of.

You have already discovered some of these differences if you have done exercise 1 in this book: a reminiscence, a family story, or an account of change. Read any story based on your private or family experience to other people, and you will notice that most of them have a lot of questions to ask before they feel that they understand what happened. Look to the left and right of you in any classroom and you are looking at people who differ from you and from each other in many ways, because they belong to different discourse communities. They root for different baseball teams, take different courses, eat different food, do different things before they get to class and after they leave it, have different jobs, strive toward different goals in life.

If people differ even in these simple, everyday ways, you can imagine how much more they differ in more complex and serious aspects of life than sports, school, food, jobs, and goals. No other member of your class was brought up quite as you were brought up, in quite the discourse communities you were brought up in. Probably none of them is a member of your family. Most don't come from your neighborhood or hometown. Some may not even have been born in your country. They or their parents do different things for a living and have different incomes. Some may be quite a bit older or younger than you. Some are of a different race, religion, or ethnic background. Probably half of them are different in gender. Some may differ from you in all these ways at once.

And the differences don't stop there. Not only do you and your classmates differ in experience, background, and gender. All of you also differ in how you feel about yourselves, how you feel about each other, and how you feel other people feel about you.

All these differences affect the way you read and write. Are you someone who knows nothing about baseball who is reading something written for baseball fans, or are you reading it as a baseball fan yourself? Are you a woman writing to other women, a woman writing to men, or a woman writing to both men and women? Are you a small-town person reading something written by a city slicker? Are you an environmentalist writing to deer hunters, or a deer hunter writing to environmentalists? Are you a farmer reading something written by a white-collar suburbanite, or a white-collar suburbanite reading something written by a farmer? Or maybe you are a scientist writing to other scientists, a scientist writing to nonscientists, or a nonscientist writing to scientists. Are there Protestants in your audience? Jews? Catholics? Muslims? How many of your readers are African-Americans, Italian-Americans, Asian-Americans, white middle-class Americans of no easily discernable ethnic background (but certainly of *some* ethnic background)?

Differences of all kinds affect you as a reader trying to understand what other people write and as a writer trying to write so that other people will understand you. They determine whether or not you feel that a writer you are reading speaks your language, and they determine the way you try as a writer to speak the same language that your readers speak.

In short, thinking about differences, between you and the writer you are reading or between you and the people who will read what you are writing, comes down to thinking about differences in language. Men tend to use different language to talk with each other about their feelings, their families, their bodies, their interests, and their jobs than women use. Chemists use different language to talk with each other about the natural world than physicists use. People in different discourse communities talk differently about their religious beliefs, their jobs, what they know, who they know, who they are, where they are, and where they're going. The language people use to talk about things, and the people they talk about those things with, define the ethnic, religious, professional and other kinds of groups they belong to.

So differences in language can be both serious and complicated. They can even cause wars. Just as people who don't understand each other can wind up fighting, nations that don't understand each other can wind up fighting too. Even at the very best, differences in language can break up friendships, keep you from learning things you need to know or would like to know, and deprive you of the pleasures of variety—which everyone knows is the spice of life.

TALKING ABOUT ELEPHANTS

To help you understand how complicated differences in language can be when you try to write across community boundaries, and understand what may be involved in thinking about those differences, consider this updated version of the story of the blind men and the elephant.

As the story goes, once upon a time a king who had heard of elephants but had never seen one wanted to explore new energy resources and thought that maybe elephants could help. So he established a task force to examine an elephant and tell him what elephants were really like. To this task force he appointed three blind men.

Duly appointed and charged, the blind men went off, found themselves an elephant, and began their investigation. The first blind man stepped up to the elephant, felt its side, and said that an elephant was like a wall. The second blind man felt the elephant's trunk and said that an elephant was like a snake. The third blind man felt one of the elephant's legs and said that an elephant was like a tree.

From the point of view of the three blind men, this research completed their investigation. They submitted a report to the king and went back to their work and their private lives.

The king, however, after one look at their report, called them back for another try. The blind men were puzzled and a bit miffed by the king's response. Each of them had reported his experience honestly in the language he normally used when he talked with people he knew. But what neither the blind men nor the king realized was that although the three task force members had a great deal in common, in many more ways they were quite different.

True, they were all blind, they were all royal appointees, none of them had ever touched an elephant before, and they had all just recently touched one. But in ways that turned out to be crucial for the task that the king assigned them to do, they were very different people indeed. The least of these differences was that each one, unknown to the others, touched a different part of the elephant. Much more important was the fact that they had never before engaged in conversation with each other about anything at all, much less elephants. Each of them was a member of a different set of discourse communities.

They all seemed to be speaking the same language—in this case, English. But in fact each one spoke a different version of English, because each one was a member of a different profession. The first blind man was a plasterer. He normally talked mostly with other plasterers. Conversation with plasterers was what he had internalized as thought. To plasterers a vertical flat surface is a wall. As a result, when the first blind man touched the side of the elephant, he thought "wall." If instead of being a plasterer he had been, say, an artist, he might have thought something quite different. Artists talk with each other a lot about the materials they use, so he might have said that an elephant was like a stretched canvas.

The second blind man was a zookeeper, and what he had internalized as thought was the conversation of zookeepers. To him a long, soft, flexible cylindrical object must be a snake. If he had been an electrical engineer instead of a zookeeper, he might have said an elephant is like a coaxial cable, or if he had been a sailor, a rope.

It is obvious by now that the third blind man was a gardener. He was not, say, an architect, in which case he would not have said that an elephant is like a tree. He would probably have said that an elephant is like a classical column, most likely Doric.

In his work on the elephant task force, each blind man used words drawn from the conversation of the professional discourse community he belonged to. So each one spoke a slightly different language. That's why their report didn't tell the king as much as he wanted to know about elephants. What it did tell him was that, so far, his task force on elephants was still a loose aggregate of political appointees talking past each other. They understood the task, but they didn't yet understand *each other* well enough to be able to make sense out of their mutual experience: touching an elephant.

To make sense out of that experience, in fact, they had to begin to talk with each other about touching the elephant. They had to discover and negotiate their differences, especially differences in the way they were using language, and arrive at some sort of consensus. They had to stop talking like plasterers, zoologists, and gardeners. They had to start talking like members of the king's task force on elephants.

So that's what they did. They talked with each other and got to know each other. Gradually their relationship changed. By talking with each other, they began to build a collective conversational history of plasterers, zookeepers, and gardeners. Each one began to remember how the others had talked before about elephants, in a variety of conversational situations. They negotiated their differences. And out of this developing conversational history they constructed a composite language common to their own particular working group: the king's task force on elephants.

They continued to use many of the words that they had been using right along, of course. But by negotiating, translating, and making conversational adjustments and compromises at the boundaries of the communities they normally belonged to, each one changed the way he used those words. And as their language and their relationship changed, so did what they knew about elephants.

Here, for example, is how their conversation went at one stage. The first blind man was still insisting rather boringly that an elephant was like a wall. He was still using the word *wall* just as he had used it in his .

part of their first report to the king. That is, he was using it as plasterers normally use it, to refer to the vertical flat surfaces they work on. But by now the two other blind men were listening harder and remembering more.

"Oh, I get it," said the third blind man, "you mean that this elephant-wall you're talking about is flat and smooth like a plastered wall."

"Right," said the first blind man. Then, thinking it over for a moment, he continued, "Well, uh, not exactly. An elephant-wall is different. It's, well, sort of bristly."

"Oh, I see," said the second blind man, "bristly like my snake."

"And like my tree?" said the third.

"Say," said the first, "I didn't know your tree and snake were bristly. That's odd. The trees and snakes I've touched around home aren't bristly, any more than the walls I plaster are."

"That's true, come to think of it," said the second. "Trees and snakes aren't bristly around my place either. Very odd. Listen, my elephant-snake is wrinkled as well as bristly. Is your elephant-wall wrinkled, too?"

"My elephant-tree is," interrupted the third.

"Well, maybe," answered the first blind man, ignoring the interruption. "It depends on what the wrinkles on your elephant-snake are like. My elephant-wall sure is wrinkled. But its wrinkles run from side to side. The wrinkles on most of the trees I've ever touched, like oak trees, run up and down."

"Come to think of it," said the third, "the wrinkles on my elephant-tree run side-to-side too."

"Wait a minute," said the second, "my elephant-snake's wrinkles also run side-to-side. Or, to be precise about it, they run around the snake, not from end to end." "Hmm," he said, "do you suppose that what really makes an elephant is bristles and side-to-side wrinkles? No wonder the king rejected our report."

"Nonsense," said the third, his nose still a little out of joint at being ignored. "It is obvious to me that, wrinkles or no wrinkles, bristles or no bristles, an elephant *is* like a tree."

"Pardon me," said the first, "but don't you mean that an elephant is like a wall, a snake, and a tree all at once?"

"Well, all right," conceded the third, mollified that the other two were finally paying attention to what he had to say.

"Hey," said the second, "I think you've really got something there. What an elephant really is, *is* a wall and a tree and a snake all at once, *with* bristles and wrinkles from side to side. What about that?"

"Well, maybe," said the third, not quite following. "By the way," he threw in, "how thick is your wall?"

"*Thick?*" said the first. "I've never thought about thickness before. How thick is your tree?"

And so on. Now this conversation among the three blind men may seem a little silly. But something is going on in it that is crucial to the task that they were assigned. Each one is getting to know how the others use certain key words *(wall, snake, tree)*, and they are all learning to use those words in new ways. They are constructing a conversational history and a composite, boundary language common to themselves.

In the process, the social relationship among them is changing. By erasing some of the community boundaries among themselves, they are becoming a new, coherent discourse community, a community of knowledgeable peers. The change in their social relationship occurs as they strive to reach a consensus about what elephants are. How the blind men are related socially, how they talk with each other, and what they know about elephants all change at the same time. It is impossible to distinguish their knowledge, their social relationships, and their language.

Starting off as an aggregation of people who made very little sense to each other or to anyone else because they were members of different language communities, the three blind men gradually became a cohesive new community of people who speak the same language. They made sense to each other—that is, they constructed sense with each other—in this case about elephants. Maybe in time they will make sense about other things too.

WRITING ACROSS COMMUNITY BOUNDARIES

As a writer, that is just exactly what you want to happen when you try to interest members of other language communities in the position you are taking in an essay. You want your readers to put aside for the time being the differences between you and them that are based on the fact that you belong to different language communities. Instead, you want them to agree for the time being to translate the language you are using into language that they normally use. You are inviting them to help you negotiate the community boundaries between you and to become, for the time it takes to read your essay and talk about it, a coherent discourse community with its own composite working language and its own conversational history.

Thinking about both the similarities and the differences between the discourse communities you belong to and those that other people belong to can be crucial to how well you get across. Members of the communities you belong to—your family, your friends, your religious or ethnic group, and so on—are likely to understand your position in one way. Members of other communities are likely to understand it quite differently, if they take enough interest in it to understand it at all. How hard you have to think about these differences depends on what you are reading or writing about, the position taken on the topic, and the depth or sensitivity of the differences you have to deal with.

If your writing course is set up collaboratively so that you can talk with other students regularly about writing, you have an opportunity to discover and negotiate differences among you that are very much like the ones that the three blind men had. You can engage in conversation directly with your readers, many of whom do not belong to the language communities you belong to, so that you can discover the differences among you and negotiate them.

But of course you may not always have that opportunity. And in some cases as a writer you may have to deal with some differences that are more serious and complicated than the differences the blind men encountered. Imagine how much more complicated and contentious their conversation would have been if they differed in other, more complex and deeply personal ways such as ethnic or religious background or in gender.

These deeper differences would certainly not make agreement impossible, but it could make it a lot harder. Everyone engaged in the conversation would have to think more carefully about the differences in language among them and the differences in experience, background, and gender that those differences in language implied.

That is exactly the kind of thinking you have to do when you try to relate the insides of an essay you are writing, to readers whose interests and opinions differ from yours. It is the kind of thinking you will have to do for most of the essays you will ever write. Most of your readers are not going to belong to all the discourse communities you belong to. Not only will they use different words, worse still they may use some of the same words you use, but in different ways. Where you talk about trees, they may talk about snakes or walls. Or where you talk about trees as growing things that bear leaves, they may talk about trees as something you stick into shoes to keep their shape.

The purpose of Part Four is to help you learn how to relate the insides of an essay you write to diverse readers. It will help you write at the boundaries between the discourse communities you belong to and the discourse communities that your readers belong to. It will help you relate what you know and value, what you think on the topic you are writing about, and what you have experienced to what other people have experienced, what they think on the topic, and what they know and value. That is, it will help you place the position you take in an essay into a context of sharable concerns, or a context of issues.

CONTEXTS OF ISSUES, SHAREABLE CONCERNS

Exercise 4 (p. 31) defines an *issue* as a *shareable concern*. Issues are the sort of things that you talk about with people you know, that people you know read about, and maybe that all of you together would like to do something about. Issues grow out of the concrete experiences that you have had in common, that you talk a lot about with each other, or maybe that you hardly ever talk about but just assume.

An issue can be expressed as a noun phrase or as a question that makes specific one or more of the relationships implied in the noun phrase. An example of an issue stated as a noun phrase is *water pollution*. This phrase may also be stated as several specific questions: "What materials are polluting the oceans? Where do these materials come from? What can we do to keep the oceans clean?" (see p. 31).

The **context of issues** of any essay you write is made up of concerns related to the position you are taking in the essay that are shareable by two or more discourse communities. One way to interest members of other discourse communities in that position is to describe, outline, or, better still, dramatize concerns that you think other people may share with you, even though they may have backgrounds and interests that differ from your own. If your readers become aware of those shared concerns, they will be more likely to consider the position you are taking, read what you have to say about it, and give it some thought even though they don't agree with it. If you point out concerns that you and your readers share, they are more likely to feel that what they are reading is worthwhile, and they are more likely to understand what you are getting at.

For example, suppose you decided to write an essay about an experience you had last summer at the beach. When you went for your first walk on the beach with some friends on the day you arrived, you saw an oil slick on the water and a "No Swimming" sign posted at your favorite place to swim. You and your friends felt really disappointed and angry. Then you came across a dead sea gull covered with a thick, sticky, tarlike substance, and you began to feel even worse. Suddenly your vacation seemed a lot less happy than you expected it to be.

Later, you noticed a poster advertising a meeting of commercial fishermen to discuss declining catches due to the oil slick, and you ran into an Audubon Society member organizing teams to save sea birds overcome by oil. Learning about the interests of both these groups made you realize that the experience you shared with your friends on the beach was not just an instance of personal misfortune and disappointment. It made you members of a much larger discourse community made up of people who are concerned for different reasons about the same issue.

This larger community included the fishermen and the Audubon people. It included the region's water commissioners. It included everyone who eats fish, drinks water, or swims in the sea. All those people, however different in other ways, have a common interest when it comes to keeping the oceans clean. So they talk with other members of their own local community about some of the very same things that members of the other communities talk about with each other, although they talk about those things for different reasons and in different ways. The fishermen talk with each other about the oil slick on the ocean because it reduces their catch, the Audubon people because it kills birds, the water commissioners because it affects the drinking water supply, you and your friends because it affects swimming.

The differences in the way the members of these communities talk with each other about keeping the oceans clean—their differences in language—are related to differences in their experience and background. The fishermen are working people living on worker's wages who talk about business in the local dialect. Audubon Society members tend to be well-paid professional or business people who talk bird watching in the dialect of the college-educated middle-class. Fish eaters and swimmers can of course be anyone who talks salmon or surf in any dialect at all, in fact in any native language.

So, when you set out to write an essay based on your vacation experience with the oil slick, the closed beach, and the dead bird, you had a large number of potential readers in a number of different discourse communities who share a concern about clean oceans. Who would you want to read the essay? Who would you want to think about the topic you are writing about and the position you are taking on that topic? Certainly the friends who walked with you along the beach that day. But they already share your interest and your feelings, and they share it in very much the same terms. You all speak more or less the same language.

How much more worth your while it would be to write the essay so that many more people than just that small group of friends would want to read it. To address more people than your immediate friends, you would have to show how it affects the interests of people in other communities besides your own. To write as a fellow beach lover to your beach-bum friends, describing the curl of a breaker and the sun on the sand would certainly make them feel the importance of what you have to say. But how would the fishermen, the Audubon Society members, and the fish eaters be likely to respond?

There is a good chance that they would reject your position out of hand without trying to understand it. They would feel that you aren't someone who speaks their language. To interest them in your position you would have to show them that you are addressing concerns that you all share by finding language that negotiates the boundary between your community and theirs. You would have to talk about declining catches swimming beyond the breakers, endangered species flying above them, and the rich taste of bluefish steaming on the beach to perfection.

Consider another example. Suppose you are a child psychiatrist writing an essay about a scene you witnessed in which two children were fighting in front of a candy store. You want to explain what the fight was all about not just to other child psychiatrists but also to parents of young children and members of the American Association of Candy Store Owners. How would you negotiate the boundaries among these three discourse communities so that few readers in these groups would reject what you say without trying to understand it?

The way you interest members of other discourse communities in what you have to say depends on your understanding of the language they normally speak. Although the members of these three groups may all talk about children, they differ widely in the language they use when they talk about them. Child psychiatrists talk with other child psychiatrists in the language of Freudian or behavioral psychology about how to treat troubled children. Parents talk with other parents about how to deal with children who misbehave in the language of parental hope and despair. Candy store owners talk with other candy store owners in the language of profit and loss about how to sell children more candy.

Given the great diversity of interest and language of these three communities, can you possibly find anything at all that child psychiatrists, parents, and candy store owners have in common? Maybe. Child psychiatrists want the troubled children they treat to behave differently. Parents want their children to behave well in public. Candy store owners want the children who visit their shops to behave politely so that the parents of potential customers will feel comfortable letting their children go there.

So, to interest members of all three groups you might try to show that knowing what any fight is all about can help control it. For example, if you know that a fight in a boxing ring between two men in shorts and puffy gloves is a profit-making business, you know that it can be controlled the way other businesses are controlled: with laws requiring that products be genuine, fairly priced, and as safe as possible for both producers and consumers. In contrast, a fight between bride and groom on their wedding day may result from nervousness or from changing their minds at the very last minute. To control that fight requires knowing something about the personal history and character of the man and woman involved and what led them to decide to marry.

If you can show this relationship between understanding any fight and controlling it, then it is likely that at least some members of all three groups—child psychiatrists, parents, and candy-store owners—would be willing to consider your position that to control a fight between two children in front of a candy store requires understanding what it is really about. Child psychiatrists, parents, and shopkeepers would all feel that you speak their language.

WHAT AN INTRODUCTION DOES

As a writer, it is sometimes possible to try to interest members of other discourse communities in what you have to say by showing that you understand the language they normally speak while you are exploring, explaining, or defending your position. But that is hard to do without confusing both your readers and yourself. You have to bring into your explanation or defense some material that, strictly speaking, does not either explain or defend your position. Mixed with the explanation or defense, it can seem extraneous. It can spoil your essay by destroying its coherence.

Trying to interest members of other discourse communities in what you have to say at the very beginning and at the very end of the essay is a lot easier. An introductory paragraph at the beginning of an essay provides an immediate or limited context of issues for the position you take, so that readers will see how your position is related to their own experience, interests, or knowledge and to those of the discourse community they are members of. (See Introductions, p. 81.)

For example, in an introduction you might have written for the position paper on cars discussed in exercise 5, p. 44, you could have placed the proposition ("Cars may be on the way out as a major means of transportation") in any one of several immediate or limited contexts: the number of cars on the road, air pollution, governmental investigations of car safety, and so on. You would decide which context to use by thinking about the interests and backgrounds of the people you were writing to.

For example, suppose you expect your readers to be the other students in your class. What do you know about their background and interests? Do they drive? Do they have to fight traffic jams on the city streets or on the freeways? Have they or their friends had a car accident recently? Are they worried about the air pollution that cars produce?

If you drew a diagram of the car essay with these interests in mind, you might show that essay as a box placed in a set of possible frames or packages. The diagram might look something like the one on page 202.

In this diagram, the essay's insides are those three little boxes inside the larger context boxes on the left (proposition and two paragraphs of explanation or defense). The diagram makes these insides look less important than their context by exaggerating the difference in size between them. That is of course not the case in the essay itself, as the blown up version of the diagram on the right shows. Context and position are roughly equal in importance. In most essays, what you have to say can be only as effective as the reception it gets by people whose interests differ from your own.

For example, it is not hard to imagine that some people might be almost totally indifferent to the proposition, "Cars as we know them

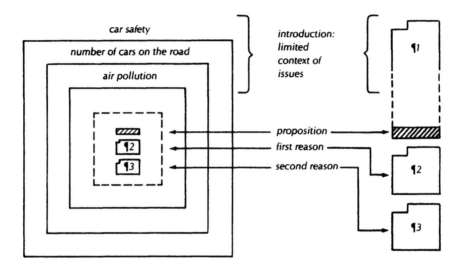

may be on the way out." Ho hum, they might say. People who feel that way are likely to belong to discourse communities in which members seldom talk with each other about cars. To interest members of those communities you have to try to understand the language that they normally speak. The position you take will make sense to them if the introduction shows that the topic, cars, and the position you are taking on that topic address one or more immediately related context of issues, that is, if the introduction shows that the topic and your position on it affect their interests, opinions, and feelings.

Or let's return to the example of the oil slick on the beach (p. 198). Suppose you wrote an essay taking the position that we should put an end to oil spills. And suppose you defended that position with two reasons: Oil spills hurt ocean wildlife (gulls, geese, and terns), and they cripple ocean-dependent industry (fishermen, lobstermen). But the people you wanted most to interest in your position were not Audubon Society members, fishermen, and lobstermen, whom you believe are already convinced that the problem is serious. The people you wanted most to interest in your position this time are some of your ecologically indifferent beach-bum surf-and-sun friends. They're the people you really want to stir up.

Since you know that your friends took a vacation walk along a polluted beach just as you did, you could establish a context of issues by reminding them about finding the "No Swimming" sign and the dead bird. That's a story that you could probably tell with a good deal of feeling. You would probably make it a compelling introduction to the position you want to take in the essay.

190

Now suppose you found out that you had convinced your beach-bum friends and you knew, of course, that the Audubon people were convinced of the need to put an end to oil spills. Instead, it is the local lobstermen and fishermen's cooperative who have lost interest in the issue. In this case you would have to guess that their background might make them become interested again in keeping the oceans clean. You would have to introduce the essay now in another way. Maybe you could tell a story that one of the fishermen told you at that meeting you attended—the story about coming home with an almost empty boat after twelve hours fishing. Or you could present some figures that show increased unemployment in the fish canning industry due to small catches. Or you could talk about how wary people are becoming about eating fish that they feel may be polluted.

In any case, what you would try to do is develop an immediate or limited context, choosing language that touches the boundary between your discourse community and the communities that the readers belong to, whom you hope to interest. And you would make that context as vivid and striking as you can. You would try to write it in a way that is likely to involve or interest people with backgrounds and interests that may overlap your own but are also somewhat different from your own.

For example, the example essay on cars takes the position that we are not going to use what we think of as cars much longer. Readers who believe that cars are a necessity of human life are not going to find an argument like that very attractive. The introduction at the beginning of that essay looks as if it was written to capture the interest of just such people.

introduction   Cars seem to be everywhere today. We find them in the desert and the mountains, the forests and the plains. They jam the city streets. They flow like rivers along our superhighways. There are more cars on the road today than ever before. Yet, there are signs that people are not entirely happy with this situation. We complain about air pollution and high accident rates. We worry when we read the news that even though domestic cars have improved a great deal in recent years still another manufacturer has had to recall thousands of cars because the brakes are defective or the gas line leaks. More and more people are traveling by plane and train. Bicycles are increasingly popular in many cities and towns. Some two-car families are selling their second car because they simply can't afford the cost of insurance and upkeep. Of course, it is hard to imagine how we could get along without cars entirely. But it is certainly reasonable to speculate that as people choose other ways of getting around, travel by car may have reached its high-water mark and has begun to recede. It seems fantastic *proposition* and unlikely, yet it is now possible to say that in the future the trend will be for people to use cars as we know them less rather than more. In fact, it looks as if cars may be on the way out as our major means of transportation.

But people who believe cars are a necessity of human life may not be the only people whose interest you want to capture if you wrote the essay on cars. Instead, you might want to interest people who think that today's cars are unique. For that purpose you could conceivably begin the essay with an entirely different introduction that goes something like this:

introduction Chevys, Fords, Toyotas, VWs, Buicks, Jeeps. Dozens of kinds of cars. And dozens of models: convertibles, range rovers, sporty two-door jobs, four-door family models, pick-ups. Each one seems to have its own special purpose and own history. As different as they are, though, all of them really have a single purpose and a single history. They can all be traced back to the old Model T. Henry Ford did not invent the automobile. But he did invent the family car, the everyday workhorse, the common travel convenience. True, the cars we see on the road today don't seem to look much like the old, rattling, clattering black box on wheels that Ford cranked out by the thousands in the early decades of the twentieth century. But take away the fancy trimmings, the devices added for special purposes, and of course the increase in power and you'd find that the differences between Ford's Tin Lizzy and your own is pretty small. Both run on gasoline fueling an internal combustion engine. Both can go anywhere you want to drive them, when they don't get stuck in the mud. They pervade our lives as though no one had ever thought of an alternative to them. But alternatives do exist, and recent, rapid changes in the world we live in may make these alternatives very attractive *proposition* indeed. In fact, it looks as if cars may be on the way out as our major means of transportation.

COLLABORATIVE LEARNING

These collaborative tasks are about acknowledging people's differences in background and coping with those differences.

Task 1   Acknowledging Differences

Divide the class according to birth order: oldest children in the family, youngest children, middle children, only children. One person in each group records the views expressed in the group and the consensus that the group arrives at collaboratively. Try to arrive at an answer to each of the following questions that most people in the group can live with, but make sure that the group's recorder makes note of differences of opinion and dissent from the consensus. Finally, review the recorder's notes. Make sure that they state accurately what the group has decided and include differences of opinion and dissent. When you have finished the task, the recorder will report the results of the group's discussion to the rest of the class.

> What was it like being a child in your birth order?
>
> How has being a child of that birth order affected your life after childhood?

In plenary session (the whole class together), recorders should report by listing answers in what the group agrees is their order of importance.

Task 2   *Doing Something About Differences as a Reader*

Return to birth-order groups.

1. Reach consensus on what you think is the *worst* aspect of being in that birth order and why.

2. Report to the class as a whole. Everyone takes careful notes on what all the other groups report.

3. Record your collective responses as a birth-order group to the other groups' reports. If you feel sympathetic to what another group has reported, explain why you feel that way. If you feel unsympathetic, that's okay too. Just explain why.

   Then concentrate on the statement made by another group that brought out your group's most unsympathetic collective response. Suppose that a statement like that turned up in something you were reading. What could you do to make sure that you understand that statement as completely as possible *before* you reject it?

4. Report on your discussion to the class. In the class as a whole, list what seem to be the best ways to try to understand statements you respond to unsympathetically.

Task 3   *Doing Something About Differences as a Writer*

Return again to birth-order groups and list three experiences, attitudes, goals, or fears that you had as a result of being born in that birth order and that you think would be hard to explain to people whose birth order was different from yours. For example, list three experiences, attitudes, goals, or fears that you had as a result of being an only child and that you think middle children would find hard to understand.

Then decide how you would approach people in each of the other birth-order categories to try to help them understand how you feel on each of those topics.

> 1. How would you get their interest or make them feel it would be worth their while to listen to what you have to say on that topic? (For example, what could oldest children say to engage the interest and get the sympathy of youngest children?)
>
> 2. How would you try to make them care about your position or feel sympathetic to it? (For example, what could middle children say to gain the sympathy of only children?)
>
> After each report, people in each birth-order category explain their reaction to each of the suggested approaches.

This whole set of "difference tasks" may be repeated with other kinds of differences in escalating levels of stress: for example, favorite holidays, why they like (or dislike) their jobs, gender differences, ethnic differences, religious differences, racial differences. To discuss topics like these in a classroom takes increasing amounts of courage, restraint, tact, tolerance, and trust on everyone's part. And yet it is just such topics as these that are most likely to divide us when we try to agree with each other or even just try to get along. Furthermore, if writers are insensitive to differences such as these, they may lose some of their readers.*

WHAT AN ENDING DOES

These issues that directly touch the lives of the members of a few communities of readers, and that you might refer to in an essay's introduction, are often called "limited" issues. There are other issues you could also refer to that affect the members of many more communities, but touch them less directly and in more general ways. Issues of that type are often caled "larger" issues. The place to show how your position is related to these larger issues is in the essay's *ending*.

For example, in contrast to the limited issues of the necessity and the uniqueness of today's cars, the position taken in the essay on cars also has several larger contexts: our changing sense of distance and space, the increasing urbanization of the world, conservation of natural resources, the need for alternative means of public transportation, concern for the environment as a whole, and so on.

---

*I am indebted to Alex Gitterman for this nonthreatening difference task involving birth order.

If you wanted to place your position in the context of one of these larger issues you would not raise it in the first paragraph, because it is probably too abstract to grab anyone. And you would not raise it while you are exploring, explaining, or defending your position in paragraphs two and three, because it would get in the way. You would devote a fourth paragraph to it. For example, if you diagrammed the car essay again, you could show its insides as three small boxes in the middle (proposition and two paragraphs of explanation) between two concentric sets of issues. The inner set of three issues are the limited ones that your introduction might refer to. The outer set of four issues are the larger ones that your ending might refer to.

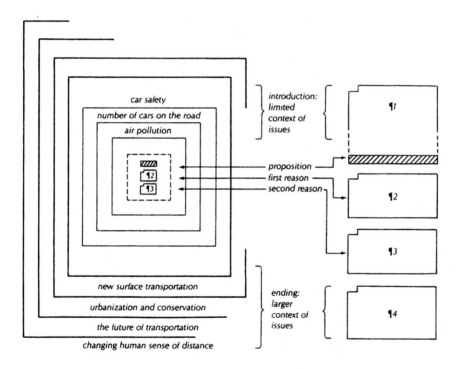

Suppose you decided that the larger issue that affects most people today is the changing sense of distance and space that almost everyone in the world now experiences through satellite-linked TV. To relate the fourth paragraph firmly to the position you take in the essay, first you would refer to the issue you brought up in the introduction. That would remind readers where they started and how your position is related to their more immediate concerns. Then in the ending you would explain the implications of your position to the larger issue. The essay (beginning with the introduction about the necessity of cars) might read something like this:

introduction

Cars seem to be everywhere today. We find them in the desert and the mountains, the forests and the plains. They jam the city streets. They flow like rivers along our superhighways. There are more cars on the road today than ever before. Yet, there are signs that people are not entirely happy with this situation. We complain about air pollution and high accident rates. We worry when we read the news that even though domestic cars have improved a great deal in recent years, still another manufacturer has had to recall thousands of cars because the brakes are defective or the gas line leaks. More and more people are traveling by plane and train. Bicycles are increasingly popular in many cities and towns. Some two-car families are selling their second car because they simply can't afford the cost of insurance and upkeep. Of course, it is hard to imagine how we could get along without cars entirely. But it is certainly reasonable to speculate that as people choose other ways of getting around, travel by car may have reached its high-water mark and has begun to recede. It seems fantastic and unlikely, yet it is now possible to say that in the future the trend will be for people to use cars as we know them less

proposition

rather than more. In fact, it looks as if cars may be on the way out as our major means of transportation.

¶2 transition

And it is high time they were. The world oil supply, which cars depend on for fuel, has been diminishing at the rate

last sentence in ¶2

of. . . . But we travel these super routes at speeds that threaten our lives no matter how safely our cars may be built.

¶3 transition

Cars will become less important in the future not only because they waste fuel and are dangerous, but also because they waste time and human energy. The man I worked for last

last sentence in ¶3

summer. . . . There are millions of conservative travelers like this in mid-century America now taking to the air.

ending
¶4 transition
reference to introduction (limited context of issues)

My conservative old friend would be shocked to find out how really up with his times he is. It is all those people jamming the nation's highways who are behind. This is an age in which you can get to London quicker than it takes me to write one of these essays. They no longer show full-length movies on some transatlantic flights. The movies last longer than the few hours it takes to get there. And now we can see things going on in Asia and Europe and Africa, anywhere in the world where

leads to a larger context of issues

they have electricity to run a TV camera, not weeks, months, or days after it happens but the very second it happens. This means that people's sense of distance and space has undergone a big change in the last hundred years. My grandfather went to church on a horse. It was the fastest way to get there. It

another
reference to
the
introduction
took him an hour to go five miles. Those people crawling along our highways at fifty-five miles an hour and sending letters by mail are almost as backward. A man-made satellite goes two-thirds of the way around the earth in the same time. We can fax a letter to Tokyo in minutes, and we can fly from New York to Boston in an hour by jet. The sacred car: How can it compete? It is already little more than an expensive luxury, and in ten years a car may be just a convenience to take vacations in, once you've gotten off the plane in Ankara and rented one for a week's safari into the bush.

On the other hand, you might have chosen to end the essay by relating your position to the interests of some other large community that is affected by some other larger context of issues. For example, you might have related it to the most concrete of the larger contexts, the need for new surface transportation. In this case, the essay would end quite differently, and this ending would catch the interest of the members of an entirely different, and much larger, set of discourse communities. Then the end of the essay might read something like this:

introduction
Cars seem to be everywhere today. We find them in the desert and the mountains, the forests and the plains. They jam the city streets. They flow like rivers along our superhighways. There are more cars on the road today than ever before. Yet, there are signs that people are not entirely happy with this situation. We complain about air pollution and high accident rates. We worry when we read the news that even though domestic cars have improved a great deal in recent years, still another manufacturer has had to recall thousands of cars because the brakes are defective or the gas line leaks. More and more people are traveling by plane and train. Bicycles are increasingly popular in many cities and towns. Some two-car families are selling their second car because they simply can't afford the cost of insurance and upkeep. Of course, it is hard to imagine how we could get along without cars entirely. But it is certainly reasonable to speculate that as people choose other ways of getting around, travel by car may have reached its high-water mark and has begun to recede. It seems fantastic and unlikely, yet it is now possible to say that in the future the trend will be for people to use cars as we know them less rather than more. In fact, it looks as if cars may be on the way out as our major means of transportation.

proposition

¶2 transition

last sentence in
¶2
And it is high time they were. The world oil supply, which cars depend on for fuel, has been diminishing at the rate of. . . . But we travel these super routes at speeds that threaten our lives no matter how safely our cars may be built.

¶3 *transition*

Cars will become less important in the future not only because they waste fuel and are dangerous, but also because they waste time and human energy. The man I worked for last summer. . . . There are millions of conservative travelers like this in mid-century America now taking to the air.

last sentence in
¶3
ending
¶4 *transition*

reference to introduction

leads to larger context of issues

Despite this new rash of private flying, though, my old boss is not really as ahead of his times as he thinks he is. People have been flying on business trips for years. The shuttle from Washington to New York is an example of the great amount of fast, daily air travel that is already lessening by thousands the number of cars on the road even in this peak year of car travel. But this tendency has held back the most important innovation that must occur soon, before our country, especially in the large urban centers, becomes one hot, smelly traffic jam. That innovation is cheap, clean rail transportation traveling at very high speeds. We must have a way of transporting masses of people medium distances, say from fifty to four or five hundred miles. The governmental machinery is already set up for this kind of transportation, and in places like Japan such systems have been in effect for several years. As soon as these trains begin running regularly and safely, the passing of the car may be inevitable. Cars may be relegated to the position of expensive luxuries. Eventually maybe, automobile transportation will be used only for vacations and Ford will be selling only one line of sedan, three lines of sports cars, and a dozen lines of station wagons—all of them run by electricity.

In the example about oil spills, in which you tried in several different introductions to get several different groups of readers to think about their personal experiences with ocean pollution, the larger context of issues that you might raise in the ending might be the effect of water pollution in rivers and lakes as well as oceans and the effect of pollution on the quality of life in general. Or stewardship: the fact that we are drinking the same water that the dinosaurs drank, but they didn't pollute it, we did. So we have a duty to clean it up.

The difference between this larger context of issues in the ending and the more limited context of issues in the introduction is not that readers are likely to feel one more deeply than the other, although of course they might. The difference is that the introduction shows the essay's relation to the interests of a limited number of discourse communities by spelling out an everyday kind of knowledge and experience and some familiar assumptions and implications (summer vacation, swimming, fishing, family income, the disappearance of favorite birds).

The ending, in contrast, shows the essay's relation to the interests of a broad range of larger discourse communities by spelling out less obvious kinds of knowledge and experience and some less familiar assumptions and implications (the need to control the environment as a whole, pollution of rivers and lakes eventually winds up in the oceans), and to systems of knowledge and value that readers may not yet be fully aware of (environmental studies, the delicate interdependence of all living beings).

In short, introductions are "why bother" paragraphs, whereas endings are "so what" paragraphs. In an *introduction* you answer the reader's question, "Why should I bother reading on?" In an *ending* you answer the reader's question, "Now that I've read all that, so what?"

The two exercises in Part Four are intended to help you learn to write endings that will affect the members of a greater number of larger discourse communities. Exercise 10 asks you, as an experiment, to write two alternative fourth paragraphs for a three-paragraph essay that you have already written. That experiment will show you how different endings can make your position accessible to different sets of larger language communities. Exercise 11 asks you to start from scratch writing a four-paragraph essay: introduction with proposition, two paragraphs of exploration, explanation or defense, and an ending.

(William Perry's "Examsmanship and the Liberal Arts," p. 343, talks about how to engage the interest of members of certain academic communities, those whom your teachers represent, such as English, history, chemistry, sociology, mathematics, and so on. Perry talks about how the language of facts and ideas is related to the language of conceptual frames of reference that gives them meaning for those communities. You may find it interesting to read and discuss this article while working on exercises 10 and 11. See also Unity and Coherence, p. 116, and Assumptions, p. 132.)

▷ EXERCISE 10   EXPERIMENT IN ENDING

The purpose of this exercise is not to produce a polished product. It is to learn something about the difference between the insides of an essay (your position explored, explained, and defended) and what's outside it, the interests of members of other language communities than your own. That is, one purpose is to learn something about the difference between taking a position and putting your position into a context of issues or shared concerns. Another purpose is to help you see that the way you end an essay can affect how seriously people take the whole essay, and for that matter whether or not they are willing to take it seriously at all.

Choose a three-paragraph essay that you wrote for essay exercises 5 through 9. Read it and list all the issues you can think of that are related to it.

Then choose two of these issues and write two alternative paragraphs, each of which could serve as an ending to the essay.

Add a section to the descriptive outline for that essay. Explain what each alternative final paragraph *does* and *says*.

To do this exercise well, you may have to change the last sentence or two of the essay as you originally wrote it. You may also have to change the introduction a little in order to give yourself the kind of phrase you need to refer to in order to write a transition to the two new endings. If you like, you can revise the whole essay.

Don't worry, though, if the product doesn't satisfy you. You started it as a three-paragraph essay. Anything you add now will almost inevitably seem tacked on. One of the alternative endings you write will probably seem better than the other, and you may never like either of them very much.

But that will be alright, because the point of this exercise is not to write a first-rate essay. The purpose is to understand the relation between your position and the several issues it may be related to. Another purpose of the exercise is to help you see that, depending on the circumstances, you always have several options for ending an essay. You always have several possible contexts of issues to choose from that will engage the interest of members of quite different language communities. You make that choice depending on the differences you are aware of between what interests you to talk about and the language you use to talk about it and what interests them and the language they use.

COLLABORATIVE LEARNING

Task 1 Practice Alternative Endings

Working in groups of two or three, choose an example three-paragraph essay from this book. Read it aloud.

Describe the essay's introduction. What immediate context of issues or shared concerns does the introduction raise? What community or communities of readers does the introduction set out to interest in the essay's position?

Describe a possible or hypothetical ending for the essay. What possible larger contexts of issues are relevant to the position taken in the essay? How are those larger issues related to the more limited issues raised in the introduction?

Draft two alternative endings to the essay. (Writing these alternative endings could be done individually as a homework assignment. In that case, the members of the collaborative working groups should reconvene in the next class, read their alternative endings to each other, and compare how each writer went about the task.)

Task 2 Reading Aloud

Follow the instructions for reading aloud on p. 55.

☐ EXAMPLE ESSAY ────────────────────

The People's Health
Antonio Rambla

Hardly a day goes by that the news does not carry a story of human drama and suffering that resulted at least in part from poor health care or lack of elementary medical knowledge or medical facilities. Urban minorities, the ghettoized—rural and urban, the jobless, the underpaid, the poorly educated in this country are constantly cheated of the bare essentials of modern health care. Unlike the rich and the middle class, who can afford private medical insurance and private doctors, these people are barred from advanced methods of treatment and from fast, efficient medical service. In a TV ad we are told by the hemophiliac son of a wealthy family that he can survive his disease because his family can afford the huge cost of regular injections of the clotting factor. In the same ad, we are told by a hemophiliac son of poor parents that his chances of obtaining the precious serum are nil. Oddly enough both these young men are equally deprived members of our advanced society. One is as neglected as the other. Both depend on private sacrifice—one by his rich parents, the other by sympathetic and generous strangers. In the end, though, you know who is most likely to survive. This inherent inequality in our system illustrates one of the many spots of social decay that now fester dangerously. To heal this sore, the prescription is simple, but painful and expensive. The remedy is free, government-sponsored national health insurance that gives us total, just, and equal health care for everyone.

Just and equal health treatment, as most city dwellers know as well as those who live deep in the rural countryside of America, is exactly what we do not have. In the country, hospital care is often simply not available at all. In the city, the poor and needy flock to public hospitals in search of care, only to be placed in long waiting lines. Doctors are overworked. Facilities and equipment are overloaded. Quality gives way to quantity. In spite of its good intentions, the medical profession cannot give proper treatment to all the people who need it under these conditions. For lack of room, patients cannot be admitted to hospitals when they need help. Care is delayed and illness aggravated. In sheer human terms, the suffering left unattended by our present medical system is untold.

Beyond the needs of individuals and the organizational, social, and moral problems raised in every local instance by the lack of medical care, there is a larger problem. That is the question of the duty of government to the people governed. Government today must begin to reassess its responsibilities, or, in the fashionable term, its priorities. We believe that one of the main purposes of government is to "promote the general welfare," as the United States Constitution puts it. One interpretation of that phrase is that a government created by a people has a duty to that people. The government is responsible for the preservation of each member of society, as well as the society in general. Of the rights that the Declaration of Independence specifically mentions, "life, liberty, and the pursuit of happiness," the first is life. Life does not mean bare subsistence. It means hale and healthy life, otherwise liberty is useless and happiness impossible to pursue. Hence one of the first duties of modern government is to ensure the health of its people, regardless of social strata or economic means. Anything else falls short of just and equitable treatment for all people, and is an abrogation of duty.

Alternative ending number 1
This abrogation of duty in health care at present is not, however, the only sore that needs healing. Everything that can be said about health can be said about education, shelter, even recreation and transportation. These are necessities of decent human life in a modern, civilized world. They are not luxuries. They are necessary services. And they are services that in fact everyone supposedly pays for through taxes. Taxes go up, bureaucracy expands, expense accounts fatten, and services decline. Politicians continually accuse each other publicly of graft and mismanagement, favoritism, and unfair practices, and yet none of them seem to grasp the central idea: their job, the purpose we elect them to office to fulfill, is increasingly left unfulfilled. In this fix, what are we to do? The answer, finally, may be to undertake a complete restructuring of governmental services. If that's what it takes to guarantee ourselves life, as monumental a task as it may seem, we may just have to do it.

Alternative ending number 2
But it is of course not just "they" who are not doing their duty. Governments can only be as good as the citizens who elect them. The real problem lies in the values of the people themselves. So long as people continue to think of doctors as members of a special social class, instead of fellow participants in a society in which all people are equally and mutually dependent, and think of medical care as a privilege instead of an essential service, the attitude of those who govern those people will not change. Today, medical students learn, in subtle but persuasive ways, that a Fifth Avenue address and a Southhampton summer practice are the proper goals of a self-respecting physician, not making house calls in Harlem or manning a county clinic. It's minding the bank account, not mending the poor, that motivates doctors today. Until we can change the values of those who enter that profession from self-seeking to service to mankind, we will continue to lack responsible health care. □

BASIC DESCRIPTIVE OUTLINE

PROPOSITION   The remedy is free, government-sponsored national health insurance that gives us total, just, and equal health care for everyone.

PLAN   Develop two reasons in defense of the proposition.

PARAGRAPH 1   *says:* Many people in this country do not get good medical care.

does: Introduces the proposition by describing a national public problem and by telling an anecdote.

PARAGRAPH 2   *says:* Public hospitals give poor treatment because they are overcrowded and the personnel are overworked.

does: Supports the proposition by describing the effect of the problem on individuals.

PARAGRAPH 3   *says:* Government has a duty to ensure the life of the people—meaning healthy life.

does: Supports the proposition by explaining the government's responsibility to solve the problem.

ALTERNATIVE ENDING NUMBER 1

PARAGRAPH 4   *says:* Because poor health service is just one of many poor services our government performs, we may have to restructure the government.

does: Shows the relationship of this problem to other governmental problems.

ALTERNATIVE ENDING NUMBER 2

PARAGRAPH 4   *says:* Health care will not change until the public's attitude toward the medical profession changes.

does: Puts the problem into the context of public attitudes toward the relevant profession.

(The difference between basic and detailed descriptive outlines is explained in Part Three: Constructive Reading. See also the example basic and detailed descriptive outlines written for the same essay on p. 77.)

▷ EXERCISE 11   FOUR-PARAGRAPH ESSAY

This essay should be six hundred to seven hundred words long and should be written in four paragraphs: an introductory paragraph ending with a proposition, two paragraphs of defense, and a final paragraph that places the position taken in the essay into a larger context of issues. And of course a descriptive outline.

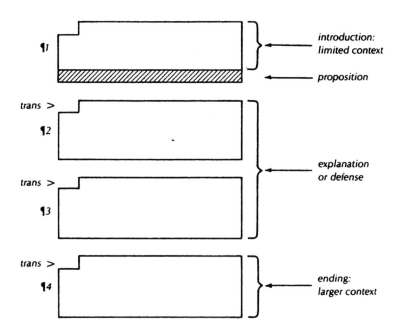

You might prepare yourself to write this essay by reviewing invention exercises 1 through 4, to find a topic closely related to your own experience and knowledge. Also, take a minute to review the instructions for exercise 5. Remember that the place to start, once you have decided on a topic, is the proposition. Then think through a way to explore, explain, or defend the position you take in that proposition. In this exercise you can use one of the forms you learned in essay exercises 5 through 9:

Two reasons

Nestorian order

Opposition plus refutation

Opposition and refutation plus one reason

Opposition and concession plus one reason

Write this essay as you wrote those three-paragraph essays. The only difference now is that you are going to plan ahead for a fourth paragraph—an ending that tries to interest members of larger, more encompassing communities. Write the ending after you have written the introduction. Think of the essay as a single working unit:

Think of a subject.

Think of a tentative proposition.

Think of a defense or explanation.

Write a proposition and defend or explain it.

Write an introduction.

Write an ending.

Check the transitions.

Write a descriptive outline and make adjustments.

Read the essay aloud and revise it.

Make the final copy.

COLLABORATIVE LEARNING

Task 1 Reading Aloud

Follow the instructions for reading aloud on p. 55.

Task 2 Essay Exchange and Peer Conference

Follow the instructions for essay exchange and peer conference on p. 75.

 EXAMPLE ESSAY ————————————————————

Proteins and Health

Sharon Owens

Protein molecules are large, complex organic compounds composed of carbon, oxygen, hydrogen, nitrogen, and sulfur. These five elements are found in all naturally occurring protein molecules. Proteins are made up of smaller units called amino acids. Hundreds of amino acids make up one protein. Just as railroad cars can be joined to make up one train, so can different amino acids be joined to make up one protein. These amino acids are classified as either essential or nonessential. Essential amino acids are those that we have to include in our diet to maintain life and promote growth. The other amino acids found in proteins are classified as nonessential. This designation tends, unfortunately, to imply that they lack importance in the body, which is not the case. Proteins containing all the essential amino acids are called "complete" proteins, and those containing an inadequate amount of one or more of the essential amino acids are called "incomplete" proteins. Proteins, both complete and incomplete, play an important part in maintaining our health.

One way proteins help maintain our health is by forming body regulators. These regulators include enzymes, hormones, antibodies, and antigens. Enzymes are complex materials that play an important part in digestion and in speeding up chemical reactions in our bodies. Enzymes are present in all cells. Without them, cells could not live. Hormones are chemical substances made by the body that control important functions, such as growth, development, reproduction, and metabolism. Antigens are proteins from other organisms that, when present in the body, may cause illness. The body fights off antigens by producing antibodies, which are substances made by living cells to combat infection.

Besides forming these body regulators, proteins also supply material for the formation of new tissues, which include epithelial, muscular, connective, and nervous tissue. Epithelial tissues are coverings, such as the skin. The skin is the tissue that covers the outside of the body. Muscular tissues allow the body to contract and relax, thus enabling movement throughout the body. Connective tissues that are fibrous, elastic, or bone bind different parts of the body together. Nervous tissues are made up of cells that carry electrochemical impulses from one part of the body to another. Whenever many of these tissues are lost due to stress, burns, or illness, the body's proteins replace them.

Proteins, therefore, are a source of our physical life. When our protein intake is low, our cells begin to waste away and we produce fewer antibodies. As a result, we are more likely to be attacked by infection. To avoid this deterioration, we should eat foods that provide substantial amounts of protein. Generally speaking, protein is found in both animal and plant foods. Animal protein sources include beef, veal, pork, lamb, fish, eggs, milk, and cheese. Plant protein is found in soybeans, navy beans, lima beans, pinto beans, and red beans. Our bodies renew themselves with the life-giving protein they get from these animals and plants. □

DETAILED DESCRIPTIVE OUTLINE

PROPOSITION   Proteins, both complete and incomplete, play an important part in maintaining our bodies.

PLAN   Develop two reasons supporting the proposition, plus an introduction and an ending.

PARAGRAPH 1   *says:* Proteins are made up of smaller units called amino acids.

          does: Introduces the proposition by defining the main term in the proposition and describing the composition of the substance it denotes. Defines another term related to the topic. Distinguishes two main categories of the substance.

PARAGRAPH 2   *says:* One way proteins maintain our bodies is by forming body regulators.

          does: Supports the proposition by explaining one function of the substance. Lists four ways that the substance works to perform this function. Explains each of the four in detail.

PARAGRAPH 3   *says:* Another way proteins maintain our bodies is by supplying material for forming new tissue.

          does: Supports the proposition by explaining another function the substance serves. Lists four products of the substance and explains the purpose of each product in detail.

PARAGRAPH 4   *says:* Because lack of proteins can make us vulnerable to sickness, we must eat enough proteins to keep up our protein supply.

does: Ends the paper by placing its scientific information into the context of maintaining life. Explains the results when the substance is lacking or when it functions improperly. Explains what to do to avoid this result, and, briefly, why.

(How to write detailed descriptive outlines is explained beginning on p. 153.)

☐ EXAMPLE ESSAY ————————————————————

What Should Patients Be Told?

Terry Hayes

In 1977, writer Susan Sontag, while recovering from a mastectomy, began to explore the ways society conceptualizes illness. Sontag was charting unknown waters, the sort that were once labeled "Here lie Dragons" on old maps. The result of her exploration was *Illness as Metaphor*, a brief, fiercely literate analysis of how and why we create myths that obscure the reality of certain fatal diseases. Although a new book by Sontag never enters the literary world unremarked, this one created waves of greater-than-usual magnitude. The overwhelming attention the book received cannot be attributed solely to the combined effects of innovative ideas and a controversial author. At a deeper level *Illness as Metaphor* speaks to us all because it is about a disease that scares us all, cancer. In our highly technological age, every one of us must eat, drink, and inhale carcinogens. As a result, one out of four people alive today will develop cancer (Epstein 8). It has therefore become more practical than fatalistic to familiarize ourselves with the old, much-debated issues surrounding this disease. How will we be treated if we contract cancer? What constitutes proper patient care? Unfortunately, there are no easy answers to such questions as these. The professionals whom we would depend on for care continue to debate, their solutions changing with the character of the times. Consequently, even the basic issue of how much to tell cancer patients about the disease remains unsettled.

Most cancer researchers and clinicians, called *oncologists*, simplify the issue by consistently taking one of two extreme positions.

208

These positions can be stated briefly as (1) tell all, and (2) tell nothing (Goodfield 224). The first, and for some time the most prevalent opinion, is that patients have a right to as much information about their condition as the doctor can supply: what illness they have, how they will be treated, and how long they can expect to live. Specialists who hold this view feel that whereas nothing can be gained by withholding bad news, telling patients the truth is at least potentially beneficial. Informed patients, they reason, can prepare themselves better for the course of the disease and can cooperate more fully with doctors. Interestingly enough, the growth of this opinion among professionals coincides not only with the increased focus on individual rights that is characteristic of the past few decades, but also with the increased incidence of cancer itself, which is reaching epidemic proportions. The second extreme position, that patients should be told nothing about the disease, is far less frequently encountered today than in the past. But physicians who still adhere to this opinion—and they are not all old-fashioned general practitioners—steadfastly maintain that the less patients know, the less they worry, and, consequently, the more energy they have to fight the illness. This attitude was fashionable during the first half of the twentieth century, a period during which the individual was expected to focus more on others, and during which cancer was less widespread.

Recently, alongside these two extremes, a third, more moderate position has emerged. This position takes into account the cancer victim's individual needs and individual rights (Abrams 44). It is an attitude held by a growing number of physicians who feel that to take a rigid stance at either extreme would be unethical, since different patients have different psychological responses to information about their cancers. Some patients do, in fact, want to know everything, and these people adjust to the disease most successfully when they are given details. Other patients prefer to know as little as possible, and may become severely depressed if told too much. And although patients will probably not state their preference explicitly, by "listening between the lines" the doctor can usually determine which message is being sent (Abrams xxii). Of course, this approach requires more of the doctor, who must listen harder and make tougher decisions. But against the clamor of our times it strikes a hopeful note. Perhaps scientific specialization and personalized attention are not as mutually exclusive as many of us had feared. At any rate, if intelligently put into practice, the moderate attitude is very good news indeed for cancer patients, who are treated in accordance with needs that are theirs and theirs alone (Abrams xxiii). □

WORKS CONSULTED

Abrams, Ruth D. *Not Alone With Cancer: A Guide for Those Who Care.* Springfield, Ill.: Thomas, 1974.

Epstein, Samuel S. *The Politics of Cancer.* San Francisco: Sierra Club, 1978.

Goodfield, June. *The Siege of Cancer.* New York: Random House, 1975.

Levit, Rose. *Ellen: A Short Life Long Remembered.* San Francisco: Chronicle, 1974.

Sontag, Susan. *Illness as Metaphor.* New York: Farrar, Straus, and Giroux, 1977.

Winick, Myron, ed. *Nutrition and Cancer.* New York: Wiley, 1977.

DETAILED DESCRIPTIVE OUTLINE

PROPOSITION	Even so basic an issue as how much to tell cancer patients about their disease remains unsettled.
PLAN	Explain two extreme views of an issue, one important and the other less important, and then explain the most important third view.
PARAGRAPH 1	*says: Illness as Metaphor* received attention because it's about cancer.
	does: Introduces proposition by describing a relevant book: why it was written and what it's about. Analyzes the book's reception. Isolates the most influential of three contributory factors. Cites facts and statistics to establish the importance of the subject matter to any reader. Names two related issues and narrows one of them.
PARAGRAPH 2	*says:* Some cancer specialists tell patients everything so that they can cope better with reality and cooperate more fully during treatment; others tell patients nothing in order to prevent unnecessary worry.
	does: Supports the proposition by supplying two contrasting views of the issue. (1) Summarizes the most popular position and gives three reasons (one negative, two positive) in support. Then relates the prevalence of this position to two factors characteristic of our time. (2) Summarizes a less popular opinion and gives one positive reason in support. Relates the former prevalence of this view to two factors characteristic of the times in which it was favored.

PARAGRAPH 3   *says:* Still other doctors hold that the issue must be decided differently for different patients, taking into account their individual psychological needs.

does: Supports the proposition by describing a third view of the issue. Gives one important reason for its growing popularity by contrasting possible effects of the most popular view. Names two drawbacks of this view. Suggests a possible meaning of this new view in terms of modern society. Makes a conditional value judgment about general benefits of this opinion.

NOTES FOR PART FOUR

PUTTING POSITION PAPERS TO GOOD USE

OTHER WAYS TO END AN ESSAY

There are several other ways to end an essay besides relating the position you take in the essay to a context of issues.

One common ending in very long essays is to **summarize**. A summary might be useful if you think that your readers may need help remembering and fitting together the several parts of your exploration, explanation, or defense and relating them to your position. And the conventional format for some kinds of papers in the sciences and social sciences requires a summary. But in most short essays, anything up to ten or twelve pages, ending the essay with a summary is a waste of time and paper.

Other options are more constructive. One of these is to **refine the proposition**. In this case, you use your exploration, explanation, or defense of the position you take at the beginning of the essay to suggest another way of stating that position. What you are saying is that, in light of the way you have been explaining your position, another way of phrasing it may seem more accurate, more useful, or more far reaching. For example, an ending that refined the proposition of the essay on cars might say something like this.

211

introduction	. . . It seems fantastic and unlikely, yet it is now possible to say that in the future the trend will be for people to use cars
proposition	as we know them less rather than more. In fact, it looks as if cars may be on the way out as our major means of transportation.
¶ 2	. . .
¶ 3	. . .
ending	In light of the complexity of all these rapid changes in the way we live, it may oversimplify the situation to say that cars
refining the proposition	may be on the way out. It may make more sense to say that the way we use cars will change so much that what we call cars then won't look at all like what we call cars today. In a hundred years we may no longer use private vehicles to get around. Instead we may use . . .

If you like, you can prepare your readers for an ending that refines your position in this way with a proposition that is hypothetical ("It may be true that . . . ," or "If X is true, then Y"). Then your ending can restate the proposition more positively.

introduction	. . . It seems fantastic and unlikely, yet it is now possible to say that the future trend will be for people to use cars as we
proposition	know them less rather than more. If our way of life changes as much in the next hundred years as it has in the hundred years just past, cars as we know them may be on the way out.
¶ 2	. . .
¶ 3	. . .
ending	So it looks as if our lives are going to continue to change
proposition restated positively	just as rapidly as they have been changing for a century or more. That being the case, it oversimplifies the situation to say that cars may be on the way out. It makes more sense to say instead that we may . . .

Similar to an ending that refines a hypothetical proposition is one that chooses one of several alternatives offered in the proposition. In this case, the proposition doesn't state one position but states two similar but alternative positions ("Either . . . or . . . "). In this case, the ending settles on one of the alternatives as preferable, more reasonable, more practical, and so on, in light of what you have said in your exploration, explanation, or defense.

introduction	. . . It seems fantastic and unlikely, yet it is now possible to say that in the future the trend will be for people to use cars
proposition	as we know them less rather than more. Either most of the technological change we are capable of has already occurred so that we will continue transporting ourselves indefinitely

pretty much as we do today, or else our lives will continue to
change and cars as we know them will simply disappear.

¶ 2

¶ 3

ending

alternative
selected and
restated

   . . .

   . . .

     So it looks as if technological change is not going to stop.
Our lives are going to continue to change just as fast as they
are changing now. That being the case, then it seems inevitable
that cars as we know them will disappear. In the future we are
much more likely to . . .

In another kind of ending you can **evaluate the essay.** This kind of
ending is useful if it turns out that you cannot explore, explain, or defend
your position conclusively, or if you see that you could explore, explain,
or defend it in two or more ways. For the essay you are writing you
choose one of these ways rather than the other. For example, you take
a personal or social approach instead of a political or scientific one.

Then, in the ending, you defend the way of exploring, explaining,
or defending your position that you chose; you defend the evidence you
used; or perhaps you even defend your decision to write the essay
at all.

Or instead, an evaluative ending might evaluate the essay in terms
of the timeliness of its argument or its position. You might want to say
that the position you have taken is true at the present moment, but
since all the evidence is not yet in, the situation may change. So the
position you have taken is subject to change.

introduction

proposition

   . . . It seems fantastic and unlikely, yet it is now possible to
say that in the future the trend will be for people to use
cars as we know them less rather than more. If fact, it looks
as if cars may be on the way out as our major means of
transportation.

¶ 2

¶ 3

ending

evaluating the
essay

   . . .

   . . .

     In light of the complexity of all these rapid changes in the
way we live, of course it oversimplifies the situation to say
that cars may be on the way out. Trying to predict the future
in this way is always futile. No one has a crystal ball. There
is some value in trying to predict the future, however, because
even though we can't know the future, we always have to plan
for it. . . .

An ending may also **suggest other possible approaches or solutions**
to the problem that you have addressed in the essay, evaluating these
alternative approaches or solutions in light of what you have written.

introduction	. . . It seems fantastic and unlikely, yet it is now possible to say that in the future the trend will be for people to use
proposition	cars as we know them less rather than more. If fact, it looks as if cars may be on the way out as our major means of transportation.
¶ 2	. . .
¶ 3	. . .
ending	Of course, using a few statistics provided by the major oil companies and some personal anecdotes is not the only way to go about making an important prediction like this. There are less direct but probably just as reliable means, and these may suggest different answers. For example, within half a century or so dozens of what we now call underdeveloped countries will be well on the way to being fully developed. In those countries millions more people will have more money to spend, and one thing they are going to want to spend it on is going places. . . .

Finally, and rarely, depending on your self-confidence as a writer and your command of the subject, the end of the essay may be the place to **go out on a limb and speculate.** You might try guessing what might happen in the future based on what you have said, or what might result from a course of action or thought implied in the position you have taken in the essay.

introduction	. . . It seems fantastic and unlikely, yet it is now possible to say that in the future the trend will be for people to use
proposition	cars as we know them less rather than more. If fact, it looks as if cars may be on the way out as our major means of transportation.
¶ 2	. . .
¶ 3	. . .
ending	So suppose it turns out that cars are on the way out as our major means of transportation—what then? Interviewed ten years ago, the president of the Ford Motor Company was asked what he thought Ford would be making in the year 2050. He didn't know, he said, but it won't be cars. So, facing the possibility that cars are on the way out, what we do is think
speculation	of what is likely to replace them. What is most likely to replace them is . . .

However wild in substance, a conservatively worded speculation that maintains the essay's topic and tone can sometimes demonstrate very effectively your ability to think through an issue.

214

WRITING ESSAY EXAMS

Once you understand the form that this book requires, *Short Course* form, you will grasp some of its practical implications. The most obvious of these is that the basic element in *Short Course* form (proposition plus exploration, explanation, or defense) can be useful in answering questions on essay examinations.

The first sentence (or two) of an exam answer should be a clear, succinct generalization that answers the question fully. This generalization is your proposition. Then in the rest of the answer you explore, explain, and defend your generalization by explaining its operative words and the key relationship it draws among those words. (See Propositions, p. 85, and Paragraph Development, p. 111.)

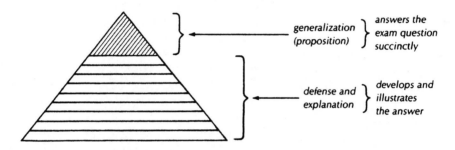

Used without an introduction in this way, *Short Course* form resembles the standard form of newspaper articles:

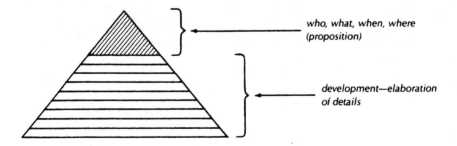

This resemblance between *Short Course* form and newspaper form is not accidental. The pressure you would feel as a newspaper reporter and the pressure you feel as an exam writer are similar. Reporters and exam writers both have limited time and space. Both have to write quickly and intelligibly.

Both also have to write in a form that will suffer the least damage if it has to be cut short abruptly and arbitrarily for lack of time or space. Reporters write in pyramid form so that the editor can snip the article off at any point to fit the space available in the newspaper, yet not lose the main point of the article. When you are writing an exam, you write in a similar form so that if the bell rings and you have to quit when you are only halfway through the essay, your answer will not lose its point. You will already have made your point, right up there at the beginning.

Short Course form without an introduction will not work for every essay exam question you write, but it will work for most of them. Also, there are hitches. One is that you may sometimes change your mind halfway through writing an exam essay, so that the proposition you wrote at the beginning no longer says what you want to say.

Of course you might change your mind no matter what form you write in, and in fact you are less likely to change your mind using *Short Course* form because the form itself encourages you to think through your answer carefully before you begin to write. You have to think through your answer to some extent in order to write a proposition sentence to begin your answer. If you do change your mind, you can still go back if you have time, scratch out the proposition you wrote in the first place, and write a new one.

One way to think through an exam answer is with an imaginary dialogue or an imaginary topic interview. Before you set pen to paper, imagine yourself explaining to a friend the answer you have tentatively decided on. Silently "talking over" the answer in this way lets you write a first draft in your head where you can change the answer without penalty. (See Topic Interviews, p. 30.)

Another hitch you may run into in using *Short Course* form for writing essay exams is that, because it makes clear what you know to both your teacher and yourself, it may also make it harder for you to hide what you do not know from both the teacher and yourself. That is a measure of self-awareness that can be painful or satisfying, depending on the way you look at it.

Short Course form leads you to discover what you know and what you don't know because the form requires you to be specific and concrete. You write an initial statement (your proposition) that can be stated as generally as the question is stated. Then you write a detailed, specific development that explores, explains, and defends the position you have taken in that initial statement.

The form is useful, therefore, because no matter how generally an examination question may be stated, it always requires a specific, concrete answer. But it means that you have to know those specifics and you have to have thought them through in order to arrive at some of the generalizations that they may suggest. In short, if you plan to use

Short Course form to write an exam, you've got to prepare yourself well to take the exam.

Finally, if you do use *Short Course* form and if you have time, you can add an ending to your answer that places it in a context of issues. One of the most effective endings you can write to an exam question suggests that you are aware of your answer's limitations and the limitations of the operative words you have used in it. These qualifications tell your teacher not only that you understand the subject matter of the course but that you also understand the way that conversation about that subject matter is carried on in the relevant discourse community.

(See Talking About Elephants, p. 193, and William Perry's "Examsmanship and the Liberal Arts," p. 343. Perry talks about relationships between what you know and the academic communities that your teachers represent, such as English, history, chemistry, sociology, mathematics, and so on. See also Unity and Coherence, p. 116, and Assumptions, p. 132.)

EXAMPLE ESSAY EXAM

Question: Gene Sharp's *Social Power and Political Freedom* is about relationships between political freedom and governments regarded as hierarchies of power. He argues that in hierarchies of political power, the people at the top are placed in that position by those at the bottom. People get the government that they deserve, that they want, or that they need. Describe the arguments that have been made against Sharp's position by political writers we have read this term and explain them.

☐ EXAMPLE ESSAY ANSWER ─────────────────

Sharp's *Social Power*

Theresa Montoya

Several of the political writers we read this term say that, contrary to Sharp's position, people obey political rulers for reasons that are anything but voluntary.

The reasons explaining people's obedience are varied, but they are all related in some way to their psychological makeup. Bertrand de Jouvenel claims, for instance, that habit is a major reason people do what they are told. He concurs with Hume, who wrote that be-

217

cause habit is acquired through culture and experience that we are not fully aware of, many people "never think of departing from that path" laid down by "their ancestors." People obey, de Jouvenel says, largely because they are apathetic, and he talks about "zones of indifference" where people "accept orders without questioning authority." Another reason people obey is because they fear sanctions or punishment, as Thomas Green points out. The state can use the criminal justice system against anyone who defies it, and it can threaten the insubordinate with extreme penalties for petty crimes. Still another reason is self-interest. The state can offer incentives such as elevation in political or social status, jobs, and privileges. Green also points out that people may feel that they gain indirectly from obedience, because obedience makes a government stable so that it can concentrate its energies on raising the standard of living of its people.

But the strongest force making people obey their government according to these writers seems to be the belief that obedience is a moral obligation. This belief may be a basic cultural value of the people being governed, or it may be a product of government indoctrination. In either case, people tend to identify psychologically with the ruler and the state, which they see as extensions of themselves and therefore not to be betrayed. Even Sharp acknowledges the power of this feeling of moral obligation. But Green puts the case much more forcefully than Sharp. He says that people feel that obedience is an individual's contribution to a good society because to resist, that is, not to obey, might bring down "greater evil" on the society and might even make the government collapse. Once again fear plays a role. Most people believe that the state provides personal security, they regard the established leadership as legitimate, whatever its history, and they condone punishment for those who disobey.

Given such strong motives to obey, people who have tried to oppose a government in power have found the belief that obedience is socially acceptable and morally just hard to undermine. Those who have used force to oppose a government and bring it down (in, for example, the French, American, or Russian Revolutions) resort to inciting fear and outrage against apathy and habit. Those who have tried to bring a government down or oppose what they regard as oppressive conditions with disobedience or passive resistance (for example, Ghandi and King) play feelings of moral justice, self-interest, even social embarrassment against apathy and habit. In the end, looking closely at these contests of will, it is hard not to agree with Sharp that people get the government they need and want. So, the revolutionary's job is, by hook or by crook, to get people to want something better for themselves and their children, and then realize that they don't just want to change it but feel it as a genuine need. ☐

Adapting Short Course *Form for Many Uses*

Essays can be written in many forms. The essay form that this book teaches you is only one of them. But it is an especially useful one and it can be adapted for many purposes. It is adaptable because it stresses the fundamental necessities of all well-planned, well-developed expository writing—focusing on a single idea and expressing relationships between subordinate ideas. It is also adaptable because it helps you discover, explore, explain, and defend your ideas.

The previous section, Writing Essay Exams, explains only one way you can adapt *Short Course* form. You can also stretch it to any length for term papers and other long writing assignments. And you can use it as an efficient format for writing letters, reports, and memos in business and the professions.

Length: Term Papers and Other Long Writing Assignments

Most essays you write in school or at work have to be a lot longer than three or four paragraphs and 500 to 750 words. Whenever you write long essays like that you can apply everything you have learned about organization in earlier parts of this book simply by stretching *Short Course* form.

The organizational principles of the form are clear, no matter how much you stretch it. You can organize a twenty- or thirty-page research paper with it just as you can use it to organize a two-page, five-hundred-word essay, because it teaches you explanatory subordination. That is, it helps you to focus on a single main idea and to make explicit relationships between that idea and subordinate ideas, and among those subordinate ideas. Whatever the length and complexity of the paper, *Short Course* form helps you discover and explore your ideas and helps you explain and defend them. You may even find that the longer and more complex your writing task is, the more helpful *Short Course* form becomes.

Short Course form is even clear when it is stretched to length of a three-hundred-page book. Imagine writing a book in which chapter one is an introduction that explains the issues addressed in the book and ends with a paragraph that summarizes the book's main point. Then chapters two through five explore, explain, and defend that point. And the last chapter places your position into a larger context of issues. Your book would be an adaptation of *Short Course* form. You would know how to make the book coherent throughout every one of its three hundred pages because you would know from writing transition sentences connecting paragraphs and parts of paragraphs in five-hundred-word, three-paragraph essays how to write transitions linking chapters and parts of chapters to each other and to the main point you are making in the book.

You can organize long essays in the same way, subdividing them into mini-chapters as you divide up a book. For example, you might begin a twenty-page term paper with two or three pages of introduction explaining the issues addressed in the essay, leading to a paragraph that summarizes the essay's main point: the essay's proposition. Then you might write several minichapters of four or five pages each that explore, explain, and defend different aspects of that point. You could organize each of these mini-chapters in *Short Course* form, too. Finally, you could end the paper with two or three pages that place the position you have taken into a larger context of issues.

In writing a long essay like that, you would take care to write transitions linking the chapters and paragraphs to each other and to the essay's main point, just as you have to take care to write transition sentences connecting the paragraphs and parts of paragraphs in a five-hundred-word, three-paragraph essay.

The following example is a research essay written by a student who had learned to write shorter essays in *Short Course* form and who adapted what she learned when she came to be doing the mature undergraduate research that she reports in this essay. Notice that the proposition of the essay occurs at the end of the introductory section of the essay, just before the first subheading, not at the end of the first paragraph (or at the end of the paper). Notice that the essay's ending puts the argument into the larger context of national attitudes toward war and violence. And notice that the essay includes transitional generalizations at the beginning of each section as well as at the beginning of each paragraph. The essay's subtitles at the beginning of each new section also help readers follow the explanation.

☐ EXAMPLE ESSAY ―――――――――――――――――――

The Inescapable Guilt of Lieutenant Calley

Michele C. Watts

The Vietnam War saw many tragedies and atrocities. One of these stands out for its brutality and scale. On March 16, 1968, Charlie Company of Task Force Barker, under the command of Lieutenant

William Laws Calley, destroyed the tiny Vietnamese hamlet that the American Army called My Lai 4 and killed most of its inhabitants, all of them unarmed, twenty-two of them while hiding helplessly in an irrigation ditch.

Calley was subsequently court-martialed and convicted of murder. In his defense, he claimed that he was just following orders when he killed most of the people in My Lai 4, and that he and his men killed in self-defense. But the jury did not find these claims persuasive. They determined that Calley himself was ultimately responsible for what happened.

As always in such a complex and threatening experience as warfare, not just one but many factors contribute to every event. Army Intelligence, having misnamed and confused Vietnamese villages, sent Calley's company to attack the wrong one. Army Intelligence also said the village would be empty of civilians that morning, so that Charlie Company could assume that anyone left there must be enemy personnel. Compounding the confusion, Task Force Barker, of which Charlie Company was a part, was a newly assembled unit with an unclear chain of command. Finally, the Vietnamese surprise attack called the Tet Offensive had just begun.

These are all mitigating factors—the conditions under which the event occurred. But even after considering every one of them carefully it is impossible to disagree with the jury's verdict. The evidence is overwhelming that Calley was responsible for the disaster, because he alone was in command.

BACKGROUND

In order to understand the atmosphere that would allow a My Lai 4 to happen, it is necessary to take a closer look at the conditions under which it occurred. Of these, the Tet Offensive was perhaps the most important, because it was the spark that lit the fire of suspicion and fear of all Vietnamese that motivated My Lai 4. The Vietnamese celebrate the religious holiday of Tet in late January. For the Vietnamese, Tet is like New Year's and Christmas rolled into one. It is a time of great rejoicing and traditionally a time of truce (Everette 11). For this reason, as the Tet season arrived in January 1968, the American troops quite reasonably breathed a sigh of relief. But their relief turned out to be premature. Tet that year marked one of the bloodiest battles of the Vietnam war. The Tet Offensive, as it came to be known, took the Americans almost completely by surprise. First, the North Vietnamese and the Vietcong infiltrated the cities that constituted American strongholds in the guise of holiday travelers, smuggling in ammunition in bodiless coffins (Everette 15, 13). As the Tet festivities began, the Vietnamese and Vietcong troops crept out of hiding, unearthed their ammunition, and attacked.

Overnight, Saigon and other Vietnamese cities went from relatively safe, peaceful enclaves to a battleground. Terror ruled the city streets and the surrounding countryside as the North Vietnamese and the Vietcong swept the cities. It took the Americans several weeks of sustained fighting to recapture hostile territory. In order to regain control, they used napalm, heavy artillery, and bombs (Everette 13). They destroyed every area that the enemy occupied, putting into effect what has been described as the American Army's principle of destroying the village to save the people. It was on this principle that My Lai 4 was destroyed.

After the Tet Offensive, the American troops remained on high alert to avoid another surprise attack of the same sort. All Vietnamese became suspect. American soldiers, already at their nerves' end from jungle warfare, were even more terrified than they had been before the Tet Offensive began. Many of them felt a thirst for vengeance. As one soldier put it, they wanted "a chance to revenge the deaths of our fellow GIs" (Hammer 111). In this atmosphere of hatred, fear, and suspicion, the village of Song My, long a Vietcong stronghold, was targeted for a search-and-destroy mission.

Song My was the base of operations from which, during the Tet Offensive, the Vietcong attacked the city of Quang Ngai, the headquarters of the second division of ARVN, the American-South Vietnamese coordinated military force (Hammer 11). The search-and-destroy mission aimed at Song My was to be carried out by the Eleventh Brigade, part of Task Force Barker of the Americal Division. Task Force Barker was "a tiny ad hoc unit composed of one company from each of the three divisions in the brigade" (Hersh 22).

This fact is significant because, newly established, Task Force Barker was a mélange of units from several independent divisions and still lacking a firm chain of command. As orders came down from above, they remained unclear, neither direct nor detailed enough to prevent them from being misconstrued. Interpretation of commands was frequently left to those in subordinate positions. This lack of clarity in the chain of command was the condition of uncertainty in which Calley could misinterpret a command and take it on himself to order his unit to kill the civilian inhabitants of My Lai 4.

Not only was Task Force Barker new, but almost all of the soldiers in its Charlie Company were green. Calley's Sergeant had been in combat before, but none of the other men in the unit, including Calley, had. They had gone straight from training in Hawaii to the bush of Vietnam and the proximity of a Vietcong stronghold. They did not know what to expect. Then, for days on end, they saw little combat and as a result became frustrated and tense. Charlie Company finally saw real action in My Lai 4. There, they overreacted because they were inexperienced, frustrated, and scared (Sack 29–30).

Army Intelligence added to Charlie Company's problems by reporting that, on Saturdays, most of the villagers at My Lai 4 would either be in the rice fields or at the market. So the attack was planned for a Saturday morning (Hammer 60). But this pattern was broken on the morning of March 16. What Army Intelligence called My Lai 4 was a subdivision or hamlet in the village of Song My. The night before, many villagers had returned to Song My after years in refugee camps because the government had told them that Song My was now safe (Hammer 115). On that Saturday morning many people did not go to work in the rice fields but stayed home to get resettled.

Army Intelligence also confused the hamlets that made up Song My, with the result that they aimed the mission at the wrong hamlet. When it arrived at My Lai, Charlie Company did not find a Vietcong emplacement and munitions dump. Instead, it found "exactly three rifles . . . some ammunition, and a couple of grenades (Hammer 144). This error occurred in part because Army Intelligence renamed hamlets in Song My to suit its own convenience, giving them instead names that were easier to recognize and classify. In place of their Vietnam place names, it labeled the several little hamlets that made up Song My village My Lai 1 through My Lai 6. Intelligence then compounded the confusion by nicknaming the six My Lais "Pinkvilles," because they were colored pink on the maps. Partly as a result of this compound confusion, Charlie Company was sent to attack Xom Lang, renamed My Lai 4, instead of My Khe, renamed My Lai 1, which was the true target of the American search-and-destroy mission that morning (Hammer 11). Ironically, the Vietnamese name for the hamlet where the mission was actually carried out, Xom Lang, means The Place Where Trouble Does Not Come (Hammer 11). Due to American arrogance and incompetence, Xom Lang turned out to be the place where trouble indeed did come.

CALLEY ON THE STAND

Despite all the errors, shortcomings, and suspicions of the American Armed Forces, however, the Army charged Lieutenant Calley, the leader of Charlie Company, with ultimate responsibility for what happened at My Lai 4. Calley was detained and charged under Articles 32 and 118 of the Uniform Code of Military Justice with 102 counts of murder. Article 32 states that with sufficient cause and after sufficient investigation, a suspect may be charged and detained. Article 118 states that a person who has "premeditated design to kill" is subject to the death penalty or life in prison (*Title 10*, United States Code 191). It was then up to Calley to defend himself against this charge.

The prosecution argued that Calley was responsible for two reasons. First, he was in command. His misinterpretation of his orders led him to order his troops to kill all the civilians they encountered and to kill them himself. And second, even if it were true that Calley was following orders, however he construed them, that fact does not excuse his actions. The universal norm accepted even in military courts martial is that it is wrong to take another person's life unless your own life is threatened. Self-defense does not excuse the slaughter of over one hundred unarmed civilians.

Calley's defense against these arguments was twofold. First, he did plead self-defense, because although in fact the My Lai villages were not armed, he believed, and had good reason to believe on the basis of Army Intelligence reports, that they were either Vietcong or Vietcong sympathizers, and as such they counted as the enemy. His task, as he understood it, was to kill the enemy in order to save American lives. And second, Calley testified that he was following orders, because, on the witness stand, he recalled specifically asking his superior officer, Captain Medina, "Do you mean [to kill] women and children too?" and remembered that Medina replied, "I mean everything" (Sack 89). In support of this argument and in Calley's defense, another soldier remembered hearing Medina utter similar words in a preattack pep talk. Vernardo Simpson, a member of Medina's company, stated that Medina told the men to "kill or burn down everything in sight" (Hammer 111).

Unfortunately for Calley, not every witness was so favorable to his case. Paul Meadlo, who was at Calley's side when he shot the villagers, was the witness most destructive to Calley's defense. Meadlo testified twice that he saw Calley reload his magazine "between ten and fifteen times" (Everette 148–149). Meadlo made no mention of the order that Medina had supposedly issued about killing everything. Meadlo's testimony was so harmful to Calley's case, in fact, because he claimed that Calley alone initiated the massacre. Another major witness for the prosecution was equally destructive. Captain Ernest Medina himself took the stand to testify against Calley. Medina firmly denied ever giving such an order as Calley credits him with (Everette 182–183). Following Medina's testimony, several more witnesses corroborated Meadlo's and Medina's stories, totally destroying Calley's defense.

CONVICTION, SENTENCE, AND THEIR IMPLICATIONS

The jury convicted Calley of twenty-two counts of murder. They did not convict him of all of the 102 counts he was charged with, because they thought that there was not enough evidence to link him directly to all the killings. The direct link that the jury decided had been established was the twenty-two people shot in an irrigation ditch. After convicting Calley, the jury had to sentence him as well. They had the choice of death or life in prison. They chose the latter, but through appeals and commutation of the sentence, in the end Calley served a total of only three years in prison.

The story of My Lai 4 and Lieutenant Calley is therefore a tragic one not only for 102 murdered Vietnamese villagers and their families and friends, but for Calley, his fellow soldiers, and for the citizens of the United States of America on whose behalf the American Army acted in Vietnam. As is always the case, many factors contributed to the atrocity. In American memory, My Lai takes its place along with a long history of atrocities perpetrated by American military and police personnel against supposed enemies: Native Americans, African Americans, trade unionists, and war protestors. It now brings to mind another atrocity of the Vietnam War much nearer home, the death of four Kent State University undergraduates at the hands of Army National Guardsmen three years later. And for those who witnessed them, Calley's trial evoked recollections of Nazi war crimes trials in Nuremberg.

But the message of My Lai and other such atrocities is not clear. Were not Calley and his men victims too, their lives destroyed by a war America never meant to wage and, waging it, never meant to win? Vietnam put the nation under enormous pressure. But more to the point it put the American men it sent to Vietnam under enormous pressure. Men under pressure can break. Armed men under pressure who break are all too likely to break others. A jury rightfully convicted Lieutenant Calley of murder. But given the chance, of what would a jury convict the nation that sent him there? □

WORKS CONSULTED AND CITED

Contesta, David R., and Robert Muccigrosso. *America in the Twentieth Century—Coming of Age.* New York: Harper and Row, 1988.

Everette, Arthur, Katheryn Johnson, and Harry F. Rosenthal. *Calley.* New York: Dell, 1971.

Hammer, Richard. *One Morning in the War.* New York: Coward-McCann, 1970.

Hersh, Seymour H. *My Lai 4—A Report of the Massacre and Its Aftermath*. New York: Random House, 1970.

Sack, John. *Lieutenant Calley—His Own Story*. New York: Viking, 1971.

United States Code, *Title 10*. Washington: Government Printing Office, 1983.

EFFICIENCY: WRITING IN BUSINESS AND THE PROFESSIONS

Because *Short Course* form teaches you to take a position clearly and in a conspicuous place in your writing, no matter what the situation or topic, anyone who reads an essay that you write in that way can get the point right away. It also teaches you to focus your ideas and make clear relationships among supporting factors and ideas and between them and the main point of the essay. This means that the form helps you yourself understand better what you have to say, as well as helping your readers understand it. It makes it less likely that you will write nonsense—or, rather, it makes it more likely that you will be able to detect the nonsense you have written before the boss does.

So *Short Course* form is an efficient form for professional or business writing as well as for essay exams and term papers. And it is also a good form for writing articles for publication in most academic journals.

Here's how the form might work, for example, if you were a professional asked to serve as a consultant to an institutional administrator. Suppose you are a guidance counselor in a high school. The parents of one of the students in the school (we'll call him Jim) have called the high school principal and told her that they are worried about their son's performance in school. They ask her why Jim is doing so poorly in his courses. The principal tells him that she will look into the problem and will call them back.

Then she calls Jim's guidance counselor. That's you. She asks you to write her a letter about Jim. She wants you to explain what you think is going wrong, so that she can explain the problem to Jim's parents. That's your professional "writing assignment."

You get ready to write the letter by doing a little research. You look over Jim's records, you interview him, and you talk to his teachers. Then you sit down to think over what you have learned, and you begin to generalize it, much as you did in the invention exercises in exercise 4. You decide that Jim's main problem is that at this time he is having some difficulty coping with reality.

You formulate this generalization and express it as the tentative proposition of your report to the principal: "Jim's major problem at the moment seems to be that he is having a little trouble coping with reality."

226

This is the position you are taking about Jim, your judgment about him as a professional guidance counselor.

But you can't leave it at that. Your professional responsibility requires you to do more than formulate an opinion. It also requires you to explain and support your opinion so that other people will understand and accept it. To explain your judgment in this case, you express it as the proposition of your report on Jim and divide your explanation into two parts, what your proposition *assumes* and what it *asserts*. This division gives you the basis of the second and third paragraphs of your report.

Your judgment, that "Jim's major problem at the moment seems to be that he is having a little trouble coping with reality," *assumes* knowledge of the reality that Jim faces. The principal and Jim's parents may not be aware of that reality. Let's say that Jim faces new competition on the football team and is having trouble learning the first principles of plane geometry. Paragraph 2 of your letter would outline these problems and the pressures that they are likely to bring to bear on a high school student's life.

Based on this assumption, your generalization also *asserts* that Jim's present way of trying to cope with this reality is inadequate. Perhaps because he did well in first-year mathematics without working very hard, Jim is trying to get by in plane geometry in the same way, putting off his homework until the last minute and then rushing through it to get the answers without thoroughly understanding the principles involved. Maybe he is trying to deal with new competition on the football team with boasting and bravado instead of facing his limitations and trying out for another position. Paragraph 3 of your report would describe Jim's behavior and explain why it is preventing him from developing as he should.

Having taken a position and explained it, you would then write an introduction. Paragraph 1 of your letter, the introduction, might outline a conceptual context. You might discuss generally what a boy of Jim's age might be expected to accomplish and to what degree a boy of his age might be expected to understand himself and the problems he faces. You might also refer to conditions at the school or in the culture at large that might be expected to make life somewhat difficult for high school students like Jim. This introductory paragraph would end with your one-sentence evaluation of this particular boy in this particular situation. This sentence would be the proposition of your report that takes a position on "Jim's major problem at the moment."

These three paragraphs—introduction and two paragraphs of explanation—would complete the task the principal assigned you. If you also felt that the principal would appreciate some suggestions about what the school and Jim's parents might do to help him through this difficult time, you might add a fourth paragraph outlining some steps they might take. Paragraph 4 would give your report an ending by placing its proposition, a judgment based on your professional expertise, into the context of possible cooperative or individual action, as you learned to do that in What an Ending Does, p. 206, and in Other Ways to End an Essay, p. 223.

The result of organizing your letter in this way would be a well-focused essay very much like the essays that the exercises in this book ask you to write. One version of the report you might have written follows. Following that is an example report in a business situation written in *Short Course* form.

☐ EXAMPLE ESSAY MEMO

KINGSGATE HIGH SCHOOL
86 Oakwood Road
Hobart, Illinois

Counseling Department

Dr. Jean Corey, Principal
Kingsgate High School
86 Oakwood Road
Hobart, Illinois

Dear Jean,

You have asked me to respond to questions Jim MacReady's parents have asked about Jim's difficulties in school this fall. I don't think the problems are terribly serious, and they can be fairly easily solved. Jim is sixteen, and a sophomore. His junior high school record is above average. He did well at Kingsgate last year. He plays basketball and football, seems very interested in science and English, and is socially active. His class elected him treasurer last spring. At sixteen, though, he is in a very difficult stage of development. He is likely to have a chaotic emotional life, a great deal of uncertainty about his relationships with girls, and still rather strong dependence on support from home. At the same time, he may have a tendency to resent that dependence. He probably wants to try new things, and prove himself by succeeding in them, and he may feel very impatient if that success is slow to come. Most of these characteristics can be found in Jim's personality at this time. The result is that, in my view, Jim's major problem at the moment seems to be that he is having a little trouble coping with reality.

The two most troublesome features of Jim's reality this fall seem to be geometry and football. The first month of Mr. Trager's plane geometry course has left Jim very much behind. He has a weekly quiz average of 68, and Trager says that Jim is inattentive in class, hands in his homework irregularly, and makes thoughtless errors in class recitation. Jim's performance puzzles Trager because he taught Jim algebra last year and knows that the boy is potentially very good in math. On the surface, it seems that the cause of Jim's difficulty in geometry may be the fact that he is trying out this fall for quarterback on the football team. But Coach Tolland says that Jim spends more time joking with the other boys than he spends practicing passes and signals. Tolland thinks Jim will probably not make Junior Varsity quarterback, and he thinks Jim knows that Billy Fazio, who moved to Hobart just this summer, is the more likely choice.

These two pressures on Jim's life at the present time have left him rather confused. In our talk yesterday morning, Jim admitted that he was afraid Billy would make quarterback. I asked him how he felt about that. He acted cocky and said that Fazio is not half as good a quarterback as he (Jim) is. If Fazio makes it, Jim said, it would be through favoritism. He couldn't tell me why he thought Tolland favored Fazio. As for geometry, I asked Jim if he liked Mr. Trager as a teacher. He brightened up at this. He said he liked Trager, and he liked algebra a lot last year. Algebra all seemed to make sense, it all fit together. When I asked about geometry, Jim became quiet. He complained that all those axioms are too hard to memorize. None of it makes sense to him. I asked if he put as much time into his homework this year as last year. He said he did—just as much, but it didn't do any good. He knew he was going to fail geometry anyway. Half an hour of homework was enough for algebra, he said, and it should be enough for geometry too. If not, he couldn't be bothered doing more.

The new reality Jim is facing here is not just the difficulty presented by these two new subjects—geometry and quarterbacking. Both have confronted Jim with higher hurdles then he has ever had to jump before, and this has led to a bit of a crisis in Jim's self-evaluation. Surely Jim can pass geometry if we can get him to realize that it is a different sort of mathematics from algebra, and requires a different approach and more study. Trager will help him with this. Jim's parents can help too. I suggest that they call Trager and talk it over with him. Football is another kind of problem entirely. Jim is a good player, but (according to Tolland and some of the boys on the team) Fazio is more than good—he's talented. Here Jim is up against real limitations in contrast with the other boy's strengths. He is going to have to learn to accept that fact. Tolland thinks that Jim would make a solid halfback, though, and he has an opening on the team in that position. He has mentioned that opening to Jim, but Jim just mumbled something and walked away. In this case it may help to remember that Jim's father got his letter as a quarterback in his day at Kingsgate. We may be able to turn that fact to advantage in helping Jim accept the situation if we talk it through together. I suggest a meeting next week with Coach Tolland, Jim's father, and myself.

Yours sincerely,

Clinton Marley
Counselor

☐ EXAMPLE ESSAY MEMO ————————————————

McKAY, TREPP Inc.
Industrial Consultants
One East Livingston Street
Remsen, California

Memorandum   Date: May 30, 1992

To: Frank Pierrepont, President
           Lisa Hicks, Vice President—Operations
           Pierrepont Manufacturing Corporation
           Basset, Illinois 97654-3210
From: Lucille McKay
Subject: Production Problems, East Basset Plant

Background
On April 12, 1992, Frank Pierrepont, President, Pierrepont Mfg. Corp., ordered a review of production methods and organization at Pierrepont's East Basset plant. McKay, Trepp was hired on May 23, 1992, to visit the plant, examine its procedures, and interview its personnel. What prompted this review was the fact a significant decrease in production at the East Basset plant during November—

February, 1991–92 (see accompanying charts). Reports from managing officers at the plant did not seem to justify the slowdown. A visit to the plant by the company president in January elicited very little useful information and failed to increase production. An educated guess by the president in consultation with the vice president for operations was that the principal cause of the poor production record might be personal friction among managerial and production personnel at the plant. Investigation by McKay, Trepp Inc. has shown, however, that although some personal problems exist, a complicated mix of internal and external factors was the main cause of the slowdown.

Causes

Our observations and interviews at the East Basset plant suggest that there has in fact been some friction among plant personnel this winter. None of it seems serious enough in itself, though, to cause the production slowdown, and most of it can be easily resolved. The major conflict occurred between the supply manager and the production line foreman over unboxing parts and supplies. This issue, however, is not just a problem of deciding who is responsible for the task. It is complicated by the possibility of increased corrosion of the surfaces of some parts if unboxed too early and left standing too long exposed to the air. Along with this technical problem, which became unnecessarily a problem in personnel relations, another personnel problem also helped cause the winter slowdown: illness. Several important highly skilled workers came down with the flu during the first week in December. This interruption not only brought production almost to a halt for that week, but also set off a chain of production difficulties lasting well into January. Then heavy snows and a boiler breakdown in January further slowed production that month.

Despite these difficulties, production should have been only slightly less than normal this winter. The major cause of the slowdown occurred not during the winter but well before winter began: the trucking strike last October. As a result of the strike, the plant ran low on several crucial supplies toward the end of November. Faced with this shortage, plant personnel behaved nobly. Pierrepont management had reason to be especially grateful, for example, to one junior manager, Mervyn Fox, who learned of a small stock of the crucial supplies set aside in the storehouse of a recently bankrupt firm in Toledo, drove there early in December to negotiate their purchase, and brought them back in his car in a single working day. At the same time, East Basset plant managers and foremen might have been somewhat more resourceful in reorganizing production around these short supplies for the time being, and thereby saving expensive downtime on production machinery.

Recommendations

Given these causes, the solution to the East Basset plant production problems lies mainly in the hands of central management. We recommend that the vice president for operations examine the corrosion problem in consultation with suppliers and make a decision about responsibility for unboxing based on the vulnerability of the materials involved. Plant management and foremen should discuss and decide upon contingency plans to minimize the effects of brief interruptions in the flow of supplies and parts. Central management should consider computerizing supply control so that plant managers and foremen can get supplies-on-hand updates and have the opportunity to revise their requisitions once a week rather than once every two weeks. Finally, we suggest that Pierrepont hire an assistant to the vice president for operations to keep management informed of impending events and trends in the economy, labor relations, and government regulations that could affect production and other company operations in the foreseeable future.

Section II

Selections from *Revising Prose,* Fourth Edition
by Richard Lanham

CHAPTER 1

ACTION

Since we all live in a bureaucracy these days, it's not surprising that we end up writing like bureaucrats. Nobody feels comfortable writing simply "Bill loves Marge." The system requires something like "A romantic relationship is ongoing between Bill and Marge." Or "Bill and Marge are currently implementing an interactive romantic relationship." Or still better, "One can easily see that an interactive romantic relationship is currently being fulfilled between Bill and Marge." Ridiculous contrived examples? Here are some real ones.

A businessman denied a loan does not suffer but instead says, "I went through a suffering process." A teacher does not say, "If you use a calculator in class, you will never learn to add and subtract," but instead, "The fact is that the use of the calculator in the classroom is negative for the learning process." An undergraduate wants to say that "Every UCLA freshman needs to learn how to cope with crowds," but it comes out as "There can be little doubt that contending with the problem of overpopulation at UCLA is one thing that every freshman needs to learn how to do." Instead of being invited "to recruit," a corporation is asked "to participate in

235

the recruitment process." A university bureaucrat wants to make a generous offer: "To encourage broadband system use, the ACAD will pay all line charges for the next two years." But instead, it comes out as: "In order to stimulate utilization of the broadband system, it is the intention of the ACAD to provide for central funding of all monthly line charges generated by attachment to the system over the period of the next two years." A politician "indicates his reluctance to accept the terms on which the proposal was offered" when he might have said "No." A teacher of business writing tells us not that "People entering business today must learn to speak effectively," but "One of these factors is the seemingly increasing awareness of the idea that to succeed in business, it is imperative that the young person entering a business career possess definite skill in oral communication."

All these people write, and maybe even think, in the Official Style. The Official Style comes in many dialects—government, military, social scientific, lab scientific, MBA flapdoodle—but all exhibit the same basic attributes. They all build on the same imbalance, a dominance of nouns and an atrophy of verbs. They enshrine the triumph, worshipped in every bureaucracy, of stasis over action. Real actions lurk furtively in each of the sentences I've just quoted—suffer, learn, cope, recruit, pay, speak—but they are swamped by lame "is" verbs, "shun" words ("facilitation," "intention"), and strings of prepositional phrases.

This basic imbalance between action and inertia is easy to cure, if you want to cure it—and this book's Paramedic Method tells you how to do it. *But when do you want to cure it?* We all sometimes feel, whatever setting we write in, that we will be penalized for writing in plain English. It will sound too flip. Unserious. Even satirical. In my academic dialect, that of literary study, writing plain English nowadays is tantamount to walking down the hall naked as a jaybird. Public places demand protective coloration; sometimes you must write in the Official Style. And when you do, how do you make sure you are writing a good Official Style—if there is one—rather than a bad one? What can "good" and "bad" mean when applied to prose in this way?

Revising Prose starts out by teaching you how to revise the Official Style. But after you've learned that, we'll reflect on what such revision is likely to do for you, or to you, in the bureaucratic world of the future—and the future is only going to get more bureaucratic, however many efforts we make to simplify it, and its official language. You ought then to be able to see what "good" and "bad" mean for prose, and what you are doing when you revise it. And that means you will know how to socialize your revisory talents, how to put them, like your sentences, into action.

PREPOSITIONAL-PHRASE STRINGS: SMEARS AND HICCUPS

We can begin with three examples of student prose:

> This sentence is in need of an active verb.

> Physical satisfaction is the most obvious of the consequences of premarital sex.

> In response to the issue of equality for educational and occupational mobility, it is my belief that a system of inequality exists in the school system.

What do they have in common? They have been assembled from strings of prepositional phrases glued together by that all-purpose epoxy "is." In each case the sentence's verbal force has been shunted into a noun, and its verbal force has been diluted into "is," the neutral copulative, the weakest verb in the language. Such sentences project no life, no vigor. They just "are." And the "is" generates those strings of prepositional phrases fore and aft. It's so easy to fix. Look for the real action. Ask yourself, who's kicking who? (Yes, I know, it should be *whom*, but doesn't *whom* sound stilted? In this book, we'll stick with *who*.)

In "This sentence is in need of an active verb," the action obviously lies in "need." And so, "This sentence needs an active verb." The needless prepositional phrase "in need of" simply disappears once we realize who's kicking who. The sentence, animated by a real verb, comes alive, and in six words instead of nine.

Where's the action in "physical satisfaction is the most obvious of the consequences of premarital sex"? Buried down there in "satisfaction." But just asking the question reveals other problems. Satisfaction isn't a consequence of premarital sex, in the same way that, say, pregnancy is. And, as generations of both sexes will attest, sex, premarital or otherwise, does not always satisfy. Beyond all this, the contrast between the clinical phrasing of the sentence, with its lifeless "is" verb, and the life-giving power of lust in action makes the sentence seem almost funny. Excavating the action from "satisfaction" yields "Premarital sex satisfies! Obviously!" This gives us a Lard Factor of 66% and a comedy factor even higher. (You find the Lard Factor by dividing the difference between the number of words in the original and the revision by the number of words in the original. In this case, 12–4 = 8; 8÷12 = 67%. If you've not paid attention to your own writing before, think of a Lard Factor (LF) of one-third to one-half as normal and don't stop revising until you've removed it. The comedy factor in prose revision, though often equally great, does not lend itself to numerical calculation.)

But how else do we revise here? "Premarital sex is fun, obviously" may be a little better, but we remain in thrall to "is." And the frequent falsity of the observation stands out yet more. Revision has exposed the empty thinking. The writer makes it even worse by continuing, "Some degree of physical satisfaction is present in almost all coitus." Add it all together and we get something like, "People usually enjoy premarital sex" (LF 58%). At its worst, academic prose makes us laugh by describing ordinary reality in extraordinary language.

Now for the third example.

> In response to the issue of equality for educational and occupa-
> tional mobility, it is my belief that a system of gender inequality
> exists in the school system.

A diagram reveals the problem and points to a lurking action:

> **In** response
> **to** the issue
> **of** equality
> **for** educational and occupational mobility,
>
> it *is* my belief that a system
>
> **of** gender inequality exists
> **in** the school system.

A string of prepositional phrases, then a form of the verb "to
be" (usually "is"), then more prepositional phrases. But sand-
wiched in the middle lurks, furtive and afraid, the real *action*
of the sentence: "it is my belief that." Change that from the
"is" form to the active voice, and we have *an action*. Somebody *believes* something. Everything before and after this action amounts to a single phrase—"gender inequality." So we
have this revision:

> I believe that gender inequality exists in the schools. (9 words
> instead of 26; LF 65%)

The drill for this problem stands clear. Circle every form
of "to be" (*is, was, will be, seems to be, have been*) and every
prepositional phrase (*of, in, by, through, from,* etc.). Then find
out who's kicking who and start rebuilding the sentence with
that action. Two prepositional phrases in a row turn on the
warning light, three make a problem, and four demand immediate surgery. Look for the real *action* hidden behind the "is"
and prepositional phrases. So here:

Original

The history of new regulatory provisions is that there is generally an immediate resistance to them.

What hides behind "is that there is"? *Resistance.* And behind that? *Resist!* Now we need an *actor.* We have to invent one, but clearly "people in general" are acting here. So:

Revision

People usually resist new regulations.

Five words instead of 16, for a LF of 69%. The two original prepositional phrases have been eliminated. The action—*resist*—stands clear. A little practice in this kind of revision and, instead of writing "There are many ways in which people resist change," you'll say "People resist change in many ways."

The action lies in an even deeper grave of prepositions in this example:

The project is likely to result in a minor population increase in the City from families relocating to the site from outside the community.

Chart first:

The project
is likely
to result
in a minor population increase
in the City
from families relocating
to the site
from outside the community.

The classic Official Style formula: an "is," an infinitive "to" phrase, then five prepositional phrases in a row. For once, we have a clear actor—"The project." We'll start there. What is the project *doing*? What verb would express "a minor population increase from outside the City to inside the City"? How about "attract"? What is being "attracted"? Families. It all falls into place.

Revision

The project will probably attract new families to the city.

Good work: (1) 24 words cut down to 10, for a Lard Factor of 58%; (2) five prepositional phrases and one infinitive phrase shrunk to one prepositional phrase; (3) above all, a clearly defined *action*—"attract."

Sometimes people go to grotesque lengths to hide the action from their readers. Look here at an undergraduate disqualifying him or herself from membership in a creative writing class: "The type of writing that I have an interest in is in the area of creative writing." To get into the class, write instead, "I want to study creative writing" (17 words into 6; LF 66%). Or take this simple example:

Original

There are several examples of this selection process present in the Listerine ad.

Revision

The Listerine ad exemplifies this selection process.

Sometimes potential actions are smeared across the whole sentence. Here's a favorite of mine:

These are disturbed habitats (e.g. roadsides, vacant lots) vegetated by weedy colonizing species which depend on repeated disturbances for their existence.

The Official Style is at its silliest in describing ordinary things like weeds. It just can't stand giving them their plain, ordinary names. A weed has to become "a weedy colonizing species." Now, Where's the Action? Well, we have a choice:

> *disturb*
> *vegetate*
> *colonize*
> *depend*
> *disturb* [again]
> *exist*

Which offers the central action? None of them. There *isn't any* central action. I think—it is a guess—that the central, though unexpressed, *action* amounts to this:

> Weeds *grow* faster in empty spaces.

If I have guessed right, we've reduced 21 words to 6, for a LF of 71%. Not bad for government work. Now another Official Style smear job:

> Perception is the process of extracting information from stimulation emanating from the objects, places, and events in the world around us.

A diagram helps:

> Perception
> **is** the process
> **of** extracting information
> **from** stimulation emanating
> **from** the objects, places, and events
> **in** the world
> **around** us.

Again, look at the possible actions:

perceive
process
extract
inform
stimulate
emanate

Actor is clear, and *action*, too: "Perception extracts information." The rest of the sentence goes into a single prepositional phrase: "from the outside world."

Revision

Perception extracts information from the outside world.

Profound? No. Clear? Yes. Instead of 21 words, 7, for a LF of 66% exactly. And a 5-to-1 prepositional-phrase kill ratio. Sometimes in revision you want so badly to emphasize the central action that you ruthlessly cut away some of the surrounding details.

Next, a sentence from an Environmental Impact Statement:

Pelicans may also be vulnerable to direct oiling, but the lack of mortality data despite numerous spills in areas frequented by the species suggests that it practices avoidance.

You want to dig out the "avoid" in the Official Style "practices avoidance." And it is clear who is doing the avoiding: the pelicans. So this:

Revision

Pelicans seem to survive oil spills by avoiding the oil.

Have I left out anything essential in getting from 28 words to 10 (LF 64%)?

Official Style sentences smother action the way foam puts out a fire. Look at these strings from a lawyer, a scientist, and an historian:

Here is an example *of* the use *of* the rule *of* justice *in* argumentation.

One *of* the most important results *of* the presentation *of* the data is the alteration *of* the status *of* the elements *of* the discourse.

Another index *of* the breadth *of* the dissemination *of* Christian literature *in* this period is the appearance *of* translations *of* Christian scriptural documents *into* a variety *of* provincial languages.

The *of* strings are the worst of all. They seem to reenact a series of hiccups. When you revise them, you can feel how fatally easy the "is" + prepositional-phrase Official Style formula is for prose style. They blur the central action of the sentence—you can't find out what is actually going on. Let's try revising.

Original

Here is an example *of* the use *of* the rule *of* justice *in* argumentation.

"Rule of justice" is a term of art, so we must leave it intact. After we have found an active verb—"exemplify"—buried in "is an example of the use of," the rest follows easily.

Revision

This passage exemplifies argumentation using the rule of justice.

Now, how about the second sentence? It represents a perfectly symmetrical Official Style pattern: string of prepositional phrases + "is" + string of prepositional phrases. Let's diagram it for emphasis:

One

of the most important results

of the presentation
of the data

is the alteration

of the status
of the elements
of the discourse.

Notice the formulaic character? The monotonous rhythm? The blurred action? Try reading it aloud: *of* dadadum, *of* dadadum, *of* dadadum. I'm not sure what this sentence means, but the action must be buried in "alteration." Start there, with an active, transitive verb—"alter." How about "Presentation of the data alters the status of the discourse elements"? Or less formally, "The status of the discourse elements depends on how you present the data." Or it may mean, "You don't know the status of the elements until you have presented the data." At least two different meanings swim beneath the formulaic prose. To revise it you must *rethink* it.

Now, the third sentence. Diagram first:

Another index
of the breadth
of the dissemination
of Christian literature
in this period

is the appearance

of translations
of Christian scriptural documents
into a variety
of provincial languages.

The standard Official Style Sandwich: "is" between two thick layers of prepositional phrases. We know what to do: generate an active, transitive verb, and get rid of those thick slices of prepositional phrases. Now, make no mistake about it; it is

245

hard to figure out the central action in this sentence. Let me take a stab at it. First, we'll select an *actor*.

> Translation of Christian scriptures into provincial languages...

Now, what is this "translation" *doing?*

> shows how broadly Christian literature is disseminated...

So how about this:

> Translations into provincial languages show how broadly Christian Scriptures were disseminated in this period.

It is not the greatest revision in the world, but we have cut the sentence length in half, and reduced the prepositional phrases from eight to two. Often in revising an academic Official Style you discover, as here, that the root assertion is blurred and confused.

One more example of action-burial, this one in a shallow grave. A police report goes this way:

> Subject officer attempted to enter his vehicle in order to report for work. He was confronted by a skunk who denied him entrance into his vehicle. An officer-involved shooting occurred, resulting in the demise of the skunk.

"An officer-involved shooting occurred, resulting in the demise of the skunk," instead of "He shot the skunk" shows the Official Style at its fullest and finest.

"Blah Blah *Is That*" Openings

The formulaic slo-mo opening often provides your first taste of the Official Style. It delays and weakens the main action verb when (or *if*) you get to it. *The fact of the matter is that* we all fall into this habit. Let's look at some typical examples of what we will call the "Blah blah *is that*" opening from students, professors, and writers at large:

What I would like to signal here *is that*...

My contention *is that*...

What I want to make clear *is that*...

What has surprised me the most *is that*...

All that really means *is that*...

The upshot of what Heidegger says here *is that*...

The first *is that*...

The point I wish to make *is that*...

What I have argued here *is that*...

The important fundamental to remember *is that*...

My opinion *is that* on this point we have only two options...

My point *is that* the question of the discourse of the human sciences...

The fact of the matter *is that* the material of this article is drawn directly from...

Finally, the result of the use of all these new techniques and methods *is that*...

The one thing that Belinda does not realize *is that* Dorimant knows exactly how to press her buttons.

Easy to fix this pattern: just amputate the mindless preludial fanfare. Start the sentence with whatever follows "Blah blah *is that*...." Cut to the chase. On a word processor it couldn't be simpler: do a global search for the phrase "is that" and revise it out each time. For example:

The upshot of what **Heidegger says** here is that...

My opinion is that on this point **we have only two options**...

My point is that the question of **the discourse of the human sciences**...

The fact of the matter is that **the material of this article is drawn directly from**...

We can even improve my favorite from this anthology:

> The one thing that **Belinda does not realize** is **that Dorimant knows exactly how to press her buttons.**

By amputating the fanfare, you *start fast*, and a fast start may lead to major motion. That's what we're after. Where's the *action?*

Writers addicted to the "blah blah *is that*" dead rocket oftentimes tie themselves in knots with it. One writes: "The position **we are at is this.**" Another: "The traditional opposite notion **to this is that there are....**" And a third, a university professor, in an article accurately titled "On the Weakness of Language in the Human Sciences," offers this spasmodic set of *thises, thats,* and *whats:*

> Now **what** I would like to know specifically **is this: what is** the meaning of **this** "as" **that** Heidegger emphasizes so strongly when he says **that** "**that** which is explicitly understood"—**that is, that** which is interpreted—"has the structure of something as something"? My opinion **is that** what Heidegger means is **that** the structure of interpretation (*Auslegung*) is figural rather than, say, intentional. [Emphasis mine.]

In escaping from this Houdini straightjacket, a couple of mechanical tricks come in handy. Besides eliminating the "is's" and changing every passive voice ("is defended by") to an active voice ("defends"), you can squeeze the compound verbs hard, make every "are able to" into a "can," every "seems to succeed in creating" into "creates," every "cognize the fact that" (no, I didn't make it up) into "think," every "am hopeful that" into "hope," every "provides us with an example of" into "exemplifies," every "seeks to reveal" into "shows," and every "there is the inclusion of" into "includes."

Then, after amputating those mindless *fact that* introductory phrase fanfares, you'll start fast. After that fast start, "cut to the chase," as they say in the movies, as soon as you can. Instead of "the answer is in the negative," you'll find yourself saying "No."

THE PM

We now have the beginnings of the Paramedic Method (PM):

1. Circle the prepositions.
2. Circle the "is" forms.
3. Ask, "Where's the action?" "Who's kicking who?"
4. Put this "kicking" action in a simple (not compound) active verb.
5. Start fast—no slow windups.

Let's use the PM on a more complex instance of blurred action, the opening sentences of an undergraduate psych paper.

> The history of Western psychological thought has long been dominated by philosophical considerations as to the nature of man. These notions have dictated corresponding considerations of the nature of the child within society, the practices by which children were to be raised, and the purposes of studying the child.

Two actions here—"dominate" and "dictate"—but neither has fully escaped from its native stone. The prepositional-phrase and infinitive strings just drag them down.

The history...
of Western psychological thought...
by philosophical considerations...
as to the nature...
of man...
...
of the nature...
of the child...
within society...
by which children...
to be raised...
of studying...

In asking "Where's the action?" and "Who's kicking who?" we next notice all the actions fermenting in the nouns: *thinking* in "thought," *consider* in "considerations," more *thinking* somewhere in "notions." They hint at actions they don't supply and so blur the actor-action relationship still further. We want, remember, a plain active verb, no prepositional-phrase strings, and a natural actor firmly in charge.

> The **actor** must be: "philosophical considerations as to the nature of man."
>
> The **verb**: "dominates."
>
> The **object** of the action: "the history of Western psychological thought."

Now the real problems emerge. What does "philosophical considerations as to the nature of man" really mean? Buried down there is a question: "What is the nature of man?" The "philosophical considerations" just blur this question rather than narrow it. Likewise, the object of the action—"the history of Western psychological thought"—can be simply "Western psychological thought." Shall we put all this together in the passive form that the writer used?

Western psychological thought has been dominated by a single question: what is the nature of man?

Or, with an active verb:

A single question has dominated Western psychological thought: what is the nature of man?

Our formulaic concern with the stylistic surface—passives, prepositional phrases, kicker and kickee—has led to a much more focused thought.

The first sentence passes its baton awkwardly to the second. "Considerations," confusing enough as we have seen, become "these notions" at the beginning of the second sentence, and these "notions," synonymous with "considerations" in the first sentence, dictate more but different "considerations" in the second. We founder in these vague and vaguely synonymous abstractions. Our unforgiving eye for prepositional phrases then registers "*of* the nature *of* the child *within* society." We don't need "within society"; where else will psychology study children? And "the nature of the child" telescopes to "the child." We metamorphose "the practices by which children were to be raised" into "child-rearing," and "the purposes in studying the child" leads us back to "corresponding considerations of the nature of the child within society," which it partly overlaps. But we have now a definite actor, remember, in the first sentence—the "single question." So a tentative revision:

This basic question leads to three others: What are children like? How should they be raised? Why should we study them?

Other revisions suggest themselves. Work out a couple. In mine, I've used "question" as the baton passed between the two sentences because it clarifies the relationship between the two. And I've tried to expose what real, clear action lay hidden beneath the conceptual cotton-wool of "these notions have dictated corresponding considerations."

Revision

A single question has dominated Western psychological thought: What is the nature of man? This basic question leads to three others. What are children like? How should they be raised? Why should we study them?

A PAUSE FOR REFLECTION

This two-sentence example of student academic prose rewards some reflection. First, the sentences boast no grammatical or syntactical mistakes. Second, they need not have come from a student. Any issue of a psychology journal or text will net you a dozen from the same mold. How else did the student learn to write them? Third, not many instructors reading this prose will think anything is wrong with it. Just the opposite. It reads just right; it sounds *professional*. The teacher's comment on this paper reads, in full: "An excellent paper—well conceived, well organized and well written—A+." Yet a typical specimen sentence from it makes clear neither its main actor nor action; its thought consistently puffs into vague general concepts like "considerations," "notions," and the like; and its cradle-rocking monotonous rhythm puts us to sleep. It reveals a mind writing in formulas, out of focus, above all a mind putting no pressure on itself. The writer is not thinking so much as, on a scale slightly larger than normal, filling in the blanks.

You can't build bridges thinking in this muddled way; they will fall down. If you bemuse yourself thus in a chemistry lab, you'll blow up the apparatus. And yet the student, obviously bright, has been invited to write this way and rewarded for it. He or she has been doing *a stylistic imitation*, and has brought if off successfully. Chances are that the focused, plain-language version I've offered would get a lower grade than the Official Style original. Revision is always perilous and paradoxical, but nowhere more so than in the academic world. Not so perilous, though, as bridges that fall down or lab apparatus that blows up. In the long run, it is better to get your thinking straight and take your chances.

WHEN "IS" IS OK

We've been practicing the first five rules of the PM. Let's put them before us again.

1. Circle the prepositions.
2. Circle the "is" forms.
3. Ask, "Where's the action?" "Who's kicking who?"
4. Put this "kicking" action in a simple (not compound) active verb.
5. Start fast—no slow windups.

At the center of this grouping stands the search for *action*. In the Official Style, action usually comes in only one flavor— "is." We've been revising "is" into transitive, active verbs that impart the breath of life.

But rules don't always work and exceptions exist, if not to disprove them, to encourage common sense in applying them. As a segue to the next chapter, which examines sentence *shapes*, let's look at two passages which take an extreme stand toward "is." The first one uses nothing else. The second abjures it entirely.

First, a passage built on "is." It is from a famous military historian's discussion of the Battle of Agincourt.

Agincourt is one of the most instantly and vividly visualized of all epic passages in English history, and one of the most satisfactory to contemplate. It is a victory of the weak over the strong, of the common soldier over the mounted knight, of resolution over bombast, of the desperate, cornered and far from home, over the proprietorial and cocksure. Visually it is a pre-Raphaelite, perhaps better a Medici Gallery print battle—a composition of strong verticals and horizontals and a conflict of rich dark reds and Lincoln greens against fishscale greys and arctic blues....It is an episode to quicken the interest of any schoolboy ever bored by a history lesson, a set-piece demonstration of English moral superiority and cherished ingredient of a fading national myth. It is also a story of slaughter-yard behavior and of outright atrocity.

The passage is built on a backbone of "is." I've supplied in **[boldface brackets]** the repetitions only implied by the text.

Agincourt is
> one of the most instantly and vividly visualized of all epic passages in English history, and

> **[is]** one of the most satisfactory to contemplate.

It is a victory
> of the weak over the strong,

[it is a victory]
> of the common soldier over the mounted knight,

[it is a victory]
> of resolution over bombast,

[it is a victory]
> of the desperate, cornered and far from home, over the proprietorial and cocksure.

Visually it is
> a pre-Raphaelite, perhaps better a Medici Gallery print battle— a composition of strong verticals and horizontals and a conflict of rich dark reds and Lincoln greens against fishscale greys and arctic blues....

It is an episode
> to quicken the interest of any schoolboy ever bored by a history lesson,

[it is]
>   a set-piece demonstration of English moral superiority and
>   cherished ingredient of a fading national myth.

It is also
>   a story of slaughter-yard behavior and of outright atrocity.

Goodness! Everything I've been preaching against! "Is" plus strings of prepositional phrases. But the prose works in this instance because it possesses a shape, a repetitive, chorus-like pattern of similar elements until, in the last sentence, the prose shape remains the same but the sense constitutes a 180-degree inverted climax. Sentence shape matters, and our exploration of the Official Style must consider it.

Now for the opposite extreme, an article from the field of artificial intelligence which makes its point by banishing "to be" completely.

> To devise a new kind of logic we must escape from the old meta-physics. I shall indicate how I have tried to do this. One valuable technique which I recommend, I shall apply in writing this essay. I shall endeavor to write this essay without using the verb "to be." By doing so, I shall subject myself, in an informal way, to an essential discipline which a logic of action should impose, formally, upon its uses. This discipline forces one to think in terms of actions and agents and deprives one of that easy way of begging epistemological questions—the impersonal assertion of truth or existence in the style we normally expect of scientific writers.

No "is"s, but no shape either, just an awkward chorus of "I"s. Again, shape matters. Shape and rhythm. To the remaining rules of the Paramedic Method, those which deal with shape and rhythm, we now turn.

CHAPTER 3

VOICE

The elements of prose style—grammar, syntax, shape, rhythm, emphasis, level, usage—all work as dependent variables. Change one and you change the rest. Rhythm and sound seem, for most prose writers, the most dependent of all: they affect nothing and everything affects them. They do affect something, though. They affect *us*. Rhythm constitutes the most vital of prose's vital life-signs. Rhythmless, unemphatic prose always indicates that something has gone wrong.

TIN EARS

Tin ears, insensitivity to the sound of words, indicate that the hearing that registers rhythm has been turned off. Tin ears have become so common that often you can't tell mistakes from mindlessness. Was this sentence written tongue in cheek or only wax in ears?

> Conflict, chaos, competition and combat combine to constitute both the labor and fertilizer of war and the fruit of this is honor.

Too resolute an alliteration, too many "c" sounds:

> Conflict, chaos, competition and combat combine to constitute both the labor and fertilizer of war and the fruit of this is honor.

"Fertilizer" and "fruit" doesn't help, either. "Conflict" is a near synonym for "combat" and overlaps with "competition"; and if you use "constitute" you don't need "combine." Nor does "this" refer to anything specific. Yet the sentence conceals a rhythm waiting for liberation. A little subtle subtraction leads to this:

> Combat, competition, and chaos constitute the fertilizer of war and the fruit of this fertilizer is honor.

One further change—"constitute the fertilizer of" = "fertilize"—yields a sentence with a sound and shape of its own:

> Combat, competition, and chaos fertilize war and produce its fruit—honor. (LF 50%)

We've kept the alliterative yoking of the opening triplet phrase and created a rhythmically emphatic place of honor for—*honor*.

The Official Style, deaf and blind, manages to create rhythm and shape only by accident. So, for example, a U.S. government attorney refuses to talk about a controversial spy case with commendable, if desperate, pertinacity:

> I can't comment. We will not comment. We are not going to comment.

This three-segment climax has been used since classical times (when it was called *tricolon crescens*, each of the three elements being slightly longer than the previous one, thus building to a climax) as part of a sentence strategy for building long rhythmic periodic sentences. Winston Churchill was especially fond of it:

Victory at all costs, victory in spite of all terror, victory however long and hard the road may be...

This is not the end. It is not even the beginning of the end. But it is, perhaps, the end of the beginning.

The Official Style creates tin ears, and when the ear atrophies, any hope of colloquial emphasis or climax goes down the drain. But when there is a voice to begin with, things are much easier to fix. Look at this flawed diamond:

There is not a sign of life in the whole damned paper (with the possible exception of line 72).

A cinch to fix. Reverse the order.

With the possible exception of line 72, there is not a sign of life in the whole damn paper.

Terrific!

CHANGE-UPS

Sometimes you can notice a colloquial voice change abruptly to an Official Style one: "This point just emphasizes the need of repeated experience for properly utilizing the various sense modalities." The sentence breaks in half after "experience." We expect a finish like, "to use all the senses," and get instead an Official Style translation. Here is a scholar doing the same thing, this time from sentence to sentence:

Official Style

The establishment of an error detection mechanism is necessary to establish a sense of independence in our own movement planning and correction.

Change-up to Plain English

Unless we know we are doing something wrong, we can't correct it.

Change-ups like this emphasize the voicelessness of the Official Style.

Voice usually gets squeezed out of student prose by the Official Style. So we should celebrate an exception, a geography paper with real ears:

> Twice daily, at sunrise and sunset, a noisy, smokeridden train charges into the stillness of the Arabian desert. Winding about the everchanging windblown sand dunes, the "Denver Zephyr" not only defies the fatal forces of the notorious deserts, but for the nonnative, offers an extraordinary encounter with the tightly closed Saudi society.

The "s" assonance—sunrise, sunset, noisy, smokeridden, stillness—works, and so does "fatal forces"; and "**forces**" echoes part of "no**tor**ious," which, with "deserts," defines those forces. The sentence allows the voice a full tonal range, a chance for pitch to rise and fall, and a chance to build a climax on "tightly closed Saudi society" as well. This expanded tonal range, alas, went unappreciated by the instructor: the paper was marked down for being too "journalistic." No good deed goes unpunished.

I'm suggesting that writers should become self-conscious about the sound of words. Once our ears have had their consciousness raised, they'll catch the easy problems as they flow from the pen—"however clever" will become "however shrewd" in the first draft—and the harder ones will seem easier to revise.

Arrhythmia Attacks

Now for some arrhythmia attacks from a recent batch of undergraduate papers. The first illustrates the power of a single verb—or lack of one.

> Reputation is also a serious consideration for native Trojans.

Why not:

> Trojans worship Reputation. (LF 66%)

The wordiness of the following sentence lends it an unintended faintly lubricious air:

> The first duty of female characters in the drama of this period is to illustrate the various dimensions of the male protagonist.

Why not:

> In drama of this period female characters must above all illuminate the male protagonist. (LF 36%)

And how about

> Both film and song ask the eternal questions of young adulthood.

as a revision of

> A good measure of this appeal can be traced to the fact that both the visual medium of the film and aural medium of the song confront the young person with eternal questions of young adulthood. (LF 69%)

The revision, by keeping the sentence short, preserves the natural ending emphasis for "young adulthood," and so gives the voice someplace to go. Try reading both aloud several times. See what I mean?

It is not only student prose which has lost its voice but business writing as well. Here a businessman tells us about his firm's new health plan:

> When the sorting of the various problems was taking place, additional vitamins were introduced, cocktails reduced to a minimum, and a regular exercise program begun.

A natural *tricolon crescens* springs forth:

> While the plan was being started up, we took vitamins, cut down on the booze, and began a regular exercise program.

Consider now two longer examples of contrasting prose voices. The first comes from a bureaucrat at the Michigan Department of Environmental Quality. In the second, the target of the bureaucrat's threat replies to it. First the threat.

> It has come to the attention of the Department of Environmental Quality that there has been recent unauthorized activity on the above referenced parcel of property. You have been certified as the legal landowner and/or contractor who did the following unauthorized activity: Construction and maintenance of two wood debris dams across the outlet stream of Spring Pond. A permit must be issued prior to the start of this type of activity....The Department has been informed that one or both of the dams partially failed during a recent rain event, causing debris dams and flooding at downstream locations. We find that dams of this nature are inherently hazardous and cannot be permitted....Failure to comply with this request, or any further unauthorized activity on the site, may result in this case being referred for elevated enforcement action....

The authentic Official Style: land becomes a "parcel of property," "rain" becomes a "rain event," and the threat of a fine turns into "elevated enforcement action." Passives, prepositional-phrase trains, a full deployment. But note the *voice*—the genuine niggling mindlessness of a bureaucrat on autopilot.

The perpetrator of this "unauthorized activity on the site" replied:

> A couple of beavers are in the (state unauthorized) process of constructing and maintaining two wood "debris" dams across the outlet stream of my Spring Pond. While I did not pay for, nor authorize, their dam project, I think they would be highly offended that you call their skillful use of natural building materials "debris."…As to your dam request [that] the beavers first must fill out a dam permit prior to the start of this type of dam activity, my first dam question to you is: are you trying to discriminate against my Spring Pond Beavers or do you require all dam beavers throughout this State to conform to said dam request? If you are not discriminating against these particular beavers, please send me completed copies of all those other applicable beaver dam permits….I seriously hope you are not selectively enforcing this dam policy—or once again both I and the Spring Pond Beavers will scream prejudice! (*Wall Street Journal*, 3/30/98; the article concludes: "The Michigan Department of Environmental Quality informs us that the case has been closed.")

The voice of common sense, but sensible enough to clothe itself in the insane logic of the bureaucracy.

THE PARAMEDIC METHOD, FULL FORM

Often, when dealing with the Official Style, we must try revising a passage even if we are not sure what it means. In these cases, we may begin to understand the special terms by trying to fathom their relationship. Practice such a "naive analysis," a "revise-to-understand exercise," on the following wonderfully arrhythmic sentence from a book about rhythm!

> Rhythm is that property of a sequence of events in time which produces in the mind of the observer the impression of proportion between the directions of the several events or groups of events of which the sequence is composed.

Look at what the prepositional-phrase strings do to the rhythm of this definition of rhythm:

> Rhythm is that property
> *of* a sequence
> *of* events
> *in* time
>   which produces
> *in* the mind
> *of* the observer the impression
> *of* proportion
> *between* the directions
> *of* the several events or groups
> *of* events
> *of* which the sequence is composed.

Can you revise in a way to show that the writer has mastered his subject as well as written about it? Can you use the revision to clarify what the writer has obscured, drag his meaning from the depths of his prose? Try it, using the full form of the Paramedic Method to help:

1. Circle the prepositions.
2. Circle the "is" forms.
3. Ask, "Who's kicking who?" "Where's the action?"
4. Put this action in a simple (not compound) active verb.
5. Start fast—no slow windups.
6. Write out each sentence on a blank sheet of paper and mark off its basic rhythmic units with a "/".
7. Mark off sentence lengths in the passage with a "/".
8. Read the passage aloud with emphasis and feeling.

Sentence length is one of the easiest PM tests to apply. Take a piece of your prose and a red pencil and draw a slash after every sentence. Two or three pages ought to make a large enough sample. If the red marks occur at regular intervals, you have, as they used to say in the Nixon White House, a problem. You can chart the problem another way, if you like. Choose a standard length for one sentence and then do a bar graph. If it looks like this,

_____
_____
_____
_____
_____
_____
_____
_____

dandy. If like this,

_____
_____
_____
_____
_____
_____
_____
_____

not so dandy. Obviously, no absolute quantitative standards exist for how much variety is good, how little bad, but the principle couldn't be easier: vary your sentence lengths. Naturally enough, complex patterns will fall into long sentences and emphatic conclusions work well when short. But no rules prevail except Avoid Monotony.

The following passage certainly obeys this inviolable rule. It comes from a brilliantly written World War II memoir by Brendan Phibbs, *The Other Side of Time*. Dr. Phibbs has been talking about the self-dramatizing, self-serving American General George Patton, and moves from there to Patton's mirror opposite, General Lucien Truscott:

> And now, we said more happily, consider...Truscott....Men like this are stamped, early in life, and the outlines of the mold spell honesty. They fill the mold without effort; it fits them and they have no question about who they are and what they can do. They're free of the need to grimace and prance; they're free to spend themselves on a cause, for an ideal, scorning advantage and chaining the ego in some remote corner to babble and shriek and rattle its shackles. Having won, they're satisfied with the achievement; they're not driven to seek their value in the gaze and the wonder of others, and they walk off into the quiet corners of history where the truth lives, grinning to watch impostors scribbling their worthless names across the walls of the public baths.

The quiet corners of history where the truth lives—what a wonderful phrase. What creates the rhythm? The sense of authentic voice? Of sentences with a shape which energizes meaning? Well, we might start with Rule 7 of the PM, sentence length. Let's graph them. Graphing is much easier when you write on an electronic screen; simple and cheap graphing programs lie ready to hand.

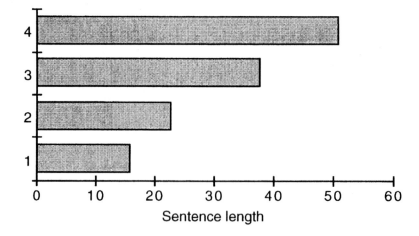

A varied, climactic sentence length. But that only begins to describe how it works. Let's apply Rule 6, and mark off basic rhythmic units.

> And now, we said more happily, consider…Truscott.…Men like this are stamped, / early in life, / and the outlines of the mold spell / honesty. / They fill the mold without effort; / it fits them / and they have no question about who they are / and what they can do. / They're free of the need to grimace and prance; / they're free to spend themselves on a cause, / for an ideal, / scorning advantage / and chaining the ego / in some remote corner / to babble and shriek and rattle its shackles. / Having won, / they're satisfied with the achievement; / they're not driven to seek their value in the gaze and the wonder of others, / and they walk off into the quiet corners of history where the truth lives, / grinning to watch impostors scribbling their worthless names / across the walls of the public baths.

What do the rhythmic units look like when diagramed?

> Men like this are stamped, /
> early in life, /
> and the outlines of the mold spell /
> honesty. /
> They fill the mold without effort; /
> it fits them /
> and they have no question about who they are /
> and what they can do. /
> They're free of the need to grimace and prance; /
> they're free to spend themselves on a cause, /
> for an ideal, /
> scorning advantage /
> and chaining the ego /
> in some remote corner /
> to babble and shriek and rattle its shackles. /
> Having won, /
> they're satisfied with the achievement; /

they're not driven to seek their value in the gaze and the wonder
of others, /
and they walk off into the quiet corners of history where the truth
lives, /
grinning to watch impostors scribbling their worthless names /
across the walls of the public baths.

I don't claim this division is linguistically correct, whatever that
might mean. Just the opposite. It is a quick and easy method
any of us can use to chart our own reading of a passage, to
imagine how our voice might embody the prose rhythm. Dia-
graming makes us specify, *become self-conscious about*, our own
rhythmic interpretation. There's no better way to spot how
sentence rhythm and shape works than to use Rules 6–8 of
the PM. Again:

6. Write out each sentence on a blank sheet of paper and
   mark off its basic rhythmic units with a "/".
7. Mark off sentence length with a "/".
8. Read the passage aloud with emphasis and feeling.

What have they told us here? Well, that the basic rhythmic units, at least as I hear them, vary markedly in length.
Second, that the passage invites stress on a series of crucial
words. Again, let me show you what I mean:

Men like this are stamped, /
early in life, /
and the outlines of the mold spell /
honesty. /
They fill the mold without effort; /
it fits them /
and they have no question about who they are /
and what they can do. /
They're free of the need to grimace and prance; /
they're free to spend themselves on a cause, /
for an ideal, /

scorning advantage /
and chaining the ego /
in some remote corner /
to babble and shriek and rattle its shackles. /
Having won, /
they're satisfied with the achievement; /
they're not driven to seek their value in the gaze and the wonder
of others, /
and they walk off into **the quiet corners of history where the truth
lives,** /
grinning to watch impostors scribbling their worthless names /
across the walls of the public baths.

The PM lends itself naturally to the typographic express-
ivity of an electronic screen. The two work together to give
anyone who cares about prose the power to analyze how a
passage works. The simple typographical diagram I've just
invented immediately tells us more about the passage. It builds
toward a definite climax in a memorable phrase, sets up a
strong emphasis on **honesty** and develops from that a meditation that ends up being about **the quiet corners of history
where the truth lives.** And did you notice how many strong
verb forms, how many actions, the passage contains?

stamped
spell honesty
fill the mold
what they can *do*
grimace and *prance*
spend themselves on a cause
chaining the ego
babble and *shriek* and *rattle* its shackles
Having *won*
driven to seen
walk off into the quiet corners
grinning to *watch* impostors
scribbling their worthless names

The passage recreates for us how history is both acted and reenacted, how it happens and how we seek its truth, waiting there for us in quiet corners. Phibbs wants to describe how we respond to social situations, how we elicit *from* them what we bring *to* them.

Now, by way of contrast, here is a passage of genuinely awesome arrhythmic unintelligibility from an American sociologist. It talks about, as the editor explains—in as much as it has been given me to understand him, much less the sociologist—the background expectancies of situations which make social interaction possible. That is to say, it covers— I think—much the same ground as the Phibbs passage.

> The properties of indexical expressions and indexical actions are ordered properties. These consist of organizationally demonstrable sense, or facticity, or methodic use, or agreement among "cultural colleagues." Their ordered properties consist of organizationally demonstrable rational properties of indexical expressions and indexical actions. Those ordered properties are ongoing achievements of the concerted commonplace activities of the investigators. The demonstrable rationality of indexical expressions and indexical actions retains over the course of its managed production by members the character of ordinary, familiar, routinized, practical circumstances.

Does it *have* to be this way? Or is Official Style prose itself a form of professional grimacing and prancing ? Using the PM as your guide, contrast the two passages. They make a revealing pair.

I've not found a satisfactory way to indicate prose rhythm in a printed book. But try reading aloud these two passages we've examined, one after the other. Don't hurry. And don't read them in a monotone. Let the pitch and timbre of your voice vary. Try out various combinations of pitch, stress, and timing. (There are several ways to read the Phibbs passage, for example.) You can mark pitch variation with a wavy up-and-down line above the text, for a start. And mark musical rests (#, ##, ###) after each phrase and sentence. Try reading each passage aloud, having someone else time you and observe where you pause and for how long. The first passage projects a recognizable voice; it is literally "readable." The second passage, academic prose at its most voiceless, is obviously meant to be read—skimmed—silently.

A Voice from the '60s

Prose varies widely in the performance instructions that it gives. Official Style academic prose gives very few. The voice has nowhere to go, no natural place to rise and fall, hurry and pause. Metronome prose: tick-tock, tick-tock, tick-tock. For extreme contrast, consider now a prose trip down nostalgia lane which offers lots of performance instructions. A sociology professor has taped a hippie guru telling us what it was like up at Big Sur in the sixties. Try marking the performance instructions; underline, double underline, use quotation marks, whatever.

> When I first got up there, it was a real romantic kind of picture. Man, it was kind of foggy. There were those really beautiful people—men, women, kids, dogs and cats, and campfires. It seemed quiet and stable. And I really felt like love was about me. I thought, "This is the place, man. It was happening. I don't have to do it. I would just kind of fit in and do my thing and that would be like a groove."
>
> After we were there about fifteen or twenty minutes, I heard the people bitching and moaning. I listened to it for awhile and circulated around to hear more about it, and, man, I couldn't believe it. Here they were secure in their land—beautiful land, where they could be free—and all these people were doing was bitching and moaning. I thought, "Oh, shit, man! Do I have to go into this kind of shit again where I gotta step in and get heavy and get ratty and get people to start talking? Do I have to get them to be open and get in some dialogue and get some communication going and

organization? What the —— is wrong with the leadership here, that this kind of state of affairs is happening? And why do I have to do it again? Man, I'm through with it. I just got through with hepatitis and double pneumonia and...—— it!" Then I really felt bad. (Lewis Yablonsky, *The Hippie Trip* [New York: Pegasus, 1968], p. 91)

This is speech, for a start. Hippie speech, heavily syncopated speech, sliding quickly over interim syllables from heavy stress to heavy stress: "first," "romantic," "foggy," "really," "love." Once you know the syncopated pattern, it is easy to mark up a passage like this. But if you don't know the pattern? Imagine yourself a foreigner trying to read this passage with a natural emphasis. It does sometimes give natural rhythmic clues. "This is the *place*, man. It was *happening*. I don't *have* to do it." The arrangement of the words underscores the sense—the scene has become the actor and the actor the scene. So, too, the alliterative repetition of "go into," "gotta step in," "get heavy," "get ratty," "get people," gives us a clear performance clue. But the passage by itself does not include a full guide to its performance. (You needed to be part of the scene to talk this talk like a native. Hippie speech was an *argot*, a special way of speaking used to dramatize a special way of living. The guru quoted above hadn't always talked this way. I know—he was in my class at Yale before the '60s "came down.")

THE TRADITIONAL WAY TO PERFORM PROSE

How can prose include a performance guide, anyway? Especially complex prose of the sort the Official Style usually embodies? In the past, it has done so by building up patterns of repetition, balance, antithesis, and parallelism. This package of systemic controls, usually called a "periodic sentence," has been the traditional way to control a long, complex sentence since classical Greece. The periodic style has been what we might call the "good" Official Style in Western stylistic history. It has striven for the Official attributes of public formality, authoritative impressiveness, solemnity even, but in a way that *emphasizes* voice rather than etiolating it. It represents true solemnity, a counterstatement to the prose we have been revising. It *designs* a long sentence under strict control, not a shopping bag stuffed with words.

Any discussion of the Official Style should consider at least one instance of its legitimate ancestor, the periodic style. Here is an example by the great master of the periodic style in English, Samuel Johnson. He speaks about his design in compiling the first great dictionary of the English language.

> When I am animated by this wish [to honor his country], I look with pleasure on my book, however defective, and deliver it to the world with the spirit of a man that has endeavored well. That it will immediately become popular I have not promised to myself: a few wild blunders, and risible absurdities, from which no work of such multiplicity was ever free, may for a time furnish folly with laughter, and harden ignorance in contempt; but useful diligence will at last prevail, and there never can be wanting some who distinguish desert; who will consider that no dictionary of a living tongue ever can be perfect, since while it is hastening to publication, some words are budding, and some falling away; that a whole life cannot be spent upon syntax and etymology, and that even a whole life would not be sufficient; that he, whose design includes whatever language can express, must often speak of what he does not understand; that a writer will sometimes be hurried by eagerness to the end, and sometimes faint with weariness under a task, which *Scaliger* compares to the labours of the anvil, and the mine; that what is obvious is not always known, and what is known is not always present; that sudden fits of inadvertency will surprize vigilance, slight avocations will seduce attention, and casual eclipses of the mind will darken learning; and that the writer shall often in vain trace his memory at the moment of need, for that which yesterday he knew with intuitive readiness, and which will come uncalled into his thoughts tomorrow. (From the preface to *The English Dictionary*, in *Johnson: Prose and Poetry*, ed. Mona Wilson [Cambridge: Harvard University Press, 1967], pp. 322-323)

When I am animated by this wish [to honor his country],
    I look with pleasure on my book,
        however defective,
    and deliver it to the world
        with the spirit of a man that has endeavoured well.
That it will immediately become popular I have not promised to myself:
    a few wild blunders, and risible absurdities,
        from which no work of such multiplicity was ever free,
    may for a time   furnish folly   with laughter,
          and harden ignorance in contempt;
but useful diligence will at last prevail,
and **there never can be wanting some**
    who **distinguish desert;**
    who **will consider**
        that no dictionary of a living tongue ever can be perfect,
          since
             while it is hastening to publication,
               some words are budding,
             and some   falling away;
        that a whole life cannot be spent upon syntax and etymology, and
        that even a whole life would not be sufficient;
        that he,
          whose design includes   whatever language can express,
            must often speak of   what he does not   understand;
        that a writer will sometimes be hurried by eagerness to the end,
            and sometimes faint   with weariness under a task,
                which *Scaliger* compares to the labours
                of the anvil, and the mine;
        that what is obvious is not always *known*,
        and   what is *known*   is not always present;
        that
            sudden fits of inadvertency   will surprize vigilance,
            slight avocations   will seduce attention,
        and casual eclipses of the mind   will darken learning; and
        that the writer shall often in vain trace his memory
            at the moment of need,
          for that which yesterday he knew with *intuitive readiness,* and
            which will come *uncalled* into his thoughts tomorrow.

Figure 7

When I am animated by this wish [to honor his country],
    I look with pleasure on my book,
        however defective,
    and deliver it to the world
        with the spirit of a man that has endeavoured well.
That it will immediately become popular I have not promised to myself:
    a few wild blunders, and risible absurdities,
        from which no work of such multiplicity was ever free,
     may for a time furnish folly   with laughter,
          and harden ignorance in contempt;
but useful diligence will at last prevail,
and there never can be wanting some
    who distinguish desert;
    who will consider
        that no dictionary of a living tongue ever can be perfect,
          since
                while it is hastening to publication,
              some words are budding,
           and some   falling away;
    that a whole life cannot be spent upon syntax and etymology, and
    that even a whole life would not be sufficient;
    that he,
          whose design includes   whatever language can   express,
             must often speak of what he does not   understand;
    that a writer will sometimes be hurried by eagerness to the end,
         and sometimes faint   with weariness under a task,
              which *Scaliger* compares to the labours
              of the anvil, and the mine;
    that what is obvious is not always *known*,
    and what is *known* is not always present;
    that
        sudden fits of inadvertency will surprize vigilance,
        slight avocations   will seduce attention,
  and casual eclipses of the mind will darken learning; and
    that the writer shall often in vain trace his memory
          at the moment of need,
    for that which yesterday he knew with *intuitive readiness*, and
        which will come *uncalled* into his thoughts tomorrow.

Figure 8

We don't write prose like this anymore, and are not used to reading it. The diagrammatic analysis in figure 7 should help a modern reader *visualize* the structure. It works by adding elements in parallel:

I look with pleasure on my book,
and deliver it to the world

The parallel elements often create a contrast:

some words are *budding,*
and some *falling away*

Or a repetitive list:

sudden fits of inadvertency will surprize vigilance,
slight avocations will seduce attention,
and *casual eclipses of the mind* will darken learning

Often the antitheses form the antithetical pattern *chiasmus*, with which we've already become acquainted.

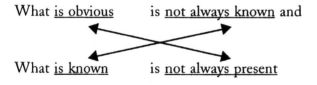

What <u>is obvious</u>   is <u>not always known</u> and

What <u>is known</u>   is <u>not always present</u>

The Official Style often embodies *lists.* The periodic style will hang its list of elements from a single lead word:

who will distinguish
who will consider

Or:

that no dictionary
that a whole life
that even a whole life

that he
that a writer
that what is obvious
that sudden fits

These clear and repeated shapes *visualize* meaning in precisely the way we considered in chapter 2. They also give the voice a set of *performing instructions.* In figure 8, simply by using three sizes of type, I indicate the obvious stresses. Notice how the *voice* plays a counterpoint over the *shape*, sometimes reinforcing it and sometimes creating a different pattern? It is the absence of this counterpoint, more often than not, which makes the Official Style so insipidly lifeless.

A PAUSE FOR REFLECTION

Whether you relish periodic prose as I do or not, you ought to try in your own writing to give equally good performance instructions. And, in your long sentences, to maintain equally good syntactic and stylistic control. For, again, that is what sentence length, rhythm, and sound are—a series of instructions, of controls, for how your sentences should be performed. And if your reader takes pleasure in performing your prose, you have her on your side. She is acting in your play.

We've seen how sentences become shapeless when the voice goes out of them. Prose that is not voiced becomes shapeless and unemphatic in the same way that an unexercised muscle loses its tone. And it works the other way, too. If we do not look at a piece of prose, attempt to perform it, we'll cease to hear real voices, our own and others', when we speak. Writing and speaking form a spiral. If they intensify each other, the spiral goes up. If they don't, each drives the other down.

APPENDIX

TERMS

You can see things you don't know the names for, but in prose style, as in everything else, it is easier to see what you know how to describe. The psychological ease that comes from calling things by their proper names has not often been thought a useful goal by modern pedagogy. As a result, inexperienced writers often find themselves reduced to talking about "smoothness," "flow," and other meaningless generalities when they are confronted by a text. And so here are some basic terms.

PARTS OF SPEECH

In traditional English grammar, there are eight parts of speech: verbs, nouns, pronouns, adjectives, adverbs, prepositions, conjunctions, interjections. *Grammar*, in its most general sense, refers to all the rules that govern how meaningful statements can be made in any language. *Syntax* refers to sentence structure, to word order. *Diction* means simply word choice. *Usage* means linguistic custom.

279

Verbs

1. Verbs have two voices, active and passive.

   An *active verb* indicates the subject acting:

   > Jack *kicks* Bill.

   A *passive verb* indicates the subject acted upon:

   > Bill *is kicked by* Jim.

2. Verbs come in three moods: indicative, subjunctive, and imperative.

   A verb in the *indicative mood* says that something is a fact. If it asks a question, it is a question about a fact:

   > Jim *kicks* Bill. *Has* Bill *kicked* Jim yet?

   A verb in the *subjunctive mood* says that something is a wish, hypothetical, or contrary to fact, rather than a fact:

   > If Jim *were* clever, he *would* kick Bill.

   A verb in the *imperative mood* issues a command:

   > Jim, *kick* Bill.

3. A verb can be either transitive or intransitive.

   A *transitive verb* takes a direct object:

   > Jim *kicks* Bill.

   An *intransitive verb* does not take a direct object. It represents action without a specific goal:

   > Lori *runs* every day.

   The verb "to be" ("is," "was," and so on) is often a *linking* verb because it links subject and predicate without expressing a specific action:

   > Elaine *is* a movie mogul.

4. English verbs have six tenses: present, past, present perfect, past perfect, future, and future perfect.

   > Present: Jim *kicks* Bill.
   > Past: Jim *kicked* Bill.
   > Present perfect: Jim *has kicked* Bill.
   > Past perfect: Jim *had kicked* Bill.
   > Future: Jim *will kick* Bill.
   > Future perfect: Jim *will have kicked* Bill.

The present perfect, past perfect, and future perfect are called compound tenses. Each tense can have a progressive form. (e.g., present progressive: Jim *is kicking* Bill.)

5. Verbs in English have three so-called infinite forms: *infinitive, participle,* and *gerund.* These verb forms often function as adjectives or nouns.
Infinitive:
To assist Elaine isn't easy.
(When a word separates the "to" in an infinitive from its complementary form, as in "to directly stimulate" instead of "to stimulate," the infinitive is said to be a split infinitive.)
Participles and gerunds have the same form; when the form is used as an adjective, it is called a *participle;* when used as a noun, a *gerund.*
Participles:
Present participle:
Elaine was in an *arguing* mood.
Past participle:
Lori's presentation was very well *argued.*
Gerund:
Arguing with Elaine is no fun.
Verbs that take "it" or "there" as subjects are said to be in an *impersonal construction:* "It has been decided to fire him" or "There has been a personnel readjustment."

Nouns

A noun names something or somebody. A proper noun names a particular being or place—Elaine, Pittsburgh.

1. *Number.* The singular number refers to one ("a cat"), plural to more than one ("five cats").
2. *Collective nouns.* Groups may be thought of as a single unit, as in "the army," and thus take a singular verb.

Pronouns

A pronoun is a word used instead of a noun. There are different kinds:

1. *Personal pronouns*: I, me, him,...
2. *Intensive pronouns*: myself, yourself,...
3. *Relative pronouns*: who, which, that. These must have antecedents, words they refer back to. "Lori has a talent (antecedent) that (relative pronoun) Elaine does not possess."
4. *Indefinite pronouns*: somebody, anybody, anything
5. *Interrogative pronouns*: who?, what?

Possessives

Singular: A *worker's* hat. Plural: The *workers'* hats. ("It's," however, equals "it is." **The possessive is "its"—no apostrophe!**)

Adjectives

An *adjective* modifies a noun: "Lori was a *good* hiker."

Adverbs

An *adverb* modifies a verb: "Lori hiked *swiftly* up the trail."

Prepositions

A *preposition* connects a noun or pronoun with a verb, an adjective, or another pronoun: "I ran into her arms" or "The girl with the blue scarf."

Conjunctions

Conjunctions join sentences or parts of them. There are two kinds, coordinating and subordinating.

1. *Coordinating conjunctions*—and, but, or—connect statements of equal status: "Bill ran *and* Jim fell" or "I got up *but* soon fell down."
2. *Subordinating conjunctions*—that, when, because—connect a main clause with a subordinate one: "I thought *that* they had left."

Interjections

A sudden outcry: "Wow!" or "Ouch!"

SENTENCES

Every sentence must have both a subject and verb, stated or implied: "Elaine (subject) directs (verb)."

Three Kinds

1. A *declarative sentence* states a fact: "Elaine directs films."
2. An *interrogative sentence* asks a question: "Does Elaine direct films?"
3. An *exclamatory sentence* registers an exclamation: "Does she ever!"

Three Basic Structures

1. A simple sentence makes one self-standing assertion, i.e., has one main clause: "Elaine directs films."
2. A compound sentence makes two or more self-standing assertions, i.e., has two main clauses: "Elaine directs films and Lori is a tax lawyer" or "Jim kicks Bill and Bill feels it and Bill kicks Jim back."
3. A complex sentence makes one self-standing assertion and one or more dependent assertions in the form of subordinate clauses dependent on the main clause:

"Elaine, who has just finished directing *Jim Kicks Bill*, must now consult Lori about her tax problems before she can start blocking out *Being Kicked: The Sequel*."

In *compound sentences*, the clauses are connected by *coordinating conjunctions*, in *complex sentences* by *subordinating conjunctions*.

Restrictive and Nonrestrictive Relative Clauses

A *restrictive clause* modifies directly, and so restricts the meaning of the antecedent it refers back to: "This is the tire *that blew out on the freeway*." One specific tire is referred to. Such a clause is not set off by commas, because it is needed to complete the meaning of the statement about its antecedent: "This is the tire"—what tire?

A *nonrestrictive clause*, though still a dependent clause, does not directly modify its antecedent and is set off by commas: "These tires, *which are quite expensive*, never blow out on the freeway." A nonrestrictive clause can be removed without changing the sense of the main clause: "These tires never blow out on the freeway."

Appositives

An *appositive* is an amplifying word or phrase placed next to the term it refers to and set off by commas: "Henry VIII, *a glutton for punishment*, rode out hunting even when sick and in pain."

BASIC SENTENCE PATTERNS

What words do you use to describe the basic syntactic patterns in a sentence? In addition to the basic types—declarative, interrogative, and exclamatory—and the basic forms of simple, compound, and complex, other terms sometimes come in handy.

Parataxis and Hypotaxis

Parataxis: Phrases or clauses arranged independently, in a coordinate construction, and often without connectives, e.g., "I came, I saw, I conquered."

Hypotaxis: Phrases or clauses arranged in a dependent subordinate relationship, e.g., "I came, and after I came and looked around a bit, I decided, well, why not, and so conquered."

The adjectival forms are *paratactic* and *hypotactic*, e.g., "Hemingway favors a paratactic syntax while Faulkner prefers a hypotactic one."

Asyndeton and Polysyndeton

Asyndeton: Connectives are omitted between words, phrases, or clauses, e.g., "I've been stressed, destressed, beat down, beat up, held down, held up, conditioned, reconditioned."

Polysyndeton: Connectives are always supplied between words and phrases, or clauses, as when Milton talks about Satan pursuing his way, "And swims, or sinks, or wades, or creeps, or flies."

The adjectives are *asyndetic* and *polysyndetic*.

Periodic Sentence

A periodic sentence is a long sentence with a number of elements, usually balanced or antithetical, standing in a clear syntactical relationship to each other. Usually it suspends the conclusion of the sense until the end of the sentence, and so is sometimes said to use a *suspended syntax*. A periodic sentence shows us a pattern of thought that has been fully worked out, whose power relationships of subordination have been carefully determined, and whose timing has been climactically ordered. In a periodic sentence, the mind has finished working on the thought, left it fully formed.

There is no equally satisfactory antithetical term for the opposite kind of sentence, a sentence whose elements are loosely related to one another, follow in no particularly anti-thetical climactic order, and do not suspend its grammatical completion until the close. Such a style is often called a *running style* or a *loose style*, but the terms remain pretty vague. The loose style, we can say, often reflects a mind *in the process of thinking* rather than, as in the periodic sentence, having already completely ordered its thinking. A sentence so loose as to verge on incoherence, grammatical or syntactical, is often called a *run-on sentence*.

Isocolon

The Greek word *isocolon* means, literally, syntactic units of equal length, and it is used in English to describe the repetition of phrases of equal length and corresponding structure. So Winston Churchill on the life of a politician: "He is asked to stand, he wants to sit, and he is expected to lie."

Chiasmus

Chiasmus is the basic pattern of antithetical inversion, the AB:BA pattern. President John F. Kennedy used it in his inaugural address:

A	**B**
Ask not *what your country*	*can do for you,* but

B	**A**
what you can do	*for your country.*

Anaphora

When you begin a series of phrases, clauses, or sentences with the same word or phrase, you are using anaphora. So Shakespeare's Henry V to some henchpersons who have betrayed him:

Show men dutiful?
Why, so didst thou. Seem they grave and learned?
Why, so didst thou. Come they of noble family?
Why, so didst thou. Seem they religious?
Why, so didst thou.

(*Henry V,* 2.2)

Tautology

Repetition of the same idea in different words. In many ways, the Official Style is founded on this pattern. Here's a neat example from Shakespeare:

Lepidus. What manner o'thing is your crocodile?
Antony. It is shap'd, sir, like itself, and it is as broad as it has breadth. It is just so high as it is, and moves with its own organs. It lives by that which nourisheth it, and the elements once out of it, it transmigrates.
Lepidus. What colour is it of?
Antony. Of its own colour too.
Lepidus. 'Tis a strange serpent.
Antony. 'Tis so. And the tears of it are wet.

(*Antony and Cleopatra,* 2.7)

NOUN STYLE AND VERB STYLE

Every sentence must have a noun and a verb, but one can be emphasized, sometimes almost to the exclusion of the other. The Official Style—strings of prepositional phrases + "is"— exemplifies a noun style *par excellence.* Here are three examples, the first of a noun style, the second of a verb style, and the third of a balanced noun-verb mixture.

Noun Style

There is in turn a two-fold structure of this "binding-in." In the first place, by virtue of internalization of the standard, conformity with it tends to be of personal, expressive and/or instrumental significance to ego. In the second place, the structuring of the reactions of alter to ego's action as sanctions is a function of his conformity with the standard. Therefore conformity as a direct mode of the fulfillment of his own need-dispositions tends to coincide with the conformity as a condition of eliciting the favorable and avoiding the unfavorable reactions of others.

(Talcott Parsons, *The Social System* [Glencoe, Ill.: Free Press, 1951], p. 38)

Verb Style

Patrols, sweeps, missions, search and destroy. It continued every day as if part of sunlight itself. I went to the colonel's briefings every day. He explained how effectively we were keeping the enemy off balance, not allowing them to move in, set up mortar sites, and gather for attack. He didn't seem to hate them. They were to him like pests or insects that had to be kept away. It seemed that one important purpose of patrols was just for them to take place, to happen, to exist; there had to be patrols. It gave the men something to do. Find the enemy, make contact, kill, be killed, and return. Trap, block, hold. In the first five days, I lost six corpsmen—two killed, four wounded.

(John A. Parrish, *12, 20 & 5: A Doctor's Year in Vietnam* [Baltimore: Penguin Books, 1973], p. 235)

Mixed Noun-Verb Style

We know both too much and too little about Louis XIV ever to succeed in capturing the whole man. In externals, in the mere business of eating, drinking, and dressing, in the outward routine of what he loved to call the *métier du roi*, no historical character, not even Johnson or Pepys, is better known to us; we can even, with the aid of his own writings, penetrate a little of the majestic façade which is Le Grand Roi. But when we have done so, we see as in a glass darkly. Hence the extraordinary number and variety of judgments which have been passed upon him; to one school, he is incomparably the ablest ruler in modern European history; to another, a mediocre blunderer, pompous, led by the nose by a succession of generals and civil servants; whilst to a third, he is no great king, but still the finest actor of royalty the world has ever seen.

(W. H. Lewis, *The Splendid Century: Life in the France of Louis XIV* [New York: Anchor Books, 1953], p. 1)

PATTERNS OF RHYTHM AND SOUND

Meter

The terms used for scanning (marking the meter of) poetry sometimes prove useful for prose as well.

> *iamb*: unstressed syllable followed by a stressed one, e.g., in vólve.
> *trochee*: opposite of iamb, e.g., úse ful.
> *anapest*: two unstressed syllables and one stressed syllable, e.g., per son nél.
> *dactyl*: opposite of anapest, one stressed syllable followed by two unstressed ones, e.g., óp er ate.

These patterns form *feet*. If a line contains two feet, it is a *dimeter*; three, a *trimeter*; four, a *tetrameter*; five, a *pentameter*; six, a *hexameter*. The adjectival forms are *iambic, trochaic, anapestic*, and *dactylic*.

Sound Resemblances

Alliteration: This originally meant the repetition of initial consonant sounds but came to mean repetition of consonant sounds wherever they occurred, and now is often used to indicate vowel sound repetition as well. You can use it as a general term for this kind of sound play: "Peter Piper picked a peck of pickled peppers"; "Bill will always swill his fill."

Homoioteleuton: This jawbreaker refers, in Latin, to words with similar endings, usually case-endings. You can use it to describe, for example, the "shun" words—"function," "organization," "facilitation"—and the sound clashes they cause.

For further explanation of the basic terms of grammar, see George O. Curme's *English Grammar* in the Barnes & Noble College Outline Series. For a fuller discussion of rhetorical terms like *chiasmus* and *asyndeton*, see Richard A. Lanham's *A Handlist of Rhetorical Terms* (second edition, Berkeley and Los Angeles: University of California Press, 1991). For a fuller discussion of prose style, see Richard A. Lanham's *Analyzing Prose* (New York: Scribner's, 1983).

Section III

Penn Student Essays, Outlines, and Reflections

Nat Ward
Two Reasons Paper
Draft One

Throughout history, stories have been an integral part of every culture. Today, stories captured as movies are an important part of our culture, making the film industry worth billions of dollars. This money has to come from somewhere, specifically, out of the pockets of the people going to see movies each week. These same people have elevated the actors and actresses in these movies to the highest social status possible and demonstrate an almost obsessive curiosity with the lives of these celebrities. Why do we invest so much of our money and emotions in these films and the people in them? The answer lies in the relation between psychology and film. More specifically, movies satisfy certain psychological needs and subconscious desires.

The relation between psychology and movies has been studied by psychologists as well as by those in the film industry. One of the major theories agreed upon is that of "The Three V's", which states that movies provide voyeuristic, vicarious, and visceral pleasures for their audiences. Humans, by nature, are "visual" beings, taking in and remembering information mainly through their vision. The visual medium of film plays upon this by showing the audience what it's like to live in a new place and witness different events. These events usually give the viewers an opportunity to live out experiences that, in reality, are unsafe or unfeasible. Therefore, audiences get to live vicariously through the characters of the film they're viewing. Horror films, as well as those films involving suspense and intense action, also illicit a physical, or visceral, response from viewers. These physical responses are evidence of the rush of excitement that comes from watching certain films, which not only makes the audience feel more "alive", but also takes them out of their everyday experiences. This temporary escape from everyday live can be an effective stress reliever.

While there is an escapist element involved in the viewing of films, watching movies can also allow the viewers to understand themselves and their problems in new ways, satisfying the need for greater self-understanding and self-improvement. I can personally attest to this, since for the past several years I have been obsessed with "The Matrix" trilogy. The feeling I got from watching "The Matrix" for the first time was like nothing I had ever experienced. It was this unexplainable rush that somehow made me feel good not only in the general sense, but about myself as well. The release of "The Matrix Reloaded" brought my growing obsession to its peak. It was shortly after the release of this movie that I finally determined the reason for my deep interest in "The Matrix" movies. The prevalent themes in "The Matrix", namely self-actualization, change, and the nature of reality, were directly related to issues I was working through at the time, and seeing Neo successfully work through those same issues gave me hope and inspiration, as well as a model through which to work on my own problems. "The Matrix" has changed the lives of thousands of others as well, as evidenced by the postings on the official movie website and on many fan websites. In addition, a light-hearted series of books on the use of films as a form "therapy" show that movies can bring hope and clarity to the life of the viewer, if they are willing to see the films as something more than just a form of entertainment.

Nat Ward
Descriptive Outline
Two Reasons Essay, First Draft

PROPOSITION: Movies satisfy certain psychological needs and subconscious desires.

PLAN: Develop two reasons supporting the preposition.

PARAGRAPH 1: *says:* Stories in the form of movies are an important part of our culture because they satisfy basic psychological needs and desires.
Does: Introduces the preposition by placing in a historical context. Gives an explanation as to why we care so much about a certain form of expression.

PARAGRAH 2: *says:* An accepted explanation for our preoccupation with film is that of "The Three V's". Movies also provide a convenient form of escapism.
Does: Supports the preposition by given an academic/theoretical explanation. Explains the meaning behind each part of this explanation. Elaborates on this by providing a similar theory that branches off the academic explanation. Explains this offshoot.

PARAGRAPH 3: *says:* Another reason for our fascination with film its potential to help us better understand ourselves and our problems. I have experienced this myself in a profound way, and others have as well.
Does: Supports the preposition by means of a personal story. Points out that this type of story is not unique to the author. Illustrates the importance of such experience to the individual and to others, relating directly back to things discussed in Paragraph 1.

Michelle Chikaonda
DESCRIPTIVE OUTLINE
Of Nat Ward's Two Reasons Essay

PROPOSITION: Movies satisfy certain psychological needs and desires.

PLAN: Develop two reasons to support this proposition.

PARAGRAPH 1

Says: Stories captured as movies are an important part of American culture.

Does: Introduces the proposition for the essay by describing the magnitude of the movie industry, with regard to the celebrities it creates and the money it generates.

PARAGRAPH 2

Says: Movies provide voyeuristic, vicarious and visceral pleasures for their viewers.

Does: Describes and explains how and why people need movies by using the framework of these "Three V's."

PARAGRAPH 3

Says: Watching movies can help viewers to understand themselves better, moving them to greater self-understanding and -improvement.

Does: Develops the second reason by discussing her own reaction to "The Matrix" trilogy and how it related to the problems in her own life that she was trying to work out.

Nat Ward
Second Draft
Two Reasons

Throughout history, stories have been an integral part of every culture. Today, stories captured as movies are an important part of our culture, making the film industry worth billions of dollars. This money has to come from somewhere, specifically, out of the pockets of the people going to see movies each week. Regardless of the genres of the films and the reviews the movies get from critics, audiences spend enough money on movie tickets and merchandise to pay the multi-million dollar salaries of the actors on the screen. Often, these audiences judge the quality of the film based on the emotions it elicits from them. Why do we invest so much of our money and emotions in these films? The answer lies in the relation between psychology and film. In particular, movies satisfy certain psychological needs and subconscious desires.

The relationship between psychology and movies has been studied by psychologists as well as by those who work in the film industry. One of the major theories agreed upon is that of "The Three V's", which states that movies provide voyeuristic, vicarious, and visceral pleasures for their audiences. Humans, by nature, are "visual" beings, taking in and remembering information mainly through their vision. The visual medium of film plays upon this by showing the audience what it's like to live in a new place and witness different events. These events usually give the viewers an opportunity to live out experiences that, in reality, are unsafe or unfeasible. Therefore, audiences get to live vicariously through the characters of the film they're viewing. Horror films, as well as those films involving suspense and intense action, also elicit a physical, or visceral, response from viewers. These physical responses are evidence of the rush of excitement that comes from watching certain films, which not only makes the audience feel more "alive", but also takes them out of their everyday experiences. This temporary escape from everyday life can be an effective stress reliever.

While there is an escapist element involved in the viewing of films, watching movies can also allow the viewers to understand themselves and their problems in new ways, satisfying the need for greater self-understanding and self-improvement. I can personally attest to this, since for the past several years I have been obsessed with "The Matrix" trilogy. The feeling I got from watching "The Matrix" for the first time was like nothing I had ever experienced. It was this unexplainable rush that somehow made me feel good not only in the general sense, but about myself as well. The release of "The Matrix Reloaded" brought my growing obsession to its peak. It was shortly after the release of this movie that I finally determined the reason for my deep interest in "The Matrix" movies. The prevalent themes in "The Matrix", namely self-actualization, change, and the nature of reality, were directly related to issues I was working through at the time, and seeing Neo successfully work through those same issues gave me hope and inspiration, as well as a model through which to work on my own problems. "The Matrix" has changed the lives of thousands of others as well, as evidenced by the postings on the official movie website and on many fan websites. In addition, a light-hearted series of books on the use of films as a form "therapy" show that movies can bring hope and clarity to the life of the viewer, if they are willing to see the films as something more than just a form of entertainment.

Nat Ward
Outline of Two Reasons Draft Two

DETAILED DESCRIPTIVE OUTLINE

PROPOSITION: Movies satisfy certain psychological needs and subconscious desires.

PLAN: Develop two reasons supporting the preposition.

PARAGRAPH 1: *says:* Stories in the form of movies are an important part of our culture because they satisfy basic psychological needs and desires.
Does: Introduces the preposition by placing in a historical context, as well as by describing its significance in everyday life. Gives an explanation as to why we care so much about a certain form of expression.

PARAGRAH 2: *says:* An accepted explanation for our preoccupation with film is that of "The Three V's". Movies also provide a convenient form of escapism.
Does: Supports the preposition by given an academic/theoretical/scientific explanation. Explains the meaning behind each part of this explanation. Elaborates on this by providing a similar theory that branches off the academic explanation. Explains this offshoot.

PARAGRAPH 3: *says:* Another reason for our fascination with film its potential to help us better understand ourselves and our problems. I have experienced this myself in a profound way, and others have as well.
Does: Supports the preposition by means of a personal story. Points out that this type of story is not unique to the author. Illustrates the importance of such experience to the individual and to others, relating directly back to things discussed in Paragraph 1.

Nat Ward
Two Reasons
Draft Three

What Really *Happens When You Buy a Movie Ticket*

"Let's go see a movie." It's a suggestion often heard at the end of a long work week. Those who make the suggestion see going to the movies as an opportunity to leave their ordinary world behind for two hours in order to experience life in the shoes of another. These people are often surprised to find themselves examining the meaning of the movie after leaving the theatre, and they can also be taken slightly by surprise at the strong feelings they had about a mere series of pictures flashed before them on the big screen. Audiences often judge the quality of the film based on the emotions it elicits from them. This causes one to question the reasons why people allow their emotions to be influenced by the stories and images presented to them at the movies. The answer lies in the relation between psychology and film. In particular, movies give their audiences certain pleasures that humans are predisposed to seek out, while providing a means for them to examine and improve their own lives

The relationship between movies and the feelings they elicit has been studied by psychologists as well as by those who work in the film industry. One of the major theories supported by psychologists is that of "The Three Vs", which states that movies provide voyeuristic, vicarious, and visceral pleasures for their audiences. The voyeuristic pleasure comes from simply watching the events on the screen. These events usually give the viewers an opportunity to live out experiences that could not happen in reality, allowing audiences to live vicariously through the film's characters. Horror films, as well as those films involving suspense and intense action, also elicit a physical, or visceral, response from viewers. Some people who saw *The Exorcist* in theatres actually screamed from fright during the film, and a few were so terrified that they were unable to sleep the night after watching the movie. These physical responses are evidence of the rush of excitement that comes from watching certain films, which makes the audience members feel more "alive" and takes them out of their everyday experiences. Depending on the genre of film, this temporary escape from everyday life can be an effective stress reliever.

While viewing films often serves as a form of escapism, watching movies can also allow the viewers to understand themselves and their problems in new ways, satisfying the need for greater self-understanding and self-improvement. For the past several years I have been obsessed with "The Matrix" trilogy. The feeling I got from watching "The Matrix" for the first time was like nothing I had ever experienced. It was this unexplainable rush that somehow made me feel good not only in the general sense, but about myself as well. The release of "The Matrix Reloaded" brought my growing obsession to its peak. It was shortly after the release of this movie that I finally determined the reason for my deep interest in "The Matrix" movies. The prevalent themes in "The Matrix", namely self-actualization, change, and the nature of reality, were directly related to issues I was working through at the time, and seeing Neo successfully work through those same issues gave me hope and inspiration, as well as a model through which to work on my own problems. "The Matrix" has changed the lives of thousands of others as well, as evidenced by the postings on the official movie website and on many fan websites.

Aubry Wand
First Draft
Two Reasons Essay

It's a good day--glassy, three to four feet--and no one else is out in the water but me and my brother. The sun is just beginning to set, and the view out into the endless ocean is just as spectacular as the scenic cliffs above covered with shades of red and orange. After an hour, the water becomes cold, and it is getting dark, so we go in. After changing in the dirty parking lot, we head to "La Fonda," a small restaurant that serves possibly the best lobster dinner you can get for twenty dollars. In short, surfing is more than just a sport; it is a lifestyle and an avenue of understanding the raw emotions which we tend to ignore in our everyday existence.

For a long time, I was under the impression that surfing is only about catching waves. But, after having gone to Mexico and experiencing a different culture, enjoying the beauty of the ocean, all without ever catching a single wave, it became apparent that surfing is more about enjoying life in its simplest form than anything else. To me, and I think this goes for my brother as well, just as good time was had driving along the coast, even sitting in traffic crossing the border listening to music, than out in the water. Surfing influences every facet of life, ranging from your friends, to where you live, and even how you dress. These are the things with which we define ourselves, and for a surfer, are inevitably linked to a life revolving around the ocean.

Surfing evokes so many emotions other than just the adrenaline of catching a good wave. While out in the water, you are inundated with conflicting feelings, which add to the overall experience, and ultimately transcend surfing as merely a sport. There is hesitance and self-doubt when the waves are bigger than they appear from shore; at the same time, there is pure confidence when standing on the board gliding through the water. Even while sitting on the board there is a duality of emotion: on the one hand, few things are more peaceful than dangling your feet in the cool water while watching the waves roll slowly in. Yet on the other, a creepy vibe can develop, which soon turns to fear--instead of looking out you are looking below, into darkness, just waiting to get eaten by a fourteen foot Great White shark. In this sense, the surfing experience allows for emotions untainted by rational thought and enriches our lives in the process.

Aubry Wand
Two Reasons Essay
Descriptive Outline

Proposition: Surfing is a way of life and an avenue of understanding the emotions which we ignore in our everyday existence.

Plan: Develop two reasons supporting the proposition.

Paragraph 1:
Says: Surfing is more than just a sport. It is a lifestyle and a source of pure emotions which often go ignored.
Does: Introduces the topic of surfing through an anecdote.

Paragraph 2:
Says: Surfing is a lifestyle and more about enjoying life in its simplest form than anything else.
Does: Supports the proposition by describing the other elements involved with surfing in order to suggest that there is more to it than the sport itself.

Paragraph 3:
Says: There are conflicting feelings and emotions that surfing evokes and ultimately ones that can enrich our lives.
Does: Describes and gives examples of the conflicting emotions that are involved with the sport and explains why they are important.

Peer Review of Aubry Wand, Two Reasons Essay
Peer Reviewer: Sahang-Hee Hahn

Proposition: Surfing is more than a leisurely activity; it is at the same time a lifestyle, a source of conflicting feelings, and a means of better understanding yourself.

Plan: Support the proposition with two reasons

Paragraph 1:
Says: Surfing is a lifestyle and means of better understanding yourself as much as it is a sport
Does: Introduces the topic of surfing using author's personal experience.

Paragraph 2:
Says: Surfing is more about enjoying life in its simplest form than anything else.

Does: Supports the proposition by describing one particular experience that demonstrates his argument.

Paragraph 3:

Says: There are conflicting feelings; which . . . add to the overall experience, and make surfing more than just a leisurely activity.

Does: Supports the proposition by describing another reason why surfing is more than just a sport.

Aubry Ward
Draft Two, Two Reasons

It's a good day--glassy, three to four feet--and no one else is out in the water but me and my brother. The sun is just beginning to set, and the view out into the endless ocean is just as spectacular as the scenic cliffs above covered with different shades of red and orange. After an hour, the water becomes cold, and it is getting dark, so we go in. After drying off in the dirty parking lot, we head to "La Fonda," a small restaurant that serves possibly the greatest lobster dinner you can get for twenty dollars. In short, surfing is a lifestyle and means of better understanding yourself as much as it is a sport.

For a long time, I was under the impression that surfing is only about catching waves. But, after having gone to Mexico, and experiencing a different culture, enjoying the beauty of the ocean, all without ever catching a single wave, it became apparent that surfing is more about enjoying life in its simplest form than anything else. To me, and I think this goes for my brother as well, just as good time was had driving along the coast, even sitting in traffic crossing the border listening to music, than out in the water. To relate this concept to the bigger picture, surfing influences every facet of life, ranging from your friends, to where you live, and even how you dress. These are the things with which we define ourselves, and for a surfer, are inevitably linked to a life revolving around the ocean.

Surfing evokes so many emotions other than just the adrenaline of catching a good wave. In many cases there are conflicting feelings; which in a sense, add to the overall experience, and make surfing more than just a leisurely activity. There is hesitance and self-doubt when the waves are bigger than they appear from shore; at the same time, there is complete confidence when standing on the board gliding through the water. Even while just sitting on the board, there is a duality of emotion: on the one hand, few things are more peaceful than dangling your feet in the cool water while watching the waves roll slowly in. Yet on the other, a creepy vibe can develop, which soon turns to fear, and instead of looking out you are looking below, into darkness, just waiting to get eaten by a fourteen foot Great White shark. In this sense, surfing maintains its intrigue indefinitely, thus making it a sport which can be enjoyed for an entire lifetime.

Revised and submitted for publication in
LAST WORD, *Penn Arts & Sciences Magazine*
Spring 2005, page 22

On the Pleasures of Surfing
by Aubry Wand

It's a good day – glassy, three to four feet – and no one in the water but my brother and me. The sun is beginning to set. The endless ocean, reflecting the last rays of light on the horizon, is just as spectacular as the cliffs above, covered with shades of red and orange. This image lasts no more than a minute, and as the colors fade, the water gets colder. Our wetsuits seem to lose their defense against the frigid Pacific, but we stay out long enough to see a pod of dolphins swim by – and get pounded by enough waves to call it a day.

Walking up a dirt trail, board under my arm and dusk enveloping the beach to my back, I've never been more at peace. At the top, we perform the standard "deck change," using a towel to cover ourselves as we struggle to remove the layer of neoprene sticking to our bodies, though none of the local campers would have cared if we had stripped down to our birthday suits right there in the parking lot. Hunger sets in, so we head to La Fonda, a nearby restaurant that arguably serves the best lobster in Mexico. Finally, we retreat to the tent. And with the help of a few margaritas, not even the rocky floor or a sweatshirt for a pillow could stop us from getting a decent night's sleep.

For a long time, I believed surfing was about catching waves and nothing else. This trip made me think otherwise. Just being out in the water gives you a chance to get in touch with feelings ignored in everyday life. There's self-doubt when the waves are bigger than they appeared from shore and pure confidence after riding a wave until it dissipates, your body losing its energy with the swell. While sitting on the board, this duality exists: on the one hand, few things are more tranquil than dangling your feet in the water, floating like kelp with the sway of the tide. On the other, a creepy vibe can develop, which soon turns to fear – instead of looking out, you're looking below into darkness, just waiting to get eaten by a 14-foot Great White.

I refer to the two days my brother and I spent south of the border on a surfing trip, even though surfing was only a part of it. We had just as good a time driving down the coast, taking in the sun and looking at the sea from the roads above. The two of us sharing the moment but lost in our own thoughts, with the Shins playing in the background and the clusters of homes built into the mountainside becoming only a memory.

Getting stuck in traffic crossing the border, heat sweltering, unable to use the AC because the tank was on empty – and the last place you want to run out of gas is the frenetic road leading out of Tijuana. Throwing health out the window and chain-smoking Camel Lights, partly as a distraction from the heat but more out of nostalgia – a bad habit, yet a brotherly tradition nonetheless. Finally, passing by the old men playing guitars and the little boys selling ice cream on the street, we both knew that we were leaving something behind, even though we weren't sure what that thing really was.

These are the experiences that encapsulate surfing, the memories I'll recall long before any wave. Appreciating the beauty and power of the ocean, traveling to an unknown place, forgetting about myself and my cares: that's what I find in surfing. The perfect wave comes around once in a lifetime, but the pursuit of it will bring years of pleasure. And as long as you keep this in mind, it doesn't even matter if you catch it.

Sophomore Aubry Wand is an English major from Portola Valley, California. He enjoys surfing even though he has only caught a few waves in his lifetime.

Michelle Chikaonda
Draft One, Nestorian

"What are we going to do tomorrow, Brain?" "The same thing we do every day, Pinky...try to take over the *world*." Two of what I consider to be the most classic lines in television animation history, yet sadly are no longer with us. Pinky and the Brain was by far one of the best cartoons of the late nineties. Indeed, most of the cartoons of that era were close to being child-sized versions of televised art. However, the cartoons that have replaced them cannot even attempt to measure up to their predecessors; they fall short in almost every dimension one could conceive of. The cartoons of the late nineties, the cartoons I grew up with, were by far superior to the cartoons that are on televisions screens today.

Currently, the cartoons that have the unfortunate privilege of gracing our televised airwaves contain no substance whatsoever. Most of them revolve around the lives of two semi-interesting characters with distracting diction and, quite frankly, terrible scripts. They constantly repeat the same story lines, with twists being rare and the heroes and villains remaining unchanged. They're all designed in the same, pseudo-futuristic style, with heavily-outlined bodies and an overly-simplistic color scheme. Their theme music lacks creativity; gone are the days of creative theme songs which quickly became the tunes you just had to know in third grade, gone are the ingeniously expressive sound effects that told stories in and of themselves. Now it is hard to tell the difference between the theme music of one cartoon and the next; they all use the same sounds and effects, and the theme songs no longer tell a story, they now just recite the name of the cartoon over and over again in slightly different pitches and keys. The characters themselves quickly become annoying after one or two episodes, expressing personality traits that not even Freud could explain away and not showing the slightest bit of intelligence in the way they choose to go about their daily existences.

However, what is the number one reason why late nineties television cartoons were better than the cartoons of the twenty-first century? They were *funny*. Cartoonists and scriptwriters of the late nineties put much effort into making the cartoons we were watching funny, intelligent and witty. Every single episode of Pinky and the Brain chronicled yet another one of Brain's plans to take over the world, yet the people who came up with the story lines made each plot so creatively different from the other – from suing a company for a shrunken head due to a malfunctioning microwave to taking over the world by starting an oyster fair – that they never got old, and were always full of humor. Tiny Toons, Animaniacs and their subsidiary cartoons like Buttons and Mindy and the Goodfeathers – all of these were examples of clever, intelligent cartoons that were difficult to get bored with. It is a shame that this tradition of cartoons has been replaced with the cartoons of late, which leave too much to be desired for me to ever decide to spend any of the lazy summer afternoons of my life with these shows.

Nargus Haroundzadeh
Peer Review of Michelle Chikaonda
Nestorian Order

Proposition Cartoons of the late 90's were far superior to cartoons of today.

Plan Support Proposition by multiple reasons in Nestorian order

P1

Says Pinky and the Brain was the best cartoon of the 90's, but is now off the air and replaced by mediocre cartoons

Does Introduces proposition by illustrating a specific example: Pinky and the Brain.

P2

Says Today's cartoons have no substance, they have the same color scheme, and mediocre music and characters.

Does Provides one big reason and three minor reasons for the proposition.

P3

Says Twenty-first century cartoons are not funny

Does Supports proposition with the main reason.

Michelle Chikaonda
Draft Two Nestorian

Pinky and the Brain: A Tribute

Overweight, doughnut-wielding laboratory guards couldn't stop them. Their combined height, a fear-inspiring nine-point-three inches, made high-powered men and women tremble with terror – or, perhaps, with hysterical laughter – as they acknowledged the plotting pair demanding their subordination. The teensy twosome's ingenious plan for taking over the world? Start an oyster fair. Or maybe con an appliance company into paying out ten million dollars in damages to a peculiarly awkward "man" (i.e. mouse-operated robot) who, while making a cup of coffee, had his abnormally stolid "face" and "head" (i.e. a Halloween accessory) inexplicably shrunken by a microwave malfunction to the size of a rodent's. So what happens when a highly intelligent mouse with a Machiavellian ethos is stuck in a cage with a scatterbrained mouse who can see clear connections between quantum mechanics and Sophia Loren, and is predisposed to yelling his trademark non-word "narf!" at ill-timed moments? One of the most creative and intelligent cartoons of the late nineties – *Pinky and the Brain*. The happily-ignorant Pinky and his narcissistic companion Brain, however, are no longer citizens of the world of Cartoonery – several years retired, they now stay enclosed in a vortex of the Cartoon Galaxy carved especially for them, like all discontinued cartoons, probably still scheming ways to take over the world but finding themselves consistently zapped back to their secluded corner in time by television networks when they do. The animation that has taken their place are cartoons like *Dexter's Lab* and *Ed, Edd & Eddy*, that, while amusing from time to time, do not measure up to the creativity and complexity of *Pinky and the Brain*. *Pinky and the Brain* was a more likeable and entertaining cartoon than *Dexter's Lab* and *Ed, Edd & Eddy*.

The problem with *Dexter's Lab* and *Ed, Edd & Eddy* is that they are not stimulating enough. While television cartoons are created with an audience of children in mind, this does not necessitate a minimalist approach to all aspects of the cartoon – *Dexter's Lab* and *Ed, Edd &*

Eddy are too simple. Their color schemes are not as elaborate as the color scheme was for *Pinky and the Brain*; and the background detail in each scene an episode of *Dexter's Lab* or *Ed, Edd &Eddy* is nothing more than what is necessary – a ball on the front lawn of Ed's house that Eddy will shortly enter the scene and play with – and what makes sense: when Dexter is outside, behind him are his front lawn and his house, and perhaps the beginnings of the next-door neighbor's house, but no random objects thrown in like bikes or toys. By contrast, in *Pinky and the Brain* there were many things included in a scene that didn't contribute to the storyline of the episode – cookie crumbs, bottle tops – that nonetheless added flavor to the scene. In line with overly simplistic visual details are uncreative episode plots: the storylines for *Dexter's Lab* and *Ed, Edd & Eddy* are less sophisticated and detail-oriented than those of *Pinky and the Brain*, making episodes of the former(s) more predictable and less engaging than those of the latter. To complete the mix of cartoon over-simplicity is inadequate use of audio stimulation – not enough use of sound that could contribute to the storyline. The sound effects, character themes and original songs of *Pinky and the Brain* were integral to each episode's story, as they helped explain events and emotions without ill-fitting words – an upbeat skipping song to express Pinky's cheerfulness in his situation, for example, rather than the words, "I'm so happy now." In contrast, the use of sound in *Dexter's Lab* and *Ed, Edd & Eddy* is sparse. The characters of these cartoons are also less developed than those of Pinky and the Brain – in *Dexter's Lab* and *Ed, Edd & Eddy* there are one or two personality traits per character that are focused on and made to ultimately define each character, which means that the characters of these cartoons quickly become boring, often annoying. For example, Dexter is smart and anal-retentive, Dee-Dee is perky and ditsy, Eddy is a loudmouth; the behavior of these characters does not ever fall outside of these restrictions. Pinky and Brain, however, had a lot more variation weaved into their characters, so that while Brain was caricatured as a heartless intellectual contemptuous of mankind, in one episode he could have burst into tears at the sight of a flower in bloom. Similarly, Pinky was crafted as "the dumb one", but in several episodes he behaved more

308

intelligently and rationally than Brain.

Michelle Chikaonda
Descriptive Outline, Draft Two
Nestorian Order

PROPOSITION: *Pinky and the Brain* was a more likeable and enjoyable cartoon than *Dexter's Lab* and *Ed, Edd & Eddy* are.

PLAN: State a proposition and develop five reasons supporting it, arranged in Nestorian order.

PARAGRAPH 1:

SAYS: Pinky and the Brain was a lot more enjoyable and creative than *Dexter's Lab* and *Ed, Edd & Eddy* are.

DOES: Introduces the proposition by describing *Pinky and the Brain*.

PARAGRAPH 2:

SAYS: Dexter's Lab and *Ed, Edd & Eddy* do not measure up to *Pinky and the Brain*.

DOES: States and develops four reasons why *Dexter's Lab* and *Ed, Edd & Eddy* do not measure up to *Pinky and the Brain*.

PARAGRAPH 3:

SAYS: The number one reason why *Pinky and the Brain* was better than *Dexter's Lab* and Ed, *Edd & Eddy* is that it was genuinely funny.

DOES: States and develops the main reason why *Pinky and the Brain* was better than *Dexter's Lab* and *Ed, Edd & Eddy*.

Nargus Harounzadeh
Draft One
Nestorian Order

"I killed her because the bitch seen my face." That was 17-year-old Christopher Simmons' justification for pushing Shirley Crook, alive and conscious, off a railroad trestle into the icy waters below. The crime was a simple, calculated one: Simmons and his accomplice entered Crook's house while she slept, smothered her in ducktape, threw her into the back of her minivan, bound her hands and feet—hog-tied fashion—and sent her plunging to her death. Simmons was sentenced to death in a Missouri court; the penalty, however, was reduced by the Missouri Supreme Court to life in prison because the Court, against precedent to which it is bound, deemed the original punishment—the death penalty-- "cruel and unusual" for a juvenile offender, and found it in direct violation of the United States' Constitution. The case was appealed to the Supreme Court where oral arguments will take place on October 13. The Supreme Court has the obligation to overrule the Missouri Supreme Court for its fully flawed decision.

The Missouri Supreme Court based its ruling on conflicting evidence, exposing only one side of the data. By including evidence from some self-appointed expert groups who condemn the death penalty for juveniles, the court wrongfully declared a national consensus based on a handful of associations' beliefs. In one instance, the (Insert Association name here) categorized juveniles as autonomous beings who were able to govern their own decisions and in another situation the same group deemed juveniles as not fully developed and not responsible for their own actions. The former was to support abortion without parental consent and the latter was to condemn the juvenile death penalty. Furthermore, the Court's review of standard indicators of societal change such as legislative action and jury verdicts was incorrect. The Court held that these two components proved evolving standards in society, allowing them to rule the way they did. In actuality, the evidence is inconclusive in that actual legislative action and jury verdicts since its brother case, *Stanford v. Kentucky*, has varied so much across the nation that no strong argument could be made in either direction.

In addition to the fact that there is no compelling argument, the Missouri Supreme Court is bound by the precedent established in *Stanford v. Kentucky* and has no authority to overrule the High Court. The Supreme Court held in *Stanford v. Kentucky* that evidence of evolving standards in society can constitute the foundation for a decision that forces the abandonment of stare decisis. However, it is for the Supreme Court, and not any lower court, to declare a ruling against precedent. The Missouri Court's action trivialized the Supreme Court's power and the command of precedent.

Nat Ward
Descriptive Outline of
Nargus Haroundzadeh's
Nestorian Order Essay

PROPOSITION: The Supreme Court has the obligation to overrule the Missouri Supreme Court for its fully flawed decision.

PLAN: State a proposition and develop reasons supporting it, arranged in Nestorian order.

PARAGRAPH 1: *says:* Due to his young age, the Missouri Supreme Court did not give Christopher Simmons the death penalty, even though he brutally killed Shirley Cook. The Supreme Court is obligated to overrule this decision.
Does: Introduces the proposition by telling the story behind it and giving specific details. The details given support the proposition.

PARAGRAPH 2: *says:* The Missouri Supreme Court based its ruling on conflicting and non-conclusive evidence, which showed only one interpretation of the data.
Does: Supports the proposition by describing two specific instances in which the topic sentence was proven true. Gives more explanation as to how the problem in the proposition came about.

PARAGRAPH 3: *says:* The Missouri Supreme Court was wrong in its ruling because it has no power to overrule the High Court, which it did by going against the precedent set in the *Stanford vs. Kentucky* case.
Does: Supports the proposition by describing the main reason why the proposition is true. Places the situation given in the proposition in a historical context. Offers legal explanation as to why the proposition is true.

Michelle Chikaonda
Descriptive Outline of Nargus Haroundzadeh's
Nestorian Order Essay

PROPOSITION:
The Supreme Court has the obligation to overrule the Missouri Supreme Court for its fully flawed decision.

PLAN:
State a proposition and develop three reasons supporting it arranged in Nestorian order.

PARAGRAPH 1:
SAYS: The Missouri Supreme Court's decision in the Christopher Simmons case – to reduce his sentence from the death penalty to life in prison – was wrong.
DOES: Introduces the proposition by describing the murder Christopher Simmons committed.

PARAGRAPH 2:
SAYS: The Court wrongfully declared a national consensus (on the death penalty being wrong for juvenile offenders) based on only a handful of associations' beliefs; the indicators the Court used to indicate societal change (that would favor the decision they made) were incorrect and inconclusive.
DOES: States two reasons why the Missouri Supreme Court decision was wrong.

PARAGRAPH 3:
SAYS: The Missouri Court's action trivialized the Supreme Court's power.
DOES: States the main reason why the Missouri Supreme Court's decision was flawed.

Things I learned from this paper:

- That it is really hard to hold juvenile offenders accountable for what they do, but if the crime is gruesome enough then it has to be done.

- That the courts are bound by precedent – each case is not treated as individually as I had thought they were

Nargus Harounzadeh
Draft Two
Nestorian Order

"I killed her because the bitch seen my face," bragged 17-year-old Christopher Simmons minutes after pushing Shirley Crook, alive and conscious, off a railroad trestle into the icy waters below. Simmons and his accomplice entered Crook's house while she slept, smothered her in ducktape, threw her into the back of her minivan, bound her hands and feet—hog-tied fashion— and sent her plunging to her death. A Missouri court sentenced Simmons to death; the Missouri Supreme Court, however, reduced the sentence to life in prison because the Court, ruling against precedent to which it is bound, deemed the original punishment—the death penalty-- "cruel and unusual" for a juvenile offender, and found that it violated the United States' Constitution. The case was appealed to the Supreme Court where oral arguments will take place on October 13. No argument, however, can justify the fact that an inferior court acted out of its bounds: the Supreme Court has the obligation to overrule the Missouri Supreme Court.

The Missouri Supreme Court presented one side of data to support its ruling, neglecting to examine conflicting data that was just as strong. By including evidence from self-appointed expert groups who condemn the death penalty for juveniles, the court wrongfully declared a national consensus based on a handful of associations' beliefs that are malleable from issue to issue. In one instance, the American Psychological Association categorized juveniles as "autonomous beings" who govern their own decisions. In another situation, the same group deemed juveniles as "not fully developed" and "not responsible" for their own actions. The former definition appeared in a brief to support abortion without parental consent; the latter surfaced in arguments condemning the juvenile death penalty, illustrating the unreliability of expert groups' testimony. Furthermore, the Court's review of standard indicators of societal change such as legislative action and jury verdicts was incorrect. The Court held that these two components mimicked evolving standards in society—the movement towards a national consensus against the juvenile death penalty—allowing them to rule the way they did. In actuality, the evidence is inconclusive in that actual legislative action and jury verdicts since its brother case, *Stanford v. Kentucky*, has varied so much across the nation that no strong argument could be made in either direction.

In addition to the fact that there is no compelling argument, the Missouri Supreme Court is bound by the precedent established in *Stanford v. Kentucky* and has no authority to overrule the High Court. The Supreme Court held in *Stanford v. Kentucky* that evidence of evolving standards in society can constitute the foundation for a decision that forces the abandonment of stare decisis. However, it is for the Supreme Court, and not any lower court, to declare a ruling against precedent. The Missouri Court's action trivialized the Supreme Court's power and the command of precedent.

Emily Previti
Draft One
Straw Man Essay

An email bounces back because I transposed a pair of letters in the address. I see the mistake and re-send the document to the correct address, but auto-BCC beats me to it, and the door a few feet behind me flies open, blinds rattling.

"Emily," she snaps. "You need to check your work more carefully."

I swivel in the chair. "Oh, I saw it. I corrected it."

"That shouldn't happen in the first place."

This interaction typifies my job during the summer following my sophomore year. My supervisor's hyper-criticism created an unhealthily stressful work environment and incited in me a dislike for the job so strong that I once cried for the entirety of my lunch hour and was often unhappy during the evenings and weekends. I consider the experience a success and proof that hate for a job leads to satisfaction.

An unrewarding work environment breeds dissatisfaction that can become consuming. I arrived at 9 am as arranged every Tuesday and Thursday during the spring. Her habit of flying in sometime between 9:20 and 9:40 permitted me to peacefully open the office. Whether sleep or clumps of mascara sealed her eyes, I knew not. I should have known, however, that she was not even in full effect during the morning shift.

"Emily, would you mind taking these books back to the library?" she asked during a snowstorm, a day on which afternoon classes were cancelled.

The due dates inside all three hundred of the books weighing down the push cart gave me two weeks leeway. "Can I take them back when it isn't snowing?"

Her countenance revealed that this request sickened her. "Why? It's just a little snow."

Shoulders hunched, I sloshed the cart to Van Pelt. The squish of my feet in my Uggs announced my presence and she bared teeth stained with Revlon Red as she handed me a stack of paperwork. I should have recognized her potential to be unreasonable, but at the end of the semester, she offered me a position that entailed committing to the summer, full-time, as her sole work-study. I accepted.

"Emily." She stood in the closet door, fake, glittery nail pointing to sweatpants and a sweater folded and stacked in the corner. "Were these left here overnight?"

"Yes, I thought that you said I could use the closet for my things."

"Not overnight."

I lugged the clothes to work and back every day for the rest of the summer. Of course, it was my own fault that I was cold in an office where the air conditioning kept the air at a balmy sixty degrees.

The view that stress on the job breeds dissatisfaction is short-sighted. Dissatisfaction induces introspection, which leads to self-discovery, the marker for the road to self-actualization. I scrutinized my associations with those whom my job performance affected, which led me to realize my strengths and regain my self-worth. I sought, and found, new employment in an arena that piqued my interest. I revere my new supervisors for their normalcy. I enjoy my responsibilities, unlike those at my old job. The new job has inspired career goals about which I am excited, not acquiescent.

Emily Previti
Descriptive Outline
Straw Man Essay

Proposition: Hate for a job leads to satisfaction.

Plan: Support the proposition in three paragraphs. The first serves as an introductory paragraph and states the proposition. In the second, explore an opposing view. In the third, refute the opposing view.

<u>Paragraph One</u>
      Says: Hate for a job leads to satisfaction.
      Does: Introduces the proposition with an anecdote.

<u>Paragraph Two</u>
      Says: An unrewarding work environment breeds dissatisfaction that can become consuming.
      Does: Supports the first reason with an anecdote.

<u>Paragraph Three</u>
      Says: Dissatisfaction induces introspection, which leads to self-discovery, the   marker for the road to self-actualization.
      Does: Supports the second reason with the narrator's experience.

316

Karen Connolly
Peer Review of Emily Previti's Straw Man Essay

Proposition:
An unpleasant work experience is important and necessary for building character and forming appreciation for future jobs.

Plan:
Support the proposition by showing how the opposing position is wrong then showing how your position is better.

Paragraph 1:
Says: tells an anecdote about an extreme situation at a bad job then states that the bad experience was important for later success.
Does: introduces the proposition by describing a situation reinforcing the opposing viewpoint then stating the opposite viewpoint in the proposition.

Paragraph 2:
Says: Tells more anecdotes about bad work experiences and states the opposing viewpoint that one must flee an unrewarding and frustrating work environment for mental health.
Does: supports the opposing viewpoint with personal examples.

Paragraph 3:
Says: The bad work experiences encouraged self-reflection and helped with finding a new, much more enjoyable and rewarding job.
Does: Supports the proposition with personal examples of how the bad work experience ended up being beneficial.

Melody Kramer
Peer Review
Emily Previti's Straw Man Essay

Basic Descriptive Outline

Proposition: Working at a terrible job will eventually lead to satisfaction.

Plan: Oppose the proposition, and then refute the opposition.

Paragraph 1 says: Emily's boss drove her nuts during her summer job, making Emily cry.

does: Introduces the proposition by giving an anecdote and discussing the circumstances.

Paragraph 2 says: Emily experienced many terrible things at the hands of her boss.

does: Opposes the proposition with one argument

Paragraph 3 says: Emily's bad job led to self-introspective thought which led to a new job.

does: Refutes the opposition by showing that there are alternatives.

Emily Previti
Draft Two
Straw Man Essay

Losing Face in Your Office Space? Stay in Place

One day, the university cancelled classes due to a snowstorm and my boss asked me to return a pushcart full of books to the library two weeks before their due dates. She refused my request to wait for the blizzard to end, so I sloshed the cart to Van Pelt. When the squish of my Uggs announced my return, she emerged to shove a stack of paperwork at me before slamming her door. I should have recognized her irrationality, but when she offered me a position for the summer, I accepted. Over the summer, the deterioration of the situation induced that of my temperament. This dissatisfaction induced introspection, which led to self-discovery, the marker for the road to self-actualization. I consider the experience a success and proof that suffering on the job ultimately leads to satisfaction.

In the interest of preserving one's self-esteem, emotional well-being, and mental health, some recommend that one flee a work environment filled with frustration. My supervisor's hyper-criticism's created such an atmosphere for me. One morning, an email once bounced back and auto-BCC alerted my boss. She flew out of her office, rattling the blinds on her door, and reprimanded me for my carelessness. When I explained that I had caught the mistake and re-sent the document, she insisted that it shouldn't have happened and couldn't again. Throughout the summer, I experienced variations on this interaction and developed a paranoia that drained me, even in the evenings and on weekends. Previously, I had jumped out of bed upon hearing the burst of static and music at 7:23 am, which now, as herald of the workday, failed to move me until the second snooze. I once cried for the entirety of my lunch hour due to my supervisor's hyper-criticism. The solutions to my shortcomings remained a mystery, as an attempt to clarify my errors solicited "Oh, but you're doing a *great* job!" which I interpreted as her hesitation to declare my incompetence for fear of destroying our semblance of civility.

A job like this dents self-image, but the recommendation to quit is short-sighted. A study conducted at Florida State University found that, in the long-run, one's career progresses from a focus on improving performance, rather than strengthening self-esteem. I found that the latter follows the former. I analyzed interactions with co-workers and found my performance met with nothing but gratitude and satisfaction, which led me to remember my strengths and regain my self-worth. Complacency at my job would have left me simmering where I sat, but my dislike for my occupation drove me to seek work that I would enjoy. I pursued new employment in an arena that piqued, and continues to hold, my interest. I bound out the door as early as 6 am instead of slamming snooze and hiding from the world beneath my comforter. I revere my new supervisors for their normalcy and revel at our mutual appreciation. Such positive reinforcement, absent from my former employer's repertoire, encourages me.

Michelle Chikaonda
Draft One, Straw Man

With the recent re-election of George W. Bush to a second term in the White House, there are several major issues he promised his voter base will be addressed in the next four years. One of the most heated topics on the table is that of same-sex marriage – Mr. Bush would like to propose a constitutional amendment banning homosexuals from the institution of marriage, and defining it as a union between one man and one woman. The possibility that homosexuals could lose rights based on what they are is frightening; marriage is something that should be open to all people, and not just people of a particular group. The proposed amendment banning same-sex marriage is wrong, and should not be allowed to pass.

The anti-gay marriage argument rests on several assertions. Firstly, that marriage was intended by God to be shared between one man and one woman, and not two people of the same sex. People who wish to have gay marriage banned also believe that the legalization of gay marriage will prove disastrous for the structure of the family – without clearly defined "male" and "female" roles in a family, children are likely to form misshapen ideas about what it means to be a man or a woman or even a human, and this makes the future of the American family a precarious one. Thirdly, people argue that two sexes are required to reproduce; if American society intends, therefore, to perpetuate itself, the institution of reproduction – marriage – needs to be prevented from becoming one where reproduction is not necessarily the result, and if gay marriage is legalized this will be the case. Finally, some people believe that homosexuality is a choice, a wrong and immoral one, and that by legalizing gay marriage Americans would be condoning sin and immorality.

However, these arguments fall apart when confronted with one thing – the constitutionality of taking civil rights away from people. The United States is supposed to be a secular state; Church and state are not supposed to be integrated with each other where laws governing the American people are concerned. If the Church wishes to keep Christian marriage as a union solely between a man and a woman, then so be it, but the Church has no place in the Constitution. To take rights away from a group of people based on what they are is blatant discrimination, and in a country that prides itself on equality for all, such an infringement on people's civil rights should not even be in consideration. Secondly, a law banning same-sex marriage based on the preservation of family roles has a host of implications – it says that there are certain personality traits that need to be present in a couple heading a family and bringing up children, which thus implies that by allowing same-sex unions one-half of this balance could be potentially eliminated, a result that proponents of this viewpoint claim could have disastrous effects for the children born of such a union. The suggestion that there are innate and unchangeable characteristics particular to men and women is a treacherous one – it is such ideas that have justified and perpetuated oppression and discrimination based on sex, a concept that most people today find repulsive. But most of all, the proposed constitutional amendment banning gay marriage dehumanizes homosexuals; it says that the existing institution of marriage is better than homosexuals, inferring therefore that heterosexuals are better than homosexuals. This is a chilling implication of this constitutional amendment; it says that only "normal" people can get married, it marginalizes gays and lesbians, and it says that they are less than human because only real humans with real sexual orientations should be allowed full recognition by the state that they wish to be united with another in matrimony.

Descriptive Outline, Michelle Chikaonda
Draft One, Straw Man

PROPOSITION: George Bush's proposed constitutional amendment banning gay marriage is wrong and should not be allowed to pass.
PLAN: Oppose the proposition, then refute the opposition.

PARAGRAPH 1:
SAYS: Marriage is something that should be open to all people regardless of their sexual orientation; Bush's proposed amendment should not be allowed to pass.
DOES: Introduces the proposition by discussing same-sex marriage with respect to recent events.

PARAGRAPH 2:
SAYS: There are several reasons why people are against same-sex marriage.
DOES: Opposes the proposition by providing several of the opposition's arguments.

PARAGRAPH 3:
SAYS: Banning same-sex marriage is unconstitutional and its banning would have very dangerous implications.
DOES: Refutes the opposition by discussing the implications of their arguments.

Nat Ward

DETAILED DESCRIPTIVE OUTLINE
Of Straw Man Essay by Michelle Chikaonda

PROPOSITION: The proposed amendment banning same-sex marriage is wrong and should not be allowed to pass.

PLAN: Oppose the opposition, and then refute the opposition.

PARAGRAPH 1: *says:* Among the issues President Bush has promised to address is that of same-sex marriages. He wishes to define marriage as a union between one man and one woman.
Does: Introduces the proposition by giving the circumstances and details surrounding it. Describes the implications of these details and their meaning with relation to the proposition.

PARAGRAPH 2: *says:* The anti-gay marriage argument is founded upon several social and religious principles, dealing with things like morality and family structure.
Does: Opposes the proposition by detailing the specific arguments against it. Gives reasons backing up each of these arguments against the proposition.

PARAGRAPH 3: *says:* The ban on gay marriage is a violation of civil rights, and it plies that homosexuals are inferior to heterosexuals. It also implies that a child must be raised by one man and one woman.
Does: Refutes the opposition by describing implications and consequences of each opposing argument.

COMMENTS: I like this essay: you describe many of the subtle (and not so subtle) implications of the anti-gay marriage argument. I also like how you refute each of the opposing arguments in detail. However, I think you need some more specific details in your second paragraph (for example: which specific institutions/organizations are making those arguments?).

Michelle Chikaonda
Draft Two: Straw Man Essay

On November 3rd, 2004 fifty-one percent of Americans joined hands to set the course of American civil rights backward. Before Election Day, George W. Bush promised his supporters that should he be re-elected, he will introduce an amendment to the constitution banning same-sex marriage; with his return to the White House, this amendment is no longer a faint possibility but a fast-approaching reality. Mr. Bush would like to define marriage as a union between one man and one woman, thereby excluding everyone who is not heterosexual from this institution. The possibility that homosexuals could be denied choices based on what they are is disturbing; any two consenting adults should be allowed to marry each other if they wish, irrespective of their sexual orientations. The proposed amendment banning same-sex marriage is wrong, and it should not be allowed to become a part of the United States' constitution.

The anti-gay marriage argument rests on several assertions, voiced mostly by members of Right-wing Christian religious communities but held widely through the population. One is that marriage was intended by God to be shared between one man and one woman, and not two people of the same sex. People who would like to see gay marriage banned also believe that the legalization of gay marriage will prove disastrous for the structure of the family – without clearly defined "male" and "female" roles in a family, children are likely to form misshapen ideas about what it means to be a man or a woman or even a human, and this makes the future of the American family a precarious one. Thirdly, people argue, two sexes are required to reproduce; if American society intends, therefore, to perpetuate itself, the institution of reproduction – marriage – needs to be prevented from becoming one where reproduction is not necessarily the result, and if gay marriage is legalized this will be the case. Finally, some people believe that homosexuality is a wrong and immoral lifestyle, and that by legalizing same-sex marriage Americans would be condoning sin and immorality.

However, these arguments fall apart when confronted with the government's duty to uphold the civil rights of the people it governs. The founders of the United States designed this country as a secular state; religion should have nothing to do with the laws governing the American people. If the Church wishes to keep Christian marriage as a union solely between a man and a woman, then so be it, but the Church has no place in the constitution. To deny a group of people the right to marry based only on what they are is blatant discrimination, and a contradiction in America's basic principles of equality for all. Secondly, a law banning same-sex marriage based on the preservation of family roles has a host of implications – it says that there are certain personality traits that need to be present in a couple heading a family and bringing up children, and that by allowing same-sex unions one-half of this balance could be potentially eliminated, a result proponents of this viewpoint claim could have disastrous effects for the children raised under such a union. The suggestion that there are innate and unchangeable characteristics particular to men and women is a dangerous one – it is such ideas that have justified and perpetuated oppression and discrimination based on sex, a concept that most people today find repulsive. But most of all, the proposed constitutional amendment banning gay marriage dehumanizes homosexuals; it says that the existing institution of marriage is better than homosexuals, inferring therefore that heterosexuals are better than homosexuals. This is a chilling implication of this constitutional amendment; it says that only "normal" people can get married, it marginalizes gays and lesbians, and it says that they are less than human, for only real humans with real sexual orientations should be allowed to unite with one another in marriage.

Michelle Chikaonda
DESCRIPTIVE OUTLINE of Draft Two, Straw Man

PROPOSITION: The proposed amendment banning same-sex marriage is wrong, and it should not be allowed to become a part of the United States' constitution.
PLAN: Oppose the proposition, then refute the opposition.

PARAGRAPH 1:
SAYS: President Bush's proposed marriage amendment should not be allowed to become a part of the constitution.
DOES: Introduces the proposition by referring to a recent event (the presidential election).

PARAGRAPH 2:
SAYS: The anti-gay marriage amendment rests on several arguments, which are voiced mostly by members of the religious right, but are held widely through America's population.
DOES: Opposes the proposition by providing several of the opposition's arguments/

PARAGRAPH 3:
SAYS: There are dangerous implications in President Bush's proposed amendment.
DOES: Refutes the opposition by discussing several implications of their

Emily Brotman
Concession Paper: First Draft

On Thanksgiving Eve, I, with my mother, my father, and my cousin dine at Smith and Wollensky Restaurant. Assuming streets and restaurants abandoned for the impending holiday, we eat our words at the steakhouse alive with patrons. My family sits in a booth, struggling to communicate over the colorful noise. Salads arrive, steaks disappear; dinner is delicious. To our waiter we note our surprise at the crowded crowd. With a laugh, he sinks to our eye level and softly says, "You know, we just found a lady passed out on the floor of the men's room. Did you know that Thanksgiving Eve is the biggest night for alcohol sales in restaurants?" We were unaware, but concerned by the evidence with which our waiter proved his point. "Is she alright?" "Yeah, she'll be fine," our waiter said, "you all just carefully make your way home." The Eve of Thanksgiving provides a reason for more people to drink in restaurants than any other night of the year.

If polled many would suppose that New Year's Eve is the most popular night for drinkers to revel in restaurants and bars, slurping their way through gallons of alcohol. New Year's Eve notoriously marks a night during which thousands of people flock to parties, bars, restaurants, and big city destinations in pursuit of fun. Some people have New Year's Eve traditions, some people spend the preceding year drafting up an exciting New Year's adventure, and some people wait until December 31st to figure out just where to head when the ball drops. Bottom line: a majority of these people anticipate intoxication when the clock strikes midnight. The desire to drink is generated by diverse reasons whether to ease the interaction with other people or to forget the debacle of the retired year. Anyone can dredge up the image of a loaded New Year's participator stumbling down the street to what is probably the next drink of a particularly long evening.

Much of this meditation on New Year's Eve activity is true; people like to eat, drink, and be merry on New Year's Eve. Whether to bring in the New Year or to wring out the Old One, people celebrate with alcoholic euphoria. Although exciting to rejoice in a bar or restaurant, on New Year's Eve the anticipation of crowds causes many people to remain home. A bulk of New Year's merriment is home-centered, in the company of friends and family. Thanksgiving generates the highest volume of traffic for a particular day; people transport themselves away from home, returning back to parents' houses or a distant relative's residence. Without a home-base, Thanksgiving transplants are forced to enjoy themselves in a public environment. A return to a childhood area promotes the reunion of friends choosing to meet at a new locale or an old haunt. Thanksgiving drinking is caused by the excitement of gathering with long-standing friends and family but also by the anxious anticipation of spending time with demanding family members.

Emily Brotman
Concession Paper
Descriptive Outline for Here's to Turkey

Proposition: The Eve of Thanksgiving provides a reason for more people to drink in restaurants than any other night of the year.

Plan: Raise arguments opposing the proposition, and then, conceding the validity of some of these arguments, offer reasons in defense of the proposition.

Paragraph One

Says: Thanksgiving Eve is a cause for heavy drinking.

Does: Introduces the proposition with a personal anecdote.

Paragraph Two

Says: New Year's Eve is the night of heaviest drinking.

Does: Gives arguments against the proposition.

Paragraph Three

Says: Thanksgiving is, in fact, the night of heaviest drinking and explains why.

Does: Concedes the validity of some criticism, and then argues in favor of the proposition.

Melody Kramer
Descriptive and Evaluative Peer Review
Emily Brotman's concession Paper

Proposition: The Eve of Thanksgiving provides a reason for more people to drink in restaurants than any other night of the year.
Plan: State the proposition. Refute the proposition, and then concede by indicating that although the other side raises good points, the proposition is still valid

Paragraph 1 says: Emily and her family go out to dinner on Thanksgiving Eve where they are told by their waiter that the day before Thanksgiving is the heaviest drinking day of the year.
does: Introduces the proposition by giving an anecdote and discussing the circumstances leading up to Emily's discovery of the proposition.
Paragraph 2 says: A majority of people might think that New Year's Eve is the time when the most people get drunk because of circumstances associated with the holiday.
does: Refutes proposition through illustrations on why another night would create more inebriation
Paragraph 3 says: Though it is true that New Year's Eve provokes a lot of drinking, the fact that Thanksgiving occurs outside the home means that people are more liable to drink more.
does: Concedes the opposition has a point but then indicates that the proposition is still more valid.

Evaluation:

Overall, your essay is a pleasure to read, Emily. You state your position clearly and your support in your paragraphs develops the main point. The essay is coherent and your sentences seem to work well in the order they are listed. The first paragraph was enjoyable to read because it added a personal element to a serious topic. Your playful use of the English language, like when you wrote *Bottom line* is an effective way to tonally guide your reader through the piece.

It seems to me, though, that a few changes would make the essay more effective.

1. I would change the location of the word I in sentence one so that the sentence reads:
   On Thanksgiving Eve, my mother, father, cousin, and I dine….
   It sounds a bit formal the way that it is right now. If you do keep it as is, you should add the word *along* before the world with.
2. Check your tenses in sentence two.
3. The word you should be capitalized in the phrase *you jut carefully make your way home* and there should be a period after the word said in the phrase *our waiter said.*
4. Although the proposition is clear, you might want to use a different verb instead of *provides* to make the proposition more succinct. A added transition would also help connect the proposition to the opening paragraph.
5. I think in your 3rd paragraph, you should focus more on Thanksgiving than New Year's Eve. Right now your focus is about equal

Emily Brotman
Concession Essay
Final Draft

Here's to Turkey

On Thanksgiving Eve, I, with my mother, my father, and my cousin dine at Smith and Wollensky Restaurant. Assuming streets and restaurants abandoned for the impending holiday, we eat our words at the steakhouse alive with patrons. My family sits in a booth, struggling to communicate over the colorful noise. Salads arrive, steaks disappear; dinner tastes delicious. To our waiter we note our surprise at the crowded crowd. With a laugh, he sinks to our eye level and softly says, "You know, we just found a lady passed out on the floor of the men's room. Did you know that Thanksgiving Eve is the biggest night for alcohol sales in restaurants?" We were unaware, but concerned by the evidence with which our waiter proved his point. "Is she alright?" "Yeah, she'll be fine," our waiter said, "you all just carefully make your way home." The Eve of Thanksgiving provides a reason for more people to drink in restaurants than any other night of the year.

If polled many would suppose that New Year's Eve is the most popular night for drinkers to revel in restaurants and bars, slurping their way through gallons of alcohol. New Year's Eve notoriously marks a night during which thousands of people flock to parties, bars, restaurants, and big city destinations in pursuit of fun. Some people have New Year's Eve traditions, some people spend the preceding year drafting up an exciting New Year's adventure, and some people wait until December 31st to figure out just where to head when the ball drops. Bottom line: a majority of these people anticipate intoxication when the clock strikes midnight. The desire to drink is generated by diverse reasons whether to ease the interaction with other people or to forget the debacle of the retired year. Anyone can dredge up the image of a loaded New Year's participator stumbling down the street to what is probably the next drink of a long evening.

Much of this meditation on New Year's Eve activity is true; people like to eat, drink, and be merry on New Year's Eve. Whether to bring in the New Year or to wring out the Old One, people celebrate with alcoholic euphoria. Although exciting to rejoice in a bar or restaurant, on New Year's Eve the anticipation of crowds causes many people to remain home. A bulk of New Year's merriment is home-centered, in the company of friends and family. Thanksgiving generates the highest volume of traffic for a particular day; people transport themselves away from home, returning back to parents' houses or to a distant relative's residence. Without a home-base, Thanksgiving transplants are forced to enjoy themselves in a public environment. A return to a childhood area promotes the reunion of friends choosing to meet at a new locale or an old haunt. Thanksgiving drinking is caused by the excitement of gathering with long-standing friends and family but also by the anxious anticipation of spending time with demanding family members.

Karen Connolly
Concession Paper Draft 1

Every Sunday morning, me and my housemates gather in our living room wearing pajamas and fluffy slippers. We all giggle in anticipation, waiting for the first of the weekend updates from the most (and sometimes least) wild members of the house. Inevitably, every story revolves around a different guy and who kissed or made out with or slept with whom. After sitting in on a Sunday morning session, any one of our parents would probably faint or take us out of school, but the promiscuity observed in my household is the norm for many Penn students. Having lived in the house for nearly a semester, I have come to the conclusion that while promiscuous behavior is popular among college students, a simple solution to the problems that may come along with it is involvement in a long-term relationship during college.

Many arguments oppose the choice to involve oneself in a long-term relationship during the college years, and legitimately so. The college years are a time of growth and expansion, and dependence on another person that often results from a long-term relationship can hinder this growth. Schoolwork is another area that can suffer when a relationship is given priority by students. Important college experiences such as travel abroad may not be fully explored when a member of a relationship does not wish to leave their significant other for a long period of time. When part of a relationship, a person often replaces the opportunity to meet other people with nights spent at home with the other half of their relationship. Along with conscious decisions to spend time with their partner, females in a relationship may subconsciously be steered towards a family life when they came into college focused on a career, positive or negative as this may be.

While all these negative effects of long-term relationships during college can be legitimate, when the problematic behavior observed at Penn is in question, a long-term relationship may be a good solution. Among the major risks associated with promiscuity are sexually transmitted infections, and being with only one partner greatly reduces these risks. Some students are more concerned with finding a guy than STI's and while a relationship takes lots of time, I have personally known many colleagues whose sole concern is preparing for hours to meet a guy for the night. A steady relationship would cut back this time dramatically. Mental health ranks among the most important reasons for students considering a long-term relationship in college to consider. Without having to worry about meeting new guys, girls can relax and enjoy their partner without stress.

Descriptive Outline for
Draft One Concession Essay
By Karen Connolly

Proposition:
 A solution to the problem of promiscuity in college lies in securing long-term relationships

Plan:
Develop my proposition by introducing the legitimate opposing idea then explaining my point of view.

Paragraph 1:
Says:
Tells an anecdote about the promiscuity observed in my household.
Does:
Introduces the proposition by telling a story.

Paragraph 2:
Says:
Involvement in a relationship during the college years hinders growth and college success.
Does:
Explains the opposing viewpoints.

Paragraph 3:
Says:
Relationships are beneficially for minimizing risks and improving mental health.
Does:
Lists reasons supporting the proposition.

330

Emily Brotman's Outline of
Karen Connolly's Concession Draft

Proposition: While promiscuous behavior is popular among college students, a simple solution to the problems that may come along with it is involvement in a long-term relationship during college.

Plan: Raise arguments opposing the proposition, and then, conceding the validity of some of these arguments, offer reasons in defense of the proposition.

Par 1 Says: Many college students have promiscuous relationships.

Par 1 Does: Introduces the proposition as a panacea to the questionable behavior of many college students; uses personal example.

Par 2 Says: Long-term relationships can hinder development at college; perhaps more so for females.

Par 2 Does: Gives arguments against proposition.

Par 3 Says: That long-term relationships are safer and can actually reduce stress.

Par 3 Does: Concedes the validity of some criticism, and then argues in favor of the proposition.

Aubry Wand
Descriptive Outline of Karen Connolly's First Draft Concession Paper

Proposition: A long-term relationship will end some of the problems that are associated with the promiscuity of college students.

Plan: Begin with a reason opposing the proposition; then concede the validity of this point of view, but explain that the one in the proposition is the stronger of the two.

Paragraph 1
Says: Many college students are promiscuous, and a long-term relationship could be a solution to some of the problems that come with promiscuity.
Does: Introduces the topic with a personal anecdote that it interesting and humorous.

Paragraph 2
Says: Serious relationships can hinder a college student's ability to grow and experience new things.
Does: Offers an opposing view to the one stated in the proposition through a variety of examples.

Paragraph 3
Says: Long-term relationships reduce the risk of sexually transmitted diseases and allow for a generally less stressful life.
Does: Gives more examples in support of the proposition, including a personal reference which strengthens the argument.

Karen Connolly
Concession Paper Second Draft

Hot Accessory of the Month

You have all seen them. Strolling smugly down Locust Walk on a day like today, at once oblivious to and keenly aware of the crowd, clinging to their latest coveted accessory. We are not referring to *Gucci* or *Prada*, but rather an adornment much harder to come by at Penn: a boyfriend. At a school like ours where attractive men stand out due to their shortage, the facially gifted can afford to date more casually or not date at all and still maintain a very active social and sexual life. This phenomenon translates to less real relationships and more casual sex for the young women seeking male attention. While the equation appears skewed in favor of securing a man when given the opportunity, the female population at Penn should scrutinize long-term relationships with the same attention they devote to shopping for handbags.

Many arguments oppose the choice to begin a long-term relationship during the college years, and legitimately so. Dependence on another person that often results from this involvement hinders personal growth that the college years provide. Schoolwork suffers when students prioritize dating. Important college experiences such as travel abroad may be overlooked when a member of a couple does not wish to leave their significant other for a semester. When entangled in a relationship, one often replaces the opportunity to meet other people with nights spent at home cuddling with their other half. Along with conscious decisions to spend time with their partner, taken females may subconsciously be steered towards a family life, opposing the focus on a career they brought into college.

All these legitimate negative effects suggest that long-term relationships during college necessitate missing out. And while couples certainly miss some experiences, we cannot overlook the opportunities for growth available in long-term relationships. Men can provide more than an accessory for Locust Walk; with the free-for-all party atmosphere at most colleges, promiscuity prevails. Among the major risks associated with promiscuity are sexually transmitted infections, and risks reduce greatly when taken with only one partner. Some students concern themselves more with finding a guy than STI's and while dating occupies time, I personally know colleagues whose sole concern is preparing for hours to meet a guy for the night. A steady relationship would cut back this time and preoccupation dramatically. More importantly, in the development of college, students construct their personal skills and can build a foundation for either positive or negative relationships later on. Dating offers an unlimited arena for testing one's likes and dislikes, and ultimate personal deal-makers and deal-breakers in a significant other. Mental health ranks among the most important issues for students considering a long-term union in college. The environment produced by casual sex relationships damages all but the hardiest girls' self-esteems, which can be mended by a deeper connection.

Sahang-Hee Hahn
Concession Paper - Draft1

While nearly everyone decries racial stereotypes in the general sense, certain stereotypes are still tolerated more than others. The 'model minority' stereotype, a term loosely applied to the even more loosely termed 'Asian-American' community is at the top of the list. At first, the 'model minority' stereotype appears one of the more flattering racial labels applied. One might even tolerate the stereotype as a complimentary if somewhat generalizing label: successfully adhering to and profiting from the existing socioeconomic order, by dint of one's diligence and reliability, is the cornerstone of the American Dream, is it not? But tolerating such a stereotype does a great disservice to this people group. The model minority stereotype limits rather than benefits members of the Asian American community. It creates a glass ceiling at the level where Asian Americans might otherwise ascend, socially and professionally, and exercise their own creative and leadership abilities.

There are those who would say that the model minority stereotype is hardly the boogeyman it is made out to be; the label is merely a reference to the quick economic stability that many Asian American groups have achieved. There is truth to this observation. Highly selective citizenship standards required immigrants from the Asian continent to possess either a professional degree or strong academic credential upon entrance into the country. As a result, a large percentage of the Asian American community arrived with skills readily transferable to the American professional arena, gaining economic stability with unprecedented speed.

It is possible that at first, the model minority stereotype only applied to the rapidity with which Asian immigrants achieved economic stability and prosperity. After all, it would seem as though this people group were 'models' in that they were 'model' immigrants, who appeared to realize their American Dream within the same generation of immigration. But what this argument ignores, however, is that in commending Asian Americans for establishing the foundation of their American Dream, this stereotype denies many the full realization of it. Ultimately, the model minority stereotype, like all stereotypes, defines and therefore limits the popular conception of a people group, in this case, Asian Americans. It limits Asian Americans to supporting, middle-management, social and professional roles where their universally regarded straits of diligence and reliability can 'shine.' By overplaying the euphemized professional abilities of working hard and obeying orders, the stereotype excludes the idea of Asian American creative and leadership potential. Recent polls discover that across the board, in the realms of politics, entertainment, and business, Americans consider Asian Americans the least suitable for leadership positions.

334

Sahang-Hee Hahn
Descriptive Outline
Concession Paper

Proposition: The model minority stereotype applied to Asian Americans is not as complimentary as it sounds.
Plan: Raise arguments opposing the proposition, and then, conceding the validity of some of these arguments, offer reasons in defense of the proposition.

Paragraph 1:
Says: The model minority stereotype limits rather than benefits members of the Asian American community.
Does: Introduces the proposition.

Paragraph 2:
Says: There are those who would say that the model minority stereotype is hardly the boogeyman it is made out to be; the label is merely a reference to the quick economic stability that many Asian American groups have achieved.
Does: Undermines the apparent threat of the model minority stereotype by pointing out its positive connotation.

Paragraph 3:
Says: But what this argument ignores, however, is that in commending Asian Americans for establishing the foundation of their American Dream, this stereotype denies many the full realization of it.
Does: Concedes the validity of some criticism, and then argues in favor of the proposition.

Nat Ward
Peer Review of
Sahang-Hee Hahn
Concession Paper

PROPOSITION: The model minority stereotype limits rather than benefits members of the Asian
        American community by limiting the ways in which Asian Americans can
        exercise their own creative and leadership abilities.

PLAN: Raise arguments opposing the proposition, and then, conceding the validity of some of
these arguments, offer reasons in defense of the proposition.

PARAGRAPH 1: *says:* While the 'model minority' stereotype for Asian Americans may seem
complimentary on the surface, it creates a glass ceiling preventing Asian Americans from
exercising their creative and leadership abilities.
        Does: Introduces the proposition by explaining how it came about. Contrasts
        the appearance of the topic in question with its reality.

PARAGRAPH 2: *says:* The stereotype of Asian Americans is a reference to the quick economic
stability that many Asian Americans have achieved. This is due to highly selective citizenship
standards.
        Does: Opposes the proposition by giving the history and facts behind the topic
        in question.

PARAGRAPH 3: *says:* While the stereotype of Asian Americans commends them for
achievingthe American Dream, it also denies many of them the full realization of it. It limits
them to roles where their diligence and reliability can "shine".
        Does: Concedes the initial validity of the stereotype. Supports the proposition
        with data from polls and statements about the general attitudes of the
        American people.

COMMENTS: I like this essay: it's well organized, and it explores the reasons for, and effects
of, the Asian American stereotype, which many people many not be totally aware of. Your third
paragraph talks about how the stereotype limits what Asian Americans can do in our society
(which supports the proposition). I think your second paragraph (refuting the proposition)
should have a few details about possible benefits (if any?) that this "model minority" stereotype
provides.

Sahang-Hee Hahn
Concession Paper- Second Draft

Stereotypes *Are* All Created Equal

The recent, cultural wave of political correctness compels many to deny the existence of stereotypes. Some nowadays might allow the possibility of their existence, albeit in some undeveloped corner of the world. A courageous few, however, will admit that stereotyping occurs and even more candidly, that not all stereotypes are created equal. Interestingly, oftentimes the subjects of a stereotype consider their racial label less negative than others, and tolerate it accordingly. Certain members of the Asian-American community believe that the 'model minority' stereotype carries a neutral, if not positive connotation. For that reason, some Asian-Americans tolerate what they consider a term testifying to how successfully they have assimilated into mainstream, American culture. Perhaps the 'model minority' stereotype is not as openly derogatory as other racial labels. But to consider the 'model minority' stereotype anything other than a racially prescribed identity is naïve and dangerous. The model minority stereotype limits rather than benefits members of the Asian-American community. This label does not indicate full-scale assimilation into American culture. Furthermore, its emphasis on Asian-American detail-orientation, obedience, and diligence, de-emphasize to the point of excluding the possibility of other, equally valid, personality traits. By tolerating this stereotype, Asian-Americans run the risk of allowing the 'model minority' idea to become a glass ceiling, that might not only prevent the future use of their creative and leadership abilities, but a genuine integration into mainstream American culture.

At first, it might appear that the model minority stereotype is not the boogeyman it has been made out to be. Some consider the label a reference to the quick economic stability that Asian American groups have achieved. After all, the rate at which Asian immigrants have achieved economic prosperity, often within the first generation of immigration, is unprecedented. There is some truth to this observation. Highly selective citizenship standards required immigrants from the Asian continent to possess either a professional degree or strong academic credential upon entrance into the country. As a result, a large percentage of the Asian American community arrived with skills readily transferable to the American professional arena, gaining economic stability with unprecedented speed. Others consider the term to apply to the diligence, obedience, and attention to details many Asian Americans bring to their jobs. Some Asian-Americans believe in both ideas, and consider the 'model minority' to describe how well Asian immigrants have assimilated into the American socioeconomic, as well as cultural fabric: after all, economic prosperity by dint of one's hard work and skill is the cornerstone of the American Dream. But even those who cannot interpret the stereotype positively will admit the seeming benefits of the model minority. Asian-Americans admit that this stereotype has socially identified them as being intelligent and hard-working. Many Asian-Americans tolerate the stereotype because they believe that the 'given' assumption of certain positive characteristics benefit them, at school and in the workplace.

It is true that the model minority stereotype often carries the traits of intelligence and diligence. But it is incorrect to believe that for this reason, the model minority stereotype is not harmful. What the previous argument ignores is that by commending Asian Americans for establishing the seeming foundations of their American Dream, this stereotype denies many the full realization of it. In the end, the model minority stereotype is like all stereotypes, limiting individuals by the presumptive act of prescribing their identity. The very act of describing an individual involves the two actions of emphasis and de-emphasis. As a result, the act of stressing intelligence, hard work, and obedience de-emphasizes and thus actively diminishes the possibility of other Asian-American traits in the public mind. The 'model minority' idea limits Asian Americans to supporting, middle-management, social and professional roles because it identifies them as the ideal candidates for such positions, and correspondingly dubious candidates for other ones. As a result, the model minority stereotype excludes the idea of Asian American creative and leadership potential. It is more than likely that the model minority label has already infiltrated the popular conception of Asian Americans and their talents. Recent polls discover that across the board, in the realms of politics, entertainment, business, and the arts, American citizens consider Asian Americans the least suitable for leadership positions.

Karen Connolly
Concession Paper Draft 1

Every Sunday morning, me and my housemates gather in our living room wearing pajamas and fluffy slippers. We all giggle in anticipation, waiting for the first of the weekend updates from the most (and sometimes least) wild members of the house. Inevitably, every story revolves around a different guy and who kissed or made out with or slept with whom. After sitting in on a Sunday morning session, any one of our parents would probably faint or take us out of school, but the promiscuity observed in my household is the norm for many Penn students. Having lived in the house for nearly a semester, I have come to the conclusion that while promiscuous behavior is popular among college students, a simple solution to the problems that may come along with it is involvement in a long-term relationship during college.

Many arguments oppose the choice to involve oneself in a long-term relationship during the college years, and legitimately so. The college years are a time of growth and expansion, and dependence on another person that often results from a long-term relationship can hinder this growth. Schoolwork is another area that can suffer when a relationship is given priority by students. Important college experiences such as travel abroad may not be fully explored when a member of a relationship does not wish to leave their significant other for a long period of time. When part of a relationship, a person often replaces the opportunity to meet other people with nights spent at home with the other half of their relationship. Along with conscious decisions to spend time with their partner, females in a relationship may subconsciously be steered towards a family life when they came into college focused on a career, positive or negative as this may be.

While all these negative effects of long-term relationships during college can be legitimate, when the problematic behavior observed at Penn is in question, a long-term relationship may be a good solution. Among the major risks associated with promiscuity are sexually transmitted infections, and being with only one partner greatly reduces these risks. Some students are more concerned with finding a guy than STI's and while a relationship takes lots of time, I have personally known many colleagues whose sole concern is preparing for hours to meet a guy for the night. A steady relationship would cut back this time dramatically. Mental health ranks among the most important reasons for students considering a long-term relationship in college to consider. Without having to worry about meeting new guys, girls can relax and enjoy their partner without stress.

Descriptive Outline for
Draft One Concession Essay
By Karen Connolly

Proposition:
 A solution to the problem of promiscuity in college lies in securing long-term relationships

Plan:
Develop my proposition by introducing the legitimate opposing idea then explaining my point of view.

Paragraph 1:
Says:
Tells an anecdote about the promiscuity observed in my household.
Does:
Introduces the proposition by telling a story.

Paragraph 2:
Says:
Involvement in a relationship during the college years hinders growth and college success.
Does:
Explains the opposing viewpoints.

Paragraph 3:
Says:
Relationships are beneficially for minimizing risks and improving mental health.
Does:
Lists reasons supporting the proposition.

Emily Brotman's Outline of
Karen Connolly's Concession Draft

Proposition: While promiscuous behavior is popular among college students, a simple solution to the problems that may come along with it is involvement in a long-term relationship during college.

Plan: Raise arguments opposing the proposition, and then, conceding the validity of some of these arguments, offer reasons in defense of the proposition.

Par 1 Says: Many college students have promiscuous relationships.

Par 1 Does: Introduces the proposition as a panacea to the questionable behavior of many college students; uses personal example.

Par 2 Says: Long-term relationships can hinder development at college; perhaps more so for females.

Par 2 Does: Gives arguments against proposition.

Par 3 Says: That long-term relationships are safer and can actually reduce stress.

Par 3 Does: Concedes the validity of some criticism, and then argues in favor of the proposition.

Aubry Wand
Descriptive Outline of Karen Connolly's First Draft Concession Paper

Proposition: A long-term relationship will end some of the problems that are associated with the promiscuity of college students.

Plan: Begin with a reason opposing the proposition; then concede the validity of this point of view, but explain that the one in the proposition is the stronger of the two.

Paragraph 1
Says: Many college students are promiscuous, and a long-term relationship could be a solution to some of the problems that come with promiscuity.
Does: Introduces the topic with a personal anecdote that it interesting and humorous.

Paragraph 2
Says: Serious relationships can hinder a college student's ability to grow and experience new things.
Does: Offers an opposing view to the one stated in the proposition through a variety of examples.

Paragraph 3
Says: Long-term relationships reduce the risk of sexually transmitted diseases and allow for a generally less stressful life.
Does: Gives more examples in support of the proposition, including a personal reference which strengthens the argument.

342

Karen Connolly
Concession Paper Second Draft

Hot Accessory of the Month

You have all seen them. Strolling smugly down Locust Walk on a day like today, at once oblivious to and keenly aware of the crowd, clinging to their latest coveted accessory. We are not referring to *Gucci* or *Prada*, but rather an adornment much harder to come by at Penn: a boyfriend. At a school like ours where attractive men stand out due to their shortage, the facially gifted can afford to date more casually or not date at all and still maintain a very active social and sexual life. This phenomenon translates to less real relationships and more casual sex for the young women seeking male attention. While the equation appears skewed in favor of securing a man when given the opportunity, the female population at Penn should scrutinize long-term relationships with the same attention they devote to shopping for handbags.

Many arguments oppose the choice to begin a long-term relationship during the college years, and legitimately so. Dependence on another person that often results from this involvement hinders personal growth that the college years provide. Schoolwork suffers when students prioritize dating. Important college experiences such as travel abroad may be overlooked when a member of a couple does not wish to leave their significant other for a semester. When entangled in a relationship, one often replaces the opportunity to meet other people with nights spent at home cuddling with their other half. Along with conscious decisions to spend time with their partner, taken females may subconsciously be steered towards a family life, opposing the focus on a career they brought into college.

All these legitimate negative effects suggest that long-term relationships during college necessitate missing out. And while couples certainly miss some experiences, we cannot overlook the opportunities for growth available in long-term relationships. Men can provide more than an accessory for Locust Walk; with the free-for-all party atmosphere at most colleges, promiscuity prevails. Among the major risks associated with promiscuity are sexually transmitted infections, and risks reduce greatly when taken with only one partner. Some students concern themselves more with finding a guy than STI's and while dating occupies time, I personally know colleagues whose sole concern is preparing for hours to meet a guy for the night. A steady relationship would cut back this time and preoccupation dramatically. More importantly, in the development of college, students construct their personal skills and can build a foundation for either positive or negative relationships later on. Dating offers an unlimited arena for testing one's likes and dislikes, and ultimate personal deal-makers and deal-breakers in a significant other. Mental health ranks among the most important issues for students considering a long-term union in college. The environment produced by casual sex relationships damages all but the hardiest girls' self-esteems, which can be mended by a deeper connection.

Reflections on the Process of Writing
By Karen Connolly

Having come into the class, I was a bit skeptical about the amount I would learn about my own writing. . . However, upon re-reading my final drafts for the portfolio, I noticed a truly dramatic change between the two most recent writings and my first two essays. My entire writing style actually changed; I used to write with a detailed outline (sometimes more extensive than the paper itself) and left very little room for revision. I felt constricted by the amount of work I had put into the first draft and often felt that changing more than one sentence would change the structure of my essay too far from the initial outline.

This process is noticeable in my first two essays. For my third and fourth essays, I decided to try a new process: I brainstormed ideas and jotted notes down as usual, but instead of extensive outlining before even writing, I just wrote. Certainly, the essays needed more revision and thinking in between drafts to really work out what I wanted to say but I feel my newer writing is much more interesting and powerful than the blander writing of before. The final paper was also my first attempt at humorous or sarcastic writing (along with some seriousness), which may or may not have been successful-- I think it was a decent first try.

More important than improving my writing and tutoring skills (which will certainly aid my bedside manner in a future medical career) this class was my favorite and most valuable class taken at Penn in terms of actual intellectual growth. Involvement in such a diverse and outstanding group of people stands out among all my other classes and distinguishes this one as a "life" class. The thinking skills and idea development I learned will stick with me, as will the personal connections we all made.

At the end of this semester I feel refreshed and excited for next semester, a first for me.

Why Write?
By Emily Brotman

I write. I struggle, however, with the idea of being a writer; a job to which I often give thought. I debate with myself the merits and the drawbacks of, for my life, *being* a writer. I know, at this point, that writing will work itself into my life: I can write, I do write, I like to write, and (I hope) I write well. To me, the life of a writer looks glamorous and exciting and fulfilling and, well, fun—in fact, I cannot think of a more ideal job. I hesitate, I think, with fear that, very simply, I will not know what to write. Or, that what I write might fail. Or, that my paycheck will barely satisfy my needs—and wants—for a month. Whenever I interact with writing, I realize the power that it possesses over my life. My experience in this writing seminar energized me; it reminded me of why—I write.

This class encouraged me to keep writing. I appreciated the method with which we learned to write. The application of writing constructively taught me how to write effectively, while maintaining my own style . . .

As I consider my options for next year, I keep spinning the wheel so that it stops on the wide-world of writing. Unsure of its meaning, I still lean closer to an occupation that allows me to work with words, to shape my thoughts with a selection of keystrokes. Writing makes me think—to think hard is rewarding. I do not feel so thoughtful and articulate as I do when I write down my ideas. To me, writing is exciting; to write well is to successfully execute art. Creatively expressing ideas allows me to feel unique, as an individual with something to say. . . as I begin to construct my future, I will look for a dock on which to land my writing. I cannot confirm how I will write or what I will write about but I realize, with this semester behind me, that whatever I do, I will write.

Reflections on the Seminar
By Emily Previti

Normally, professors assign students topics and leave the form up to them. The fact that this class reversed this procedure helped me as a writer much like varying a workout achieves greater physical results than sticking with the same regimen. My writer's "muscles" were challenged and strengthened by the variation.

I think that outlining helped us to learn how to evaluate the clarity of the essay without muffling a writer's voice, or taking it over with our own, which we emphasized throughout the course. I became more aware of how each sentence supported the paragraph and the whole essay. . .Doing outlines for my classmates developed that skill.

I do not enjoy choosing my own topic and never have, but the fact that I had to do it for this course helped me as a writer because it forced me to truly write what I know.

The brevity of the assignments allowed me to focus, and improve, on style. . .I now know firsthand the impact of drafting and revising on writing. The course taught me revision strategies. . . My favorite: cleaning out the adjectives and adverbs.

The descriptive outline format objectifies the peer review. I felt less vulnerable when receiving the reviewer's feedback and grateful for the opportunity to check the clarity of my writing. . . I realized the value of having a "fresh eye" to look at one's writing.

The professor's feedback is always thoughtful and insightful. . . Her comments are crafted in such a way that, as writers, we crave positive feedback and hurry home after class to edit drafts in order to receive it.

I am introspective as a rule and will observe or experience something and think, 'I have to write about this.' Keeping a journal helped me as a writer more than anything else.

After taking this course, playing with words to improve the efficiency of writing (mine and others') truly is like playing for me. More importantly, it helps me to improve. . .my own writing. We spent a great deal of time on a small amount of writing, and this really increased my appreciation for, and aspiration to acquire, the skill of the published writers that we examined in class.

I learned that the more you write, the better you are at it and the more comfortable you become with it. Another thing: my vocabulary has improved, as if by flexing the writing muscles I've recalled words that were never even in my repertoire before.

Melody Kramer

A Chair is a Chair is a Chair

Is the first sentence of this essay impressive? No, it's not. I might wake up with a better version tomorrow, and discard this sentence. Or maybe sentence one will drastically change, and sentence four will shift down to replace sentence eight. The first sentence of this personal statement evolved six times, but only one version of that sentence appears here, in the final edition of this paper. The other five versions, in fact, never even appeared in print. In fact, if I had an observer watching me type, she might think I did not edit my first sentence at all because she could not observe any tangible changes on screen. Where, then, were these first five sentences if they never were physically written down? Clearly, I'm no magician. It's not some trick involving invisible ink and slight of hand. And it's not that I don't edit my essays because I do, almost compulsively.

The first five drafts of sentence one never left my mind, though they were created, examined, and eventually discarded. When I write, I edit constantly in my head, whether I have a pen, paper, or computer in front of me or not. No matter what I am doing, then, I am writing. I write as I walk down the block to the grocery store, thinking of the best way to start a paragraph. I write when I shower, trying to determine the best word choice for a particular phrase. I write when I'm eating, exercising, working, even drifting off to sleep. Writing consumes me. It forces me to perceive the world as I would put it into words. It is me. I cannot distance myself from my writing any more than I can distance myself from my appearance. The difference lies in the fact that my appearance is unedited; my writing is not.

This semester, though, I have had to work to really distance myself from my writing. Without distance, I realized at some point in October, there is no room for improvement. It is

347

necessary to take a step back and examine which eventually allows the room needed for the review and reassessment. My proximity to my writing prevented me from explaining my writing style in the beginning of the semester. I could not verbalize how I wrote and I realized that explaining my writing process is actually harder for me to put into words than the actual process of writing. As the semester progressed. . . I began to realize that I do indeed have a process. It's not a process where I need a certain color of ink or I need to eat first or I can only write in a certain room. I realized that my writing process is continually editing and reediting in my head before actually taking the step and writing the piece.

Realizing I had a writing process and being able to verbalize it was perhaps the most important thing I learned about my own writing. . .Of course, this was not the only thing I learned as a writer or in my dual role as a tutor, but verbalizing my writing process is something that will enable me to think more about the process of writing, instead of the actual writing itself. As soon as I began to look at writing this way, my sentences became crisper, my paragraphs became tighter, and I saw that I did have a vision for what I wanted to get down on the page.

. . . At the beginning of the semester, Val instructed us to look at a chair. The point of the exercise was to realize that not all chairs are the same, just like not all writing is the same. Everyone envisioning a chair will most likely be thinking about something different. There are ordinary chairs and there are flamboyant chairs. Some chairs are well-constructed and sturdy. Some might collapse. Others are mass-produced and unoriginal. When I look at a chair now, I see the material sitting on the floor, ready to be molded into a piece of furniture. I see the furniture-maker, huddled over the material, crafting it into something unique or ordinary, depending. I wonder how many times his vision has evolved. A chair is not a chair is not a chair.

I feel the same way about my writing. Over the course of this semester, my writing has evolved from ordinary and somewhat thoughtless to something where I examine every nut and bolt before handing in a piece. If I had to design a chair to represent my writing, it would be something comfortable, something well-constructed, and something with a little flair. I'd probably never be fully happy with the final product, but it's much harder to edit a chair than it is to edit an essay.

Connecting
By Nat Ward

Real writing happens when you tell the whole truth about some situation or aspect of yourself. . .that is when a writer really connects with the reader. If no such connection is made, then there is no real benefit in writing the work or reading it.

Part of establishing the connection between writer and reader is to eliminate the "noise" in one's writing: those words and structures that cloud the true meaning of what the writer intends to convey. Examples of noise frequently found in my own writing at the beginning of this course are passive voice, excessive adjectives and adverbs, and imprecise word choice.

When we got our first essays back with comments, Val told us that while we were all great writers, we had the potential to become even better writers. As she went through all of the things that were wrong with our papers, I found that I was guilty of just about every mistake she mentioned. While this realization was initially disheartening, I realized that in order to improve as a writer, I needed to see the truth of how I was really expressing myself. I also realized that the things she talked about. . .applied not only to writing, but to everyday life as well. To live a full life, we shouldn't feel as if we need to constantly legitimize certain aspects of ourselves or try to hide them. Rather, we should have confidence in ourselves and share our thoughts and feelings with others, even if they are different from [. . .others'] thoughts and feelings. Each person has something of value to contribute, and should feel free to do so.

I sincerely hope that being a Writing Advisor will allow me to help others express their true selves and enable them to contribute all they can to a given social discourse community, and that I can continue to rise "beyond my expectations," or, more appropriately, become my true, complete self.

The "A" Paper

In English 135, students collaboratively developed the criteria for evaluating whether a paper should receive an A. Below is an example of the criteria one group produced.

About this experience, one of the participants wrote:

> I was more pleased than perturbed when Val announced that, according to our standards, no one received an "A" on the first paper. This demonstrated that our standards for ourselves and our peers are high, as they should be. . .It also helped me as a writer because some of the criteria [our class developed] addressed issues of which I was unaware, or that I ignored.
> --Emily Previti, "Course Analysis"

Criteria for an "A" Paper
by Michelle Chikaonda, Karen Connolly, Sahang-Hee Hahn, Natalie Ward

Coherence:
1. Clear position
2. Logical progression of sentences and ideas
3. Strong supporting paragraphs directly relating to the thesis
4. Smooth flowing transitions

Effective/Communicative Style
1. Distinct and appropriate voice (for topic)
2. Consistent tone
3. Engaging introductory paragraph
4. Appropriate word choice
5. Varied (and interesting) sentence structure
6. Expressive punctuation

Miscellaneous: No semantic distractions

About Our Contributors

Contributors Notes

With her family just over the bridge to Center City and an apartment on 40th and Spruce, **Emily Brotman** is that scarce native-born Philadelphia Penn student, with no relation to the other tri-state area. She majors in Comparative Literature and minors in English, and has always loved to read and write. Although Emily is not certain of her post-college plans, she considers law school and the publishing world exciting possibilities.

Kenneth A. Bruffee is Professor of English and Director of the Scholars Program and the Honors Academy at Brooklyn College, City University of New York. A graduate of Wesleyan University with a Ph.D. in English from Northwestern University, he has taught at the University of New Mexico, Northwestern University, the University of Virginia, Columbia University, Cooper Union, and the University of Pennsylvania. He directed a FIPSE-funded Institute in Peer Tutoring and Collaborative Learning in 1979-82. He has held a Broeklundian Professorship at Brooklyn College, 1991-94, and was a Wolfe Institute Faculty Fellow, 1991-92. His publications include *Elegiac Romance: Cultural Change and Loss of the Hero in Modern Fiction* (Ithaca: Cornell U P, 1983*); A Short Course in Writing*, 4th edition (New York: Addison Wesley Longman, 1992); and *Collaborative Learning: Higher Education, Interdependence and the Authority of Knowledge*, 2nd edition (Baltimore: Johns Hopkins U P, 1990).

Michelle Chikaonda is an International Relations major in her third year at the University of Pennsylvania. Of a multinational background, Michelle was born in Philadelphia, but has spent her life in Massachusetts, Canada, Wales and Malawi (the country from which her family originates, situated in South-east Africa). She has many extracurricular commitments, the most peculiar of which is her position as Treasurer of Penn's Philomathean Society, where she is required to sing – yes, sing – the budget report at each of the Society's general meetings. Michelle plans to attend graduate school for a master's degree or perhaps even a Ph.D. in International Relations.

A junior at the University of Pennsylvania, **Karen Connolly** is preparing for a career in medicine with a Biological Basis of Behavior major and a minor in French. Her list of activities is a testament to her dedication to the Penn community as a student; she is a member of the Penn American Red Cross Team, Chi Omega Fraternity, a volunteer at HUP, and a tour guide for Penn. Karen is also a loyal Penn football fan and loves the arts and the beach. Originally from East Hanover and Long Beach Island, New Jersey, Karen has been a vegetarian for eight years.

Sahang-Hee Hahn is an English major from just outside of Philadelphia. One of the many pre-law seniors, she does not intend to go to law school directly after graduation. She hopes instead to spend one or two years pursuing entertainment industry-related projects. A jack-of-all-trades, she has participated in various student organizations at Penn while remaining beholden to none: Without a Net (improvisational comedy troupe), Full Measure *(*a capella), Asian American Students' Association, Undergraduate Advisory Board, The Center for Community Partnerships Student Advisory Board, the Student Council for Undergraduate

Education, and dramatic productions when she could fit them in. She also spent a semester abroad, studying in London.

Nargus Harounzadeh is a junior at the University of Pennsylvania majoring in Philosophy, Politics, and Economics; she is also working towards a minor in English. An avid athlete, Nargus is a former member of the Penn Women's Swimming Team; presently she trains for multi-sport events including competition that features any biking, running, or swimming combination. Though the nature of her athleticism hints at an independent nature, she truly is a team player, working as a Peer Advisor, CWIC Advisor, and Writing Tutor. Nargus was raised in Lebanon, Pennsylvania—a small suburb bordering Hershey, the "Sweetest Place on Earth!" Her background is Persian; both her parents fled Iran in the tumultuous year preceding the Revolution.

A junior from Cherry Hill, New Jersey, **Melody Kramer** transferred to Penn last year after a year at the University of Rochester, where she took lots and lots of pre-med classes. After deciding that perhaps medicine was not the correct career choice for her, mainly after she had to dissect a sheep brain and nearly passed out, Melody decided to switch gears and declared herself an English major with a concentration in Creative Writing. After a semester of four literature classes, however, Mel unfortunately OD'd on Shakespeare, and decided to double major in Bioethics, preventing a probable death-by-Milton tragedy. Mel is also very involved on campus, and currently has a weekly humor column running on Wednesdays in the DP, attempts to play trumpet in the Penn Band, and is an editor of the *Punchbowl,* Penn's only intentionally funny publication.

From 1965 to 1994 **Richard A. Lanham** taught in the English Department of the University of California, Los Angeles, where he is now professor emeritus. He is the president of Rhetorica, Inc., a consulting and editorial services company. Although his teaching career found its center in Chaucer, Shakespeare and literary rhetoric, he founded the UCLA Writing Program and directed it from 1979 to 1986. Recently Allyn & Bacon published new editions of his two composition textbooks, *Revising Prose* and *Revising Business Prose.* Lanham has written several books of literary criticism and prose stylistics. His latest book, *The Electronic Word: Democracy, Technology, and the Arts,* was published, in both printed and electronic form, by the University of Chicago Press in 1993. To read an excerpt, go to http://ccat.sas.upenn.edu/jod/texts/lanham.sample. Since 1971, Lanham has acted as a literary consultant and expert witness in copyright disputes, working on cases involving such films and television shows as *King Kong, Jaws, Shampoo, Star Wars, The A-Team* and *Falcon Crest.*

Emily Previti is unique among the students at Penn. Along with being unique, she pursues degrees in English and Environmental Studies, and works for WXPN (88.5 FM), the Penn radio station that mixes creative and intelligent shows with a wide variety of music spanning all genres and time periods. A native of Linwood, New Jersey, Emily hopes to leave the East coast after graduation to teach underprivileged children.

Aubry Wand comes from a small suburb virtually unknown to anyone living outside of the San Francisco Bay Area called Portola Valley, a somewhat provincial little town near Stanford University about forty minutes south of the city. Whether out of boredom or sheer love for the game, Aubry began playing tennis at the age of eight and has ever since practiced nearly every day, sacrificing social life and other activities to play. He spent last summer giving tennis lessons to spoiled little kids at a local club; a job that in hindsight wasn't bad considering the reasonable pay, comfortable environment, and relatively easy hours. To conclude his summer vacation, Aubry went to Hawaii with his family--three weeks spent surfing and lying on the beach--and a much-needed rest from the intensity of California life. Though he has not put much thought into his post-graduate plans, and has yet to even declare a major, Aubry is considering attending law school.

Natalie Ward, or Nat as she prefers to be called for various reasons, is a senior in the Engineering School at Penn with a major in Computer Science and minors in English, Math, and Electrical Engineering. She's switched majors on more than one occasion, hence the Electrical Engineering minor, so if you find yourself having problems deciding on a major Nat's a good person to talk to. She hails from Somerset, New Jersey, but resides at Stouffer College House. A technological intellect, Nat is Computing Manager in Stouffer, having been an ITA since her freshman year. She also supports her fellow engineering students as an Engineering Peer Advisor. In her free time, Nat enjoys reading and writing; her favorite books readings include Shakespeare, Ayn Rand's *The Fountainhead,* and Jean Baudrillard's *Simulacra and Simulation.* She also spends a large part of her leisure time watching movies, particularly *The Matrix* trilogy because she's obsessed with it.

About the Writing Program

The Center for Programs
in Contemporary Writing and
The Critical Writing Program

For the first time in Penn's history, the
university's writing programs have been brought
together -- the Critical Writing Program, the
Creative Writing Program, and the Kelly Writers
House -- and made part of the Center for Programs
in Contemporary Writing (CPCW). Pooling our
collective energy, resources, and passion for
writing, the Center can help you find a writing
course, workshop, reading circle, outlet for
performing your writing, manuscript exchange group,
writing tutor, online discussion, editorial
apprenticeship, or creative mentor. Whatever your
writing needs, we have something to suit them.

CPCW: The Writing Neighborhood

When you arrive at Penn, we hope you will visit the
writing neighborhood, in the heart of Penn's
campus--the 1895 Victorian twin at 3808 Walnut
Street and, just behind it to the south, the 1851
Tudor-style cottage at 3805 Locust Walk. These two
beautiful spaces are CPCW's homes -- and yours,
also, if you are a Penn writer, student of writing,
teacher of writing, supporter of the writing arts;
if you have an unexplored passion for writing, feel
the need to improve the clarity and force of your
prose, or want our help with a writing project.

The Critical Writing Program

The Critical Writing Program (CWP) administers
Penn's university-wide writing program, rostering
the writing seminars that fulfill your Writing
Requirement and that are described in this booklet.
The Critical Writing Program also runs the Penn
Writing Center, providing writing tutoring and
other writing-related support services for
undergraduate and graduate students. Two
undergraduate journals are also sponsored by CWP:
3808: A Journal of Freshman Writing and *res: a*

journal of undergraduate research. CWP also evaluates writing courses for possible transfer credit. For information about any of these CWP programs and services, visit our website at http://www.writing.upenn.edu/critical/, email critwrit@writing.upenn.edu, or stop by the Center at 3808 Walnut.

The Creative Writing Program

The Creative Writing Program in the English Department offers workshops in fiction, poetry, playwriting, screenwriting and creative non-fiction. These courses are open to any interested student, as well as English majors who concentrate in creative writing. Throughout the year, the program invites locally and nationally recognized writers to Penn to read their work and talk informally with students about writing and literature. Many of these readings take place at the Kelly Writers House. For more information about the Creative Writing Program's courses or events, contact Gregory Djanikian at djanikia@writing.upenn.edu. You may also consult the website at http://www.writing.upenn.edu/cw/ (Please note: creative writing courses, including ENGL 010, do not fulfill the Writing Requirement.)

The Kelly Writers House

The Kelly Writers House is devoted to writers and writing activities of all sorts. Open from noon until 11:00 p.m. most days, the Writers House sponsors readings by professional and student writers, workshops, and other writing-related activities. Many campus literary magazines meet in the House to review submissions and plan their publications. Students initiate and oversee all House events, and space is available for any campus group planning a writing-related program.

Writers House students come from across the University: the College, Wharton, Engineering, Nursing and many graduate schools. They major in many different departments and read and write in many different genres. Their enthusiasm for writing brings them together, giving them a base for shared experiences and an audience for their work. Students are welcome to stop by any time to attend events, share a bag lunch, study or just hang out.

The Writers House is located at 3805 Locust Walk.
For information email wh@dept.english.upenn.edu or
call 573-writ. For events and descriptions of
student groups visit
http://www.writing.upenn.edu/~wh/

Fulfilling Your Writing Requirement

The University of Pennsylvania regards writing as
an integral part of your education. Charged with
this mission, the Critical Writing Program
serendipitously provides undergraduates across all
four schools with their only shared academic
experience: the critical writing seminar.

Recognizing that writing improves with practice,
and that pleasure along with discipline drives
practice, our writing seminars are among the most
exciting and innovative in the nation. Carefully
selected and rigorously trained, our instructors
are a diverse, enthusiastic community of standing
faculty, accomplished post-doctoral fellows,
published practitioners, professional writers,
journalists, and advanced doctoral candidates.
Penn's Critical Writing Program is committed to
teaching students how to write across, and beyond,
the university.

Timing

Most students satisfy the Writing Requirement
during their freshman year by enrolling in a
critical writing seminar. If your schedule does not
permit this, do complete the requirement by your
sophomore year. Many of the courses offered in the
fall will be repeated in the spring, so do not
panic if you cannot get into a seminar in the fall
term. We will offer a number of seminars in the
spring.

A writing seminar should be only the beginning of
your writing career at Penn. Writing improves with
study and practice; take advantage of your time at
Penn to get writing experience and feedback. You
may not know where life will take you, but you can
be reasonably certain that it will include plenty
of writing.

The Critical Writing Seminar: What to Expect

Critical writing seminars are small, intensive seminars taught by instructors knowledgeable and enthusiastic about their topics and about writing. Enrollments are capped at 16 so that faculty can work with you individually and so that you can get to know other students. Writing seminars are often the source of lifelong friendships. Be prepared to do more than make friends, however: these seminars are demanding. They require frequent writing and revision, reading in the disciplines, discussion, analysis, collaboration, and peer review. Attendance and participation matter, for as you hone your skills as a writer you will also be immersing yourself in the practices of intellectual inquiry. You can expect to spend more time on your writing seminar than on most of your other classes.

The College House Writing Seminar

A few writing seminars take place in the college houses, taught by the College House Deans, Faculty Associates, or the Critical Writing Fellows in Residence. Along with teaching writing seminars, Writing Fellows work with their residents to foster writing community, projects and programs as part of the "writing neighborhood."

Writing for International Students

If you are multilingual or a non-native speaker and need practice in reading, speaking and writing in English, please enroll in ENGL 011: Writing for International Students. English 011 fulfills the Writing Requirement and is described in the freshman handbook as well as on our website: www.writing.upenn.edu/critical (link to "Courses")

Penn Writing Center

The Critical Writing Program gives undergraduates as well as graduate students many ways to get feedback on their writing. Our Writing Center is staffed with tutors who work by appointment, during drop-in evening hours, and online. Many students use the Penn Writing Center, whether to get help on an application, a particular assignment, or a difficult paper. Some students want to work on a particular writing problem -- from grammar to organization and thesis - while others simply need a pair of fresh eyes. "Does this make sense?" is the question our tutors most frequently hear. One of the best-kept secrets at Penn is that our top students take full advantage of Penn's resources, especially the Writing Center. Students like the Center's writerly ambiance; it's a comfortable place. The undergraduate and graduate students who work in the Center genuinely enjoy meeting other students, talking about writing, and sharing what they know and continue to learn from each other's experiences at Penn and as writers. To find out more or to make an appointment visit http://www.writing.upenn.edu/critical and link to "Help with Your Writing.

"

Becoming a Peer Tutor

If you like to write, enjoy helping others, and have the maturity and temperament to be a writing tutor, we hope you will look into becoming a tutor. Along with providing writing feedback, tutors may also serve as teaching assistants in writing seminars and as peer review trainers. Penn Peer Tutors spend a semester in English 135, aka Writing Bootcamp, taught by the Director of Critical Writing. Tutors proclaim this course and their tutoring work as among their most rewarding and transformative college experiences, as well as excellent preparation for their future careers or graduate studies.

Student Publications

The Critical Writing Program sponsors two undergraduate publications, *3808: A Journal of Freshman Writing* and *res: a journal of undergraduate research*. Publication in *3808* is open only to freshman writing produced in the critical writing seminar and nominated by the student's writing instructor. *Res* is a peer- and faculty-reviewed journal of research open only to upperclassmen. CWP also offers two publication internships each year. Interns work on the two journals as well as edit the Arts & Culture Review Blog.

In addition to these journals, Penn sponsors a variety of undergraduate publications, including the *Peregrine, Penn Review, Philomel* (the literary magazine of the Philomathean Society), *Pandora's Box* (a voice for creative women), *Mosaic* (Penn's Asian-American literary journal), *Ma'ayan* (A Journal of Jewish Creativity), and *Local Access* (Penn's on-line magazine featuring Penn student writing). Writers and editors for all publications are always needed and welcome. For more information, consult http://www.writing.upenn.edu/critical/ and link to "Contests and Publications."

Writing Tutoring

Whether you need a fresh pair of eyes, a second opinion, or an extreme makeo

we can help you:

> - proofread your papers
> - identify and correct errors of grammar & syntax
> - define your topic and audience
> - plan research strategies
> - develop a sound thesis
> - analyze texts
> - organize material and revise drafts
> - cultivate a distinct and masterful writing voice

DROP IN: Sunday through Thursday, 7:00 to 10:00 pm

*The Writing Center 3808 Walnut or
*Kelly Writers House 3719 Locust Walk

SEND IT ONLINE: critwrit@writing.upenn.edu

MAKE AN APPOINTMENT ONLINE:
Weekdays, 11 a.m. to 9:00 pm
www.writing.upenn.edu/critical (link to "Writing: Help"

For more info
 Visit www.writing.upenn.edu
 email critwrit@writing.upenn.edu
 or call 215.573.CPCW (2729)

Critical Writing Program
3808 Walnut Street
www.writing.upenn.edu
itwrit@writing.upenn.edu
215.573.CPCW